"*Engaging Globalization* delves in shape our contemporary world. concern for God's shalom, continu with his earlier volume, *Walking wi.* missiologist, which perhaps more than anything else makes this book so critical."

—**Gregg A. Okesson**, E. Stanley Jones School of World Mission and Evangelism, Asbury Theological Seminary

"Christian leaders, teachers, and ministers have a responsibility to provide accurate historical, biblical, and theological reflections on globalization rather than regurgitating uninformed, biased media reports. In this essential text, Myers offers a vision of human flourishing that emerges from careful study and thoughtful pastoral reflection."

—**Soong-Chan Rah**, North Park Theological Seminary; author of *The Next Evangelicalism* and coauthor of *Return to Justice*

"God wants our hearts and heads, our hands and feet, to partner in transforming a messy and complex world. Loving God and loving neighbor in our age of globalization requires new dimensions of discipleship, attentive discernment, and intentional spiritual formation. Myers shares a compelling vision for how ordinary laity, church leaders, and people of goodwill are called to partake in God's work of restoration and redemption."

—**Krisanne Vaillancourt Murphy**, coauthor of Advocating for Justice: An Evangelical Vision for Transforming Systems and Structures

"After more than half a century of usage, the term *globalization* is experiencing a crisis of meaning and significance. For people of faith, the concept poses daunting questions; perhaps especially for the global Christian family, since the Christian movement is both impacted by and deeply implicated in the processes of globalization. But Christian perspectives or responses tend to narrowly focus on one dimension or the other. In *Engaging Globalization*, Myers provides a comprehensive and astute appraisal. The complexities of globalization (understood as 'a deeply embedded historical process') are carefully navigated; entrenched myths regarding its value, promise, and outcome are interrogated; and the ambiguities, not to mention unresolved dilemmas, of its myriad processes are laid bare. This engaging exploration of what it means to be the church in a new global age is both timely and instructive."

—**Jehu J. Hanciles**, Candler School of Theology, Emory University

"For Christians desiring to engage the joys and trials of globalization with inspired, faith-centered, and effective responses, Myers marks the path. Insisting on the essential connection between a deep spiritual relationship with God and commitment to justice in the world, *Engaging Globalization* calls Christians everywhere to the redemptive task of appreciating the good of secular theories and practices of globalization, while at the same time revising and reforming these theories and practices with our deep awareness of God, our image-bearing humanity, and the purpose God has given us."

—**Roland Hoksbergen**, Calvin College

MISSION
in Global Community

SCOTT W. SUNQUIST
AND AMOS YONG,
SERIES EDITORS

The Mission in Global Community series is designed to reach college students and those interested in learning more about responsible mission involvement. Written by faculty and graduates from Fuller Theological Seminary, the series is designed as a global conversation with stories and perspectives from around the world.

ENGAGING GLOBALIZATION

The Poor, Christian Mission, and Our Hyperconnected World

BRYANT L. MYERS

Baker Academic
a division of Baker Publishing Group
Grand Rapids, Michigan

© 2017 by Bryant L. Myers

Published by Baker Academic
a division of Baker Publishing Group
PO Box 6287, Grand Rapids, MI 49516-6287
www.bakeracademic.com

Printed in the United States of America

Library of Congress Cataloging-in-Publication Data
Names: Myers, Bryant L., author.
Title: Engaging globalization : the poor, Christian mission, and our hyperconnected world / Bryant L. Myers.
Description: Grand Rapids, MI : Baker Academic, a division of Baker Publishing Group, [2017] | Series: Mission in global community | Includes bibliographical references and index.
Identifiers: LCCN 2017004701 | ISBN 9780801097980 (pbk.)
Subjects: LCSH: Globalization—Religious aspects—Christianity. | Poverty—Religious aspects—Christianity. | Missions.
Classification: LCC BR115.G59 M94 2017 | DDC 261.8—dc23
LC record available at https://lccn.loc.gov/2017004701

Scripture quotations are from the Holy Bible, Today's New International Version®. TNIV®. Copyright © 2001, 2005 by Biblica, Inc.™ Used by permission of Zondervan. All rights reserved worldwide. www.zondervan.com

17 18 19 20 21 22 23   7 6 5 4 3 2 1

With love and appreciation to

Lisa
Brooke, Casey, and Samantha Grace
James, Laurel, and Evelyn Angelica

Contents

Section 1: Setting the Stage

Section 2: Introducing Globalization

Section 3: The Two Eras of Globalization

Section 4: The Impact of Globalization

Section 5: Globalization and the Poor

Sidebars

Series Preface

A mission leader in 1965, not too long ago, could not have foreseen what mission looks like today. In 1965 nations in the non-Western world were gaining their independence after centuries of Western colonialism. Mission societies from Europe and North America were trying to adjust to the new global realities where Muslim nations, once dominated by the West, no longer granted "missionary visas." The largest mission field, China, was closed. Decolonization, it seemed, was bringing a decline to missionary work in Africa and Asia.

On the home front, Western churches were in decline, and the traditional missionary factories—mainline churches in the West—were struggling with their own identities. Membership was then—and remains—in decline, and missionary vocations were following the same pattern. Evangelical and Pentecostal churches began to surpass mainline churches in mission, and then, just when we thought we understood the new missionary patterns, Brazilians began to go to Pakistan and Malaysians began to evangelize Vietnam and Cambodia. Africans (highly educated and strongly Christian) began to move in great numbers to Europe and North America. Countries that had been closed began to see conversions to Christ, without the aid of traditional mission societies. And in the midst of this rapid transformation of missionary work, the alarm rang out that most Christians in the world were now in Asia, Latin America, and Africa rather than in the West.

What does it mean to be involved in mission in this new world where Christianity has been turned upside down in less than a century?

This series is directed at this new global context for mission. Fuller Theological Seminary, particularly through its School of Intercultural Studies (formerly School of World Mission), has been attentive to trends in global mission for over half a century. In fact, much innovation in mission thinking and practice has emanated from Fuller since Donald McGavran moved from Oregon to California—as the first and founding dean of the then School of World Mission—to apply lessons about church growth learned in India to other areas of the world. Since that time many creative mission professors have provided global leadership in mission thinking: Ralph Winter (unreached people groups), Paul Hiebert (anthropology for mission), Charles Kraft (mission and spiritual dynamics), and Dudley Woodberry (Islamics), among others.

This series provides the most recent global scholarship on key themes in mission, written for a general audience of Christians committed to God's mission. Designed to be student, user, and textbook friendly, each volume contains voices from around the world speaking about the theme, and each chapter concludes with discussion questions so the books can be used for group studies. As the fields of mission are changing, shifting, or shrinking, the discussions connect the church and the world, East and West, North and South, the developed and developing worlds, each crossing cultural, political, social, and religious boundaries in its own way and knitting together people living and serving in various communities, both of faith and of other commitments—this is the contemporary landscape of the mission of God. Enjoy the challenges of each volume and find ways to live into God's mission.

Scott W. Sunquist

Amos Yong

Acknowledgments

I have just finished ten years as a professor of transformational development in the School of Intercultural Studies (SIS) at Fuller Theological Seminary. I describe myself as an accidental academic as I never dreamed about teaching at the graduate level when I completed my thirtieth year at World Vision International with every intention of retiring there. I am indebted to Doug McConnell, then dean of SIS, who saw an opportunity for me and the seminary, and then patiently coaxed me into changing careers.

As a new professor with no history in academics, I discovered that I was expected to develop a portfolio of courses to teach. The first choice was obvious. I developed a course based on my earlier book, *Walking with the Poor*, a book deliberately limited to the grassroots aspects of transformational development, the topic most directly connected to my experience at World Vision.

I then decided that I needed to develop a course on poverty and development that provided a global, sweeping overview of the field. This was largely a new area of interest for me and thus represented a far greater challenge. The first few versions of this course were pretty rough, as I had a great deal to learn. So my first acknowledgment goes to all the students who suffered through the initial versions of the course and yet kept encouraging me. What surprised me was that most students reported that the topic of globalization in Christian perspective was new to them. Apparently, they had not been exposed to the idea of a Christian engagement with globalization in either their churches or their Christian colleges. This discovery was one of the reasons I decided to write this book.

As I developed the course, I was helped greatly by my faculty colleague, Jehu Hanciles, a brilliant professor of world Christianity whose primary research at that time was on migration, globalization, and mission. His book

Beyond Christendom: Globalization, African Migration, and the Transformation of the West was foundational in shaping my views, and you will find his fingerprints repeatedly in this book. Jehu was also part of a team at the Lausanne 2004 Global Forum that wrote the Lausanne Occasional Paper on globalization and the gospel.[1] This seminal thinking on globalization from a missiological perspective was also an important part of my formation.

Jehu taught his own course on globalization and Christian mission, and our courses proved to be complementary. When Jehu saddened us all by taking up a new challenge at the Candler School of Theology at Emory University, I revamped my course to include more world Christianity and Christian mission. Thus the shape of what became this book began to take form. Jehu also reviewed chapters 5 and 6 on the history of globalization; the chapters were greatly enriched by the critical eye of a real historian.

As strange as it may seem for a seminary professor, I have never taken a formal class in theology. I learned my theology "on the road" in bits and pieces. My ten years as the director of World Vision's MARC ministry (Missions Advanced Research and Communications) allowed me to engage with the larger evangelical and ecumenical mission movements and to attend many Lausanne Movement and WCC Commission on World Mission and Evangelism conferences. Through the kind auspices of Vinay Samuel and invitations to conferences that he orchestrated, I was introduced to many members of the International Fellowship of Evangelical Mission Theologians (now International Fellowship of Mission as Transformation). Listening to papers by Vinay, René Padilla, Kwame Bediako, Mercy Oduyoye, Valdir Steuernagel, Miroslav Volf, Melba Maggay, Ron Sider, Raymond Fung, Kosuke Koyama, and others—and then reading their work on an endless series of long plane flights—resulted in a slow accumulation of theological perspectives on global issues relating to mission and transformation.

I am also particularly indebted to Bill Dyrness, a theologian of global reach, and his brilliant activist wife, Gracie, who are friends and mentors, and have been for a long time, in terms of a broad range of issues of theology and social ethics. Bill and I have taught together, and Bill has reviewed and commented on most of my theological writing. Conversations here at Fuller with Bill, Mark Lau Branson, Love Sechrest, Oscar García Johnson, Howard Loewen, Amos Yong, and others have extended and deepened my theological thinking. But, of course, all the bad theology in this book is mine.

I am also indebted to colleagues at World Vision International who worked with me from time to time over the years and introduced me to

1. LCWE, "Globalization and the Gospel."

broad perspectives on poverty and development as well as some of the major international development institutions. Stephen Commins, a lecturer in urban planning at UCLA and a frequent consultant to the World Bank, introduced me to the world of international advocacy over thirty years ago and was kind enough to comment on an earlier version of a chapter in this book. Manfred Grellert, a Brazilian Baptist pastor with strong roots in liberation theology and World Vision's regional vice president for Latin America for many years, pushed and prodded many of us who were much slower in understanding the systemic causes of injustice and poverty at that time. In the 1990s, I hired Alan Whaites to restart and expand World Vision International's global advocacy efforts.[2] Highly experienced in international NGO advocacy work and deeply familiar with global policy issues, Alan provided me with a rigorous, if informal, education into globalization, global institutions, and poverty. Finally, I am indebted to Jeff Thindwa, a former director of World Vision Malawi and now an expert on governance with the World Bank. Together and separately, these friends educated a somewhat naive American on his journey toward a deeper and more nuanced understanding of God's globalizing world.

This book was completed only because the current dean of SIS, Scott Sunquist, pushed me to turn my globalization course into a book that would become part of Baker Academic's Mission in Global Community series. Constantly surprised and sometimes overwhelmed by the challenge of writing about something so inchoate and complex as globalization, I received much encouragement and many accommodations from Scott that made this book possible. Scott also reviewed my history chapters.

I also need to acknowledge my colleagues at Baker Academic, all of whom have been a pleasure to work with. Jim Kinney has been a continuing source of encouragement while tolerating an unending series of questions and corrections. My editors, Eric Salo and his team, did a very careful and thorough job of catching my many errors and making the manuscript readable.

Finally, I must salute my family and their tolerance for what became known as the "stupid book." "Is Dad still working on the stupid book?" "Your Dad can't come over this weekend, he's working on his stupid book." Even my three-year-old granddaughter Sammy got in the act: "Hi Babu, can you read me your stupid book?" "Sammy, it has no pictures." After a puzzled silence, "Oh well, never mind."

2. Alan left World Vision to work in Nepal on governance for the UK Department of International Development and then with the OECD in Paris where he has become a respected global expert.

My wife, my best friend and love of my life, tolerated my daily disappearances into my study without complaint and supported and encouraged me on the long journey down the rabbit hole that is book writing. My children Brooke and James did the same, accepting less grand parenting with graceful understanding.

At the end of the day, I am grateful to God. God took an ex-hippie and saved him from himself a little over forty years ago. God gave me a godly woman of depth, perseverance, and courage and two wonderful children. God brought me, totally unqualified, into World Vision and a long and satisfying career at the service of the poor, accompanied by good leadership and great friends. Somehow in that process, God managed to find a book in me. And now, after my unexpected sojourn into the academy, God has managed to find another one. I just went along for the ride and did the best I could to do what I was told. God be praised.

Abbreviations

AfDB	African Development Bank
ASEAN	Association of Southeast Asian Nations
CIDA	Canadian International Development Agency
DFID	Department for International Development
EU	European Union
FAO	Food and Agriculture Organization
FDI	Foreign Direct Investment
GDP	Gross domestic product, measure of total goods and services produced
IBMR	*International Bulletin of Missionary Research*
ICT4D	Information and Communication Technology for Development
IFAD	International Fund for Agriculture Development
ILO	International Labour Organization
IMF	International Monetary Fund
INGO	International nongovernmental organization
ISIS	Islamic State
LCWE	Lausanne Committee for World Evangelization
MDGs	Millennium Development Goals
NAFTA	North American Free Trade Agreement
NGO	Nongovernmental organization
OECD	Organisation for Economic Co-operation and Development
UN	United Nations
UNCTAD	United Nations Conference on Trade and Development
UNDP	United Nations Development Program
UNFPA	United Nations Population Fund
UNHCR	United Nations High Commission on Refugees
UNICEF	United Nations Children's Fund
UNODC	United Nations Office on Drugs and Crime
USAID	United States Agency for International Development
WFP	World Food Programme
WHO	World Health Organization
WTO	World Trade Organization

Section 1

SETTING THE STAGE

1

Introduction and the Path Forward

We live in interesting times.

In the last twenty years, things have been changing with increasing speed in God's world. Economically, the world's gross domestic product (GDP) more than doubled to almost $78 trillion in spite of a number of recessions in major economies and the global recession of 2008–9.[1] Twenty years ago, the world's largest economies in terms of comparative purchasing power[2] were the United States, Japan, and Germany; today they are China, the United States, and India. In the last twenty years, global trade increased from $2 trillion to over $18 trillion a year.[3]

This has brought some good news to the poor. The proportion of the world's population living in extreme poverty has been cut in half over this twenty-year period. Deaths of women giving birth have been reduced by almost half, as have deaths of children under the age of five. In developing countries, life expectancy increased by almost nine years. More children are in school, and the greatest increase is among girls.[4]

1. IMF, *World Economic Outlook*.
2. Purchasing Power Parity is used worldwide to compare the income levels in different countries by making adjustments to the exchange rates of two currencies to make them equivalent with the purchasing power of each other.
3. WTO, *World Trade Report 2013*, 55.
4. UNFPA, "Last 20 Years."

Technologically, the first website was launched in 1991, and seventeen years later Google indexed one trillion websites. Internet users reached three billion in 2015.[5] In the last twenty years, we have witnessed the launch of Google, Facebook, YouTube, Twitter, and a host of new social media. The iPhone was launched in 2007, and four years later 1 billion people were using smart phones around the world and 4.6 billion people were using mobile phones. These and more technological innovations are available to this generation of adolescents and youth, which is the largest in history and represents almost one-third of the world's population. These young people will have little memory of a world without smart phones, instant messaging, and the internet.

Since the beginning of time, people, plants, and animals have been going global. But it is only in the last two hundred years that going global was turbocharged by the ability of people to get connected and get closer to each other. As we will see later in more detail, the modern era of globalization began with the economic development of Britain in the beginning of the nineteenth century, followed by Europe, the United States, and Japan. This new form of globalization began sweeping the world after World War II and especially with the end of the Cold War in the late 1980s. The drivers of globalization are deep and continuing changes in economics, technology, culture, and human self-understanding.

But there is more to globalization than just getting closer and better connected. It is changing us as individuals, not just our societies. We are meeting people previously too distant to know. Not so long ago, our neighbor usually looked like us or spoke our language; now our neighbor can be a Sudanese mother with a hungry child, or a Syrian girl fleeing the destruction of her home country. Their images and stories are readily available on our digital devices, and we are responding compassionately to these stories.

Yet there is a sense that we are letting globalization and its processes flow over us, unaware that we are being pulled into a new world. I am concerned that we as Christians are not asking the question "Are we and is the world becoming what God intends?" When we see the growth in global compassion, the answer is "maybe." When we see the materialism, the patterns of consumption, and the increase in the abuse of the weak and the environment, the answer is far less clear. These are theological questions for God's people. This leads me to my main point.

With the exception of some within the Christian academy who think we need to resist globalization, the larger Christian community seems to be ignoring globalization or fearing it. When was the last time you heard a

5. Internet World Stats, "Internet Users of the World—2016."

sermon series, a Bible or book study, or a retreat topic focused on a Christian understanding and response to globalization? How many churches or denominations have globalization as a focus of their discipleship and mission strategy? I have been teaching a course on this topic at Fuller Theological Seminary for almost ten years, and every year I experience the surprise of students when they begin to engage—"We've had our heads down; there is so much about this we did not know. This has not been on our radar." While Christians seem to be willing to use the technological tools of globalization for church and mission, there is little evidence that Christians and their churches are devoting much energy to understanding globalization, biblically assessing its values and promises to us, and preparing our people to respond.

I suspect there are three broad reasons for this. First, globalization as a topic seems too big and complicated, too involved with economics, technology, and politics. This is technical stuff best left to experts, and maybe it's a bit worldly for our taste. Second, we Christians have been socialized into quietly accepting our relegation to the private realm of spiritual things, leaving the world of economics, politics, and technology to the West's materialist and secular humanism. We no longer seem to believe that we are to be signs of the coming kingdom of God and that God has made us partners in God's plan to redeem and restore creation. Third, in the aftermath of the passing of Christendom, we have lost our nerve a bit. We are not sure that we are worthy of a place at the public table when it comes to assessing and engaging the globalization of economics, finance, technology, and the like. We are not sure that we will be welcome and, worse, that we have anything of value to offer. We seem to have forgotten that the gospel is true and secular humanism is not.

But it was not always this way. While the traditional account of the emergence of a modern economy and a democratic state in Britain at the beginning of the nineteenth century is summarized as the coalescing of the new economics of Adam Smith with the Industrial Revolution and the development of modern science, there is more to the story, as we shall see later in this book. Christian theology provided much of the philosophical and values foundation for what emerged.[6] Furthermore, it was churches and individual Christians who worked for protection of children and who cared for the poor in the era of rapid urbanization when people began working in factories unregulated by humane rules. The nineteenth century was the first century of modern economic and technological globalization, but it also came to be called the

---

6. Gillespie, *Theological Origins of Modernity*.

"humanitarian century"[7] and the "age of benevolence"[8] largely as a result of the work of Christians. The Christians of the nineteenth century had not yet learned that they needed to leave the public square to others.

We need to remember that Victorian evangelicals imagined redeeming the world, not just ruling it.[9] Voluntary mission societies responded to British colonialism with a commitment to share the gospel—the whole gospel—humanizing the empire in some places and challenging its excesses in others. Missionaries were critical in promoting religious liberty, mass education, mass printing, newspapers, voluntary organizations, most colonial reforms, and the rule of law, including legal protections for nonwhites.[10]

In addition, Victorian evangelicals launched the world's first national advocacy campaign as a prophetic rebuke directed at the emerging British Empire. The slave trade could not be the backbone of the modern global economic system of the day for the simple reason that slavery was immoral. So were cultural practices such as female infanticide and suttee[11] in India. Whatever the weaknesses or presumptions of cultural superiority, we must acknowledge that the launch of the modern era of globalization was accompanied and challenged by a Christian moral perspective. Christians in Britain and throughout the empire acted theologically and missionally.

And so the church and Christians today need to make a choice. Will we ignore globalization and remain closeted in the spiritual realm with our backs to the world? Will we resist globalization as some kind of second fall, as if God has been surprised by globalization and the staying power of capitalism? Or will we instead engage globalization as a mixture of God's grace and human sin and question its promise of a particular kind of better human future by offering a more complete vision of human flourishing as understood from Scripture? Are we willing to call out and attempt to change the darker aspects of globalization? Will the church decide to engage globalization missionally and work to shape it ethically? Are we willing to fulfill our mission of making disciples of Christ who vote, consume, and volunteer in ways that correct the evil and enhance the good in globalization? Globalization is going to the ends of the earth with its version of good news. What are we doing?

7. Pinker, *Better Angels of Our Nature*, 168. Steven Pinker is a cognitive psychologist and professor of psychology at Harvard University.

8. Himmelfarb, *Roads to Modernity*, 131. Gertrude Himmelfarb is professor emerita at the Graduate Center of the City University of New York.

9. Ferguson, *Empire*, 113. Niall Ferguson is professor of history at Harvard University and a senior fellow at the Hoover Institution, Stanford University.

10. Woodberry, "Missionary Roots of Liberal Democracy."

11. Self-immolation of a Hindu widow on her husband's funeral pyre.

We need the courage to act as if it were true that the kingdom of God is the only kingdom that will be left standing at the end of time. We need to act as if it were true that God is working now in human history toward that end. Furthermore, we need to act as God's partners in this task for the simple reason that working through flawed human beings is the way God has chosen to act in the world. Walter Brueggemann reminds us that, in the Old Testament, God's resolve always translates into human action.[12] God met Moses at the burning bush and announced God's resolve to free Israel from Egypt and then said to a surprised Moses, "I am sending you to Pharaoh to bring my people the Israelites out of Egypt" (Exod. 3:10). This mode of God's action also appears again in the Gospel of John. Jesus announced that he had come that the world might have life and have it in full, and then he told the disciples, "As the Father sent me, I am sending you. . . . Receive the Holy Spirit" (John 20:21–22). Acting theologically and missiologically in God's world is our mission.

But we do not appear to have globalization—as a value system, as a collection of principalities and powers, as an offering of a better human future—in our sights. We need to be making ourselves aware of the missing parts of the globalization story. We need to be informing and forming ourselves about how to witness to the kingdom in the midst of today's globalization in terms of how we consume, volunteer, and vote. Christians and the church need to contribute to the development of a moral ecology powerful enough to shape and correct globalization in favor of values that support both human dignity and human flourishing—kingdom values. Issues of idolatry and false promises need to be named and alternatives provided. Bottom line: The church needs to get back in the game. We have a God, a gospel, and a truth that a materialist and secular globalization simply cannot provide. It is to contribute to this call to action that I decided to write this book.

What Is Being Proposed?

The intent of this book is to introduce the subject of globalization to students, pastors, and church leaders, to invite them to go before God and seek their individual and collective callings to be faithful witnesses within the sprawling and complex world of twenty-first-century globalization. The book will end with an exploration of the possible missional roles of the church in today's world of economic, technological, and social change. My proposal rests on four affirmations that I will explore in some depth.

12. Brueggemann, *Journey to the Common Good*, 12.

First, globalization is an emergent, highly ambiguous global phenomenon of technological, economic, and social change that is now working itself out in history. Globalization's underlying values and assumptions are modern, involving a material world with no transcendent dimension and with human beings as the sole actors in history. This world is a source of anxiety and distress since, as individuals and even as nations, we feel powerless in the midst of globalization's increasingly rapid pace of change, its numerous contradictions, and its mixture of good and not so good outcomes. The future is unclear since all we know about globalization is what we learn by looking back at its history, and the past sheds little light on the future of emergent social systems. Looking forward leaves all of us with an uncomfortable sense of uncertainty—seemingly adrift in a world of rapid and unpredictable change.

Second, globalization has been good news to the poor, although not for all the poor and certainly not at all times in its history. Furthermore, globalization birthed a process whereby compassion became globalized in the form of an increasingly worldwide response to victims of wars and natural disasters in the late nineteenth and early twentieth centuries and in the growing global poverty eradication efforts since the end of World War II. Although resting on the thin basis of secular human rights theory, the idea that all human beings are entitled to be able to stay alive and live a life worth living has become a normative global ethic. A shared concern for the poor is a point of potential connection between the church and the secular domains of globalization.

Third, I will argue that the values and processes of globalization fail in three critical areas. First, their understanding of who human beings are and why we are here is reductionist and thin. The result is a crisis of meaning. With no theology of sin, the secular humanist lacks an adequate account for greed, poverty, and injustice, and hence suffers from a major diagnostic blind spot. Second, globalization's assumptions about the role and purpose of power are flawed, and this is the main reason for the dark side of globalization. Third, globalization fails to provide a compelling spiritual and ethical architecture that enables human beings to understand who they are, why they are here, and how they should live. We are back to a crisis of meaning.

The final offering of this book is an exploration of the many possible missional roles of Christians and of the church in today's world of economic, technological, and social globalization. I do not offer a single program. The multifaceted and complex world of globalization requires an equally broad family of Christian responses. Discovering the particular missional call for yourself or your community of faith is a question of discernment whereby gifts and calling are matched to that part of globalization in which God has placed you and thus created an opportunity for you to witness to Jesus Christ and the values of the kingdom of God in those places.

How Will We Get There?

Before we delve into the topic of globalization, chapter 2 presents a family of theological affirmations that will keep reappearing as we explore globalization. First and foremost, I will state my belief that God is not surprised by globalization and has a place for it in God's ongoing project of redeeming us and restoring creation. Second, I will show how creation theology has much to offer to this discussion if we are willing to think deeply about it. Finally, I will summarize what I believe God intends in terms of human life and flourishing.

The second half of chapter 2 introduces the idea of complex adaptive social systems, which I will argue has useful explanatory power. This idea will help us as we think about responses to globalization that call for directing or managing globalization. It also provides a useful way to make sense of the history of globalization and of the Christian church in mission, a topic I address in chapter 11.

In chapter 3 I begin trying to help us understand globalization today, although as you will see, the question of definition is a bit muddled. The chapter will examine a few perspectives on what some call "globalization from below" and also expose the dark side of globalization—an empowered and enabled world of illicit activity. The final section will explore the five interacting domains of globalization: technology, economics, governance, culture, and human beings in large numbers.

Chapter 4 further underscores the ambiguities of globalization as I examine its emergent or dynamic nature as a complex adaptive social system. I will then explore some areas of deep concern regarding the impact of globalization: asymmetries of power, income inequality, economic disruption, the environmental threat, and the reduction of what it means to be human. I will close with a brief note on the challenge of globalization for the church in mission.

Before outlining the other chapters in this book, it may be helpful to introduce the historical schema I will use. I describe the history of globalization as taking place in two broad eras (see fig. 1.1).[13] The First Era began with creation and is still under way. This is an era whose central driver is

---

13. I chose to divide the history of globalization into two eras to help me describe the globalization story for the purposes of this book. Other scholars frame the history of globalization differently. Some see it as a single, ongoing phenomenon from creation to today. Others see globalization as starting in the 1800s. Still others claim it is a new phenomenon that began with the fall of the Berlin Wall in 1989 and the concomitant explosion in technological innovation.

FIGURE 1.1 The two eras of globalization

migration. Plants, animals, and people—traders, adventurers, warriors, and missionaries[14]—moved over the face of God's earth. These migrations were driven partly by the need to flee scarcity or danger, partly by curiosity, and, in time, by a desire to extend the reach of empires and religions.

The Second Era of Globalization was an augmentation and extension of the First Era. This turbocharging of globalization began in Britain at the beginning of the nineteenth century with the unbidden and unplanned emergence of two discoveries. First, individuals and nations discovered that it was possible to create wealth, to make the economic pie bigger. Second, they discovered that creating an environment that rewarded and democratized technological innovation sped up innovation, which in turn increased the capacities of national economies to grow. These two discoveries led to people, economies, and cultures becoming better off materially, more closely connected, and increasingly globally aware. Together, the combined effect of these two eras resulted in today's contemporary globalization and its confusing, rapidly changing, still transforming world. This is the world in which we are to act theologically and missiologically as faithful witnesses.

Chapter 5 explores the First Era of Globalization, from creation to the beginning of the nineteenth century. This is an era of migration, empire, and mission. The chapter closes with an account of Britain's unexpected and emergent economic and technological transformation, which resulted in the dramatic augmentation of the First Era of Globalization.

Chapter 6 then explores how the Second Era of Globalization unfolds as an extension and an expansion of the First Era. The Second Era can be thought of as having three parts: Globalization I, the Great Disruption, and Globalization II (see fig. 1.2). Globalization I, covering the period between 1800 and World War I, was a largely Western phenomenon of rapidly growing international trade, modernization, European empires, and economic growth in Britain, Europe, the United States, and Japan.

14. Terms are taken from Chanda, *Bound Together*. Nayan Chanda is the consulting editor of *YaleGlobal Online* at the Yale Center for the Study of Globalization.

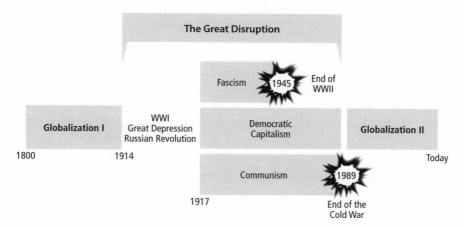

FIGURE 1.2 The Second Era of Globalization

Globalization I came to an abrupt end with the start of World War I. During what I call the Great Disruption, competing political and economic systems emerged—Marxism-Leninism or communism in Russia and national socialism or fascism in Germany. Then the world went to war for a second time. Coming out of World War II, the only free market democracies in the world were Great Britain and the United States. Globalization was on the brink of extinction.

With the end of World War II, fascism receded as an economic and political option. But communism and the Soviet Union remained an immovable alternative to the capitalism and democracy of the West. It was not until the Cold War ended in the late 1980s that capitalism and democracy prevailed and Globalization II emerged in full force seemingly without a rival.

In the last twenty-five years, Globalization II saw much of the developing world in the Global South adopt market systems and connect to global markets, leading to rapid increases in economic growth, a stunning increase in world trade, and a whole new generation of technology that resulted in what many call the "death of distance."[15] Over one billion of the world's poor became middle class, mostly in China and India.

Chapter 7 describes the impact of two hundred years of the Second Era of Globalization. To better understand globalization today, we must understand how extensive were the economic, political, and technological transformations during that period. The material lives of a large number of people improved,

15. "Death of distance" is a phrase describing how technology has made geographical distance less of a factor in terms of cost or response times.

and mass education emerged as a norm, as did modern public health. More foundationally, people and cultures underwent significant shifts in how they understood the role and agency of human beings.

Chapter 8 provides an assessment of the impact of these two hundred years of change. It begins by examining the effect of this era on the poor. There is a lot of good news on the material front but also some not so good news. The chapter closes with a summary of differing assessments of globalization. There are optimists who believe that the answer to the world's ills, especially for the poor, is more globalization, not less. There are skeptics who are not sure we really understand what we are talking about when we talk about globalization, and they wonder if the impact and future of globalization will be ambiguous and possibly disappointing. One author uses the telling metaphor of a "false dawn."[16] Finally, there are those who see a deeply troubled future that is bad news for almost everyone—a world of increasing fundamentalism, tribalism, and systemic violence for most and a sequestered, wealthy world for those who can afford to keep themselves safe. There are Christians in all three camps.

Chapter 9 examines globalization's response to the poor. While the poor have been greatly helped in material terms over the last two hundred years, there is still a lot left to do. I will trace the ideas of development and poverty eradication as they emerged in the West. We will look at the slow shift from development as economic growth to a new, more holistic formulation—development as freedom. I will report what the poor have to say when asked what makes them poor and what well-being would look like for them. The chapter closes by describing the globalization of the world's response to the poor and the many kinds of institutions working to help the poor.

Chapter 10 continues the theme of chapter 9 by examining three major poverty eradication strategies competing for followers and funding—those of Jeffrey Sachs, William Easterly, and Paul Collier. I will briefly introduce the work of Lawrence Harrison on culture and development and then I will describe some important contributions by Hernando de Soto, Muhammad Yunus, and Abhijit Banerjee and Esther Duflo. The technological innovation of globalization is also affecting our global response to the poor in the form of what is called Information and Communication Technology for Development (ICT4D). The chapter closes with a discussion of the increasing interest in the intersection of faith and development in the secular world of development

16. Gray, *False Dawn.* John Gray, formerly a supporter of neoliberal capitalism, became disillusioned in the face of its human cost. He is professor emeritus of European thought at the London School of Economics and Political Science.

studies. This is creating an opportunity for the church to contribute to what has been up to now a largely secular discussion on poverty.

In the next three chapters, I shift my focus to globalization and the church. In chapter 11, I begin by pointing out that Christianity has an agenda when it comes to globalization. The first nine chapters of Genesis, the Psalms, and Revelation make clear the universal claim of God over the whole earth and God's global intentions for all humankind. We worship a global God who is at work through all of history. Thus, Christianity offers a normative interpretation of what is happening and how things are meant to be. This makes Christians and the church seem suspicious to many who are also attempting to shape globalization. At the same time, the church is also being shaped by the processes of globalization. Understanding the church's unfolding history of adaptive change is highly relevant to our investigation. We will examine the changing nature of the church as well as how the church has changed the way it thinks about mission. We will look at Pentecostalism and the startling fact that by late in the twenty-first century over three-quarters of the people on this planet will be either Christian or Muslim. Learning to love our Muslim neighbor may be the biggest and most important missiological frontier Christians face in this century.

In trying to understand how the church might respond missionally to globalization, I examine the three main theological failings of globalization that I enumerated earlier in this chapter: its flawed anthropology, its misunderstanding of power and its purpose, and its inability to tell us who we are, why we are here, and how we should live. The result is globalization's most fundamental failure: it cannot offer a compelling and satisfying answer to the human need for meaning. This is the work of chapter 12.

Chapter 13 explores two proposals for addressing these limitations of globalization. First, I describe a proposal from Max Stackhouse and his multiyear investigation into globalization. Stackhouse calls for the development of a public theology that offers a spiritual and ethical framework to meet the human need for meaning and also provides a way for the values and processes of globalization to be shaped and corrected. The delivery system for this public theology, according to Stackhouse, is global civil society. I then introduce Catholic social teaching and a proposal from Daniel Groody. Groody's offering parallels Stackhouse's in a number of important ways, but Groody proposes an alternative delivery system: the missional formation of the laity as a result of a discipleship and formation process that is rooted in worship, the sacraments, and spiritual disciplines. While not necessarily disagreeing with Stackhouse on the church's important role in civil society, Groody calls for missionally formed laity whose faith shapes how they vote, consume, and volunteer as Christians. I close with a brief description of James Davison Hunter's observations on how cultures change, and then connect his proposal for cultural change to our discussion of globalization and the work of Groody and Stackhouse.

The final chapter addresses the missiological challenge of globalization. We are used to a missiology of going from here to a place that has not heard the good news, and we assume our good news is the best news there is. I make the observation that, in today's world, the twin globalisms of globalization are making a competing offer of "good news," and, in a sense, globalization is "evangelizing" us. Globalization's good news is material—it can be seen, touched, and taken to the bank. And it is seductive good news, a tempting offer of a better human future with more of everything one could desire. This means that today's mission field is first of all inside our churches. We need to find ways to form and empower adults and children in the pews or in the parish to first recognize the seductions and then resist this alternative "good news." Only by doing this well can we address the mission field just outside the doors of our churches. Each member of our congregation works, lives, and volunteers in a number of institutions, some of which have the power and influence to change culture. They need to be prepared and sustained as "faithful witnesses within" those institutional locations.[17] We need to inoculate and then equip and release the faithful to be witnesses wherever God has placed them.

Questions for Discussion

1. Where would you place your church on a continuum with "disengaged, no interest in globalization" on one extreme and "deeply engaged theologically and missionally with globalization" on the other?

2. What factors might be contributing to your church's location on this continuum?

3. Are you in agreement with your church's current position? What, if anything, would you like to see changed?

---

17. Hunter, *To Change the World*, 197. James Davison Hunter is professor of religion, culture, and social theory at the University of Virginia.

2

Twin Foundations

Before we begin our exploration of globalization, it is helpful to look at two sets of material that are foundational to the argument of this book. These core ideas shape and inform my descriptions of both the trajectory and the impact of globalization. The first is a set of theological affirmations. The second is an introduction to the idea and behavior of complex, adaptive social systems and their importance in helping us make sense out of social change and the process of history unfolding.

Theological Affirmations

The purpose of this section is to lay out some theological affirmations that I will repeatedly draw upon in the course of this book. I make no attempt to offer a systematic theology but rather select those theological insights that will enable us to delve deeply, critically, and Christianly into the topic of globalization.

I write this book from an evangelical perspective. I use the word *evangelical* to describe those who affirm the uniqueness of Christ and the efficacy of his death and resurrection; the need for personal conversion; the importance of the Bible as the narrative about God's work in and intention for the world, and hence as a definitive guide for life; and a commitment to witnessing to the good news of Christ by word, deed, life, and sign. I do not use the word *evangelical* to imply a conflation with conservative political views or to signify a narrow and exclusive set of moral boundaries that are so important that all other ethical issues are to be ignored.

Globalization and God

As will become clear in the next two chapters, we don't yet fully know what we are dealing with when it comes to globalization. A historical process began accelerating in the nineteenth century, picked up speed toward the end of last century, and is accelerating still. Everything we thought we knew and understood about globalization is being disrupted and demands to be reimagined.

I take it for granted that God is the God of history, all of history, and that God's story has an end and a purpose. I take it on faith that God is working on a project of redemption and restoration and thus that nothing in history or in the lives of human beings is outside the scope of God's project.

It follows, then, that I am convinced that God was not and is not surprised by globalization. Nor do I believe that globalization is outside God's project of redeeming and restoring creation. I take it as a given that God's living word and God's church in the world have something to contribute, something important. I hasten to say that making a contribution is not the same as claiming ownership or expecting to have the final say; the time of Christendom is past. Finally, I believe that proclamation by word must always be part of the church's mission, but I wonder if the part about the kingdom, about loving our neighbors and even our enemies, needs some serious renovation.

I should also declare my suspicion toward the assumptions of modernity and postmodernity in the West. It is not true that human beings are the only actors in history, as the modern secular frame assumes. Our choices for understanding human identity cannot be limited to being either autonomous rational actors seeking only what is valuable to us or socially constructed beings with no individual value other than playing our assigned roles in society and living up to societal norms.[1] In addition, while we are grateful for the material improvement in incomes, health, and education during the last two hundred years, there is no evidence that we are improving the human condition when it comes to greed or misuse of power or being driven by our desires to do things that diminish other human beings. Said another way, I do not believe in modernity's myth of inevitable human progress.

---

1. This false choice creates problems in two ways. First, both choices reduce human identity to something unacceptably thin and incomplete, and second, this in turn renders impossible any attempt at imagining a moral ecology.

The Creation Narrative

Two central claims of biblical anthropology are critical for our engagement with globalization and its history—the truth about God and the truth about humankind.[2] This requires three things of us. First, we need to know who God is and what God is doing. Second, we need to understand who human beings are and why we were created, and we need an account of the human condition. Third, we need a clear understanding of what God intended for creation and where God is going as God redeems and restores creation.

We begin with the truth about God. The Bible reveals that God is the creator, sustainer, redeemer, and restorer of creation (Gen. 1:1–2; John 1:1–3; Heb. 1:2–3). Furthermore, God is a relational God—Father, Son, and Holy Spirit—a God whose being and actions are characterized by communication, love, and peace.

What is God doing? Since our great disobedience, God has been carrying out a work of grace that will ultimately redeem and restore God's creation and us, if we so choose, to God's original intent. God is actively working in human history today. This truth about God is a direct challenge to the materialism of globalization and its underlying theology of secular humanism.

Now let's turn to the biblical truth about human beings. A number of observations will serve us well in later parts of this book. The first important truth about human beings comes from the creation account: "So God created human beings in his own image, in the image of God he created them, male and female he created them. God blessed them and said to them, 'Be fruitful and increase in number; fill the earth and subdue it'" (Gen. 1:27–28). God created all human beings in God's image. This truth about human beings has a number of important contributions to make to our conversation about globalization.

We are relational beings. Being made in the image of a relational God means that human beings are intrinsically relational too. There is no warrant in the creation narrative for unbounded individualism. Our identity and vocation are embedded and expressed most fully in our relationships—with God, with each other, with those we call Other, with the natural world in which we live, and within ourselves. We are socially embedded beings intended by God to embody and express love, justice, and peace. Any theological investigation of globalization begins with its implied anthropology, which must be tested against the biblical view of human beings as relational beings.

There are two other important consequences of our being created as relational beings. First, socially embedded human beings create culture as a

2. This is the organizing frame of Catholic social teaching. I find it a useful place to start.

way to help members of the group understand who they are and why they are here. Richard Middleton asserts that "the human calling as *imago Dei* is itself developmental and transformational and may be helpfully understood as equivalent to the labor or work of forming culture or developing civilization."[3] Andy Crouch argues that we are meaning-making and culture-producing beings; both are part of our nature.[4]

Second, relational beings aspire for things that go beyond the needs and desires of an individual alone. Margaret Archer, reflecting on Catholic social teaching, points out that it is only through our relationships, our sociality, that our deepest human needs can be met, including our needs "to love and be loved; to give, to receive and to share; to trust and become worthy of trust; to be recognized for oneself and to confer recognition of the value of the 'other'; to be cared for and to be caring."[5] These relational capabilities are important to individual well-being and are indispensable to a good society. Thus, the presence or absence of these kinds of relational values is a legitimate test of the outcomes of globalization. We will return to Archer's point in chapter 12 as we explore three of the theological failings of globalization.

We have a vocation. God's assertion that we are made in God's image was immediately followed by a statement of what God intended human beings to do—our vocation or mission. We were created to be something and to do something. The mission of all human beings is to contribute to making God's creation productive and fruitful. We were and are intended to partner with God in developing God's creation toward its intended purpose, making it a place where people love God and love their neighbors, with the result that all human beings are able to flourish.

Genesis 2 expands the idea of vocation. The cosmic God in the first chapter of Genesis is now revealed as a hands-on, working, creation-improving God. God formed *adam* from the dust of the ground and later determined that *adam* should not be alone—our relational nature again. God placed *adam* in the garden to nurture it and make it productive—our vocation again. Finally, *adam* was given the ability to recognize the rational order in what God had created and then name the animals accordingly. God stepped aside and allowed us to participate in the productive work of organizing God's world. Culture creating again.

3. Middleton, *Liberating Image*, 89. J. Richard Middleton is professor of biblical worldview and exegesis at Northeastern Seminary.

4. Crouch, *Culture Making*, 22. Andy Crouch is executive editor of *Christianity Today*.

5. Archer, "*Caritas in Veritate*," 289. Margaret Archer is a leading theorist in the critical realist strand of sociology and professor at the École Polytechnique Fédérale de Lausanne (Switzerland). In 2014, Pope Francis named her as president of the Pontifical Academy of Social Sciences.

We are rational. Being made in the image of a rational, order-making God means that we were created with the ability and the responsibility to observe God's world and use our reason to figure out how it works. This element of the creation narrative provides the origin of all modern science—rational human beings figuring out how God's world was created and seeking to make it fruitful for all.

We are creative. In a similar vein, being made in the image of a creator God means that we are able to imagine and create new things. This is the foundational source of the human ability to innovate, which is so critical to the history of human development. From the development of tools and agriculture to the technology that emerged over the last two hundred years, the exploding number of inventions in human history is a result of human creativity that reflects the image of God. We are clever and creative because we are made in the image of a clever and creative God. Thus, part of our vocation is to use imagination, reason, and investigation in ways that make the world more conducive to human flourishing.

We are moral beings. Upon completion of creation, God announced that creation was very good. At the simplest level, this means that creation works as God intended and that God was pleased with God's work. But there is more. The idea of creation being very good also alerts us to the fact that God is a moral agent whose creation reflects this fact. This moral agency raises two additional issues relevant to our engagement with globalization.

First, our being made in the image of a moral God means that we are moral beings too. Being righteous matters to human flourishing, it seems. This also accounts for our moral intuition in favor of fairness, justice, and just behavior. This is one part of the foundation for what ultimately becomes known as the rule of law, a critical element of the emergence of modern globalization and economic growth. The topic of the rule of law will come up again in chapter 5.

Second, our nature as moral beings means that we are neither fully human nor flourishing in the absence of a framework of moral right and wrong. In today's relativistic, postmodern world, the very idea of a moral order has been declared unreasonable and even oppressive. The assessment of globalization is impoverished by this lack. Christians and adherents of other world religions share a concern for what kind of moral order or moral ecology should be employed in assessing the process and outcomes of globalization. We will return to this question in some depth in chapters 13 and 14.

We are part of a covenant. The final time that our being made in the image of God is mentioned in Genesis is instructive. God tells Noah and his children that God is making a covenant with human beings, and then God connects an admonition against killing human beings with the fact that "in the image of

God has God made humankind" (Gen. 9:6). The idea that our relationship with God includes things God will do and things we will do or not do is a second part of the foundation for the rule of law.[6] This rule of law is based on rules inherent in God's moral order.

Furthermore, God's admonition not to take human life implies that God's moral order is centered on preserving or enhancing human life. This is the focus of the Ten Commandments and also Christ's commandment that we are to love God and our neighbor. This suggests that one test of any human institution is the degree to which its actions enable and enrich human life or diminish and destroy human life. This brings us back to human flourishing, which we will explore in a moment.

We are unequally gifted and thus must be interdependent. Often overlooked in the creation account is that creation was not created equal everywhere. Some parts of creation are better suited for farming than others. Some climates are more conducive to human health than others. Furthermore, while every human being is made in the image of God and thus equally valued and loved, everything else about us and our particular contexts seems to reflect an unequal distribution of gifts, talents, and resources. Nothing in the creation account indicates that this was not God's intention.

We all know that some people are smarter or stronger or more relational than others. Not all of us have the gift of leadership. Not all are called and equipped for a life of the mind. Not everyone has the skills and mental gifts necessary to build a home or an artificial knee. James Davison Hunter asserts that these differences in giftedness, intelligence, or physical skill "means that human relations are inherently power relations." He argues this is a good thing, as it forces us toward interdependence; it is a driver for relationality or solidarity.[7]

Accepting inequality of outcomes among humans as normative helps us understand why some people create wealth better than others, why some innovate more effectively, or why some are better at building houses or creating poetry or art. But it must not be used as an argument for inequality so extreme that some struggle to stay alive or to live a life worth living. Inequality among human beings is counterbalanced by the fact that all human beings are made in the image of God, which creates a moral demand that no one, however disabled or lazy or unlucky, no matter how humble their gifts, should have to struggle simply to survive or be denied the opportunity to flourish as much as their gifts allow. We are relational beings commanded to love all our neighbors.

6. Sacks, "Dignity of Difference," 39. Jonathan Sacks is former Chief Rabbi of the United Hebrew Congregations of the Commonwealth and the author of many books.
7. Hunter, *To Change the World*, 178.

Explaining the Human Condition

Sadly, the creation account from which I have derived this Christian anthropology ends with the story of human disobedience and our separation from God and from each other. The consequences of the great disobedience are clearly described. A formerly fruitful creation reluctantly sustains life (Gen. 3:17), and only by hard, backbreaking work (Gen. 3:19). Human life now ends in death (Gen. 3:19). The relationship between men and women is disrupted and becomes unjust (Gen. 3:16). Violence and murder enter the human story (Gen. 4:8), as does the hunger for revenge (Gen. 4:23). Human well-being is now a struggle and beyond the reach of human effort alone. Bad human choices disrupted our relationships with God, with each other, with nature, and within ourselves. We no longer know who we truly are, nor do we faithfully live up to our vocation of tending and improving God's creation.

The story of this great disobedience also provides an explanation for why social institutions and structures fail to live up to their missions, why a ministry of justice too often fails to provide either ministry or justice, or why a church becomes co-opted by its culture or some human ideology. They are fallen too. According to the prophets, these relational failures at the societal level result in both the worship of false gods and the presence of injustice, oppression, and violence in a fallen creation.

There are two more positive lessons in the aftermath of the great disobedience. First, we must recognize the importance of human freedom in this story. Adam and Eve were free to disobey, even though their choice ultimately led to the death of the Son of God. God gives us the freedom to use our reason and creativity for good or for ill, for enhancing life or for diminishing it. The value that God places on human liberty cannot be understated. If our liberty is that valuable to God, so it should be for us.

Second, we must remember that God's love and grace remained in creation after the fall. God gave Adam and Eve clothes and made them leave the garden, thereby preventing them from making the fall permanent (Gen. 3:22). God continued to speak of humans as made in God's image (Gen. 5:1), and after the flood, God reaffirmed the human vocation to be fruitful and productive stewards in creation (Gen. 9:1, 6). Therefore, we must always remember that the human community is an inseparable mixture of original sin and original good.[8] The image of God remained in us even after our great disobedience,

---

8. By original good, I am referring to the God-given ability of human beings to be creative, improve the material world, and act on instincts for the common good. Original sin explains the human propensity toward greed, hunger for power, hedonism, and selfish choices. Our Roman Catholic brothers and sisters are much better at acknowledging our original good than we Protestants are, especially those of us of the Reformed variety.

and as a consequence, God made it possible for us to figure out how to miti-gate the impact of sin and to work for some degree of the common good. Our vocation remains unchanged, while our sin makes us flawed partners working alongside a faithful God.

What Does God Intend?

The question of God's intention for creation is central to our thinking biblically and critically about globalization. Globalization is a set of pro-cesses and outcomes that promises a better human future as well as a way to get there. In a sense, globalization is making human beings in its image. To assess and respond biblically, we have to be clear on what God intends for us and for God's world. Shalom is the theological concept that helps us answer this question. Four aspects of shalom are germane to our discussion of globalization.

First, shalom is a relational idea. Nicholas Wolterstorff describes shalom as "the human being dwelling in peace with all of his or her relationships: with God, with self, with fellows, with nature."[9] Humans flourish when their relationships are peaceful and just, a stance consistent with what we have already noted in the creation narrative.

Second, relationships that are not just are usually not peaceful. In Psalm 85:10 we read, "Mercy and truth have met each other: justice and peace have kissed" (Douay-Rheims). Shalom means having just relationships (living justly and experiencing justice) and enjoying harmonious relationships.

Third, our relationships must be more than just and peaceful; they are intended to be enjoyable as well. God's shalom incorporates the ideas of de-light, enjoyment, and even fun. Wolterstorff argues that shalom at its highest "is *enjoyment* in one's relationships. To experience shalom is to *enjoy* living before God, to *enjoy* living in one's physical surroundings, to *enjoy* living with one's fellows, to *enjoy* life with oneself."[10]

The Bible gives us three sets of images that make God's vision of shalom concrete. The eschatological vision of Isaiah 65 speaks of the restoration of joy and of no more weeping and mourning. Infants do not die young, and the old live out their years. Mothers do not bear children doomed to misfortune. God answers even before people call out. The lamb and the wolf lie down together. The ministry of Jesus was framed in similar terms when he announced that he came to preach good news to the poor and proclaim

9. Wolterstorff, *Until Justice and Peace Embrace*, 69. Nicholas Wolterstorff is former professor of philosophy at Calvin College and former professor of philosophical theology at Yale University.
10. Ibid., 69 (emphasis added).

freedom to prisoners and recovery of sight to the blind (Luke 4:18–19). In Jesus's clearest statement on the connection between salvation and social change, Jesus declares his intention "that they [the people of the world] may have life, and have it to the full" (John 10:10). The vision of John in Revelation is similar. In an urban world, there is no more death, mourning, or pain. God dwells once again among God's people. The seemingly valuable jewels and gold we fight over today are simply beautiful building materials, used for paving streets and decorating walls. In the new Jerusalem, there is life-giving water and healing for the nations. There is no temple; the presence of God and the Lamb is enough. Together these images provide a concrete expression of God's intention for human beings and the world.

Missiologist Lesslie Newbigin reminds us that the church is to be the sign of God's kingdom in the world and that working for shalom is part of that sign.[11] Making the same point in eschatological terms, John Howard Yoder argues that the church is "called to be now what the world is called to be ultimately . . . a foretaste of the peace for which the world was made."[12] Wolterstorff articulates again: "Shalom in the world is both God's cause in the world and our human calling. . . . We are not to stand around, hands folded, waiting for shalom to arrive. We are workers in God's cause, his peace-workers."[13]

This brings us to the issue of how God is doing with God's project of redemption and restoration. From the day we were driven from the garden, God has been at work to find a way home for human beings that satisfies the requirements of both God's love and God's justice. This work culminated in the birth, life, death, and resurrection of Jesus Christ, the Son of God. The kingdom of God embodied in the Son of God entered human history, and the Father, Son, and Holy Spirit are working toward God's final victory. Through Christ, the potential now exists to restore all our broken, strained, unjust, and unhealthy relationships—with God, within ourselves, with our community, with those we call Other, and with nature.

One last note about shalom. This comprehensive idea of peace, justice, and delight is also used in the Bible to convey images of wholeness, unity, and harmony—of something that is complete and sound. Thus, relationships that reflect shalom should include prosperity, health, and human fulfillment.[14] This leads us to some reflections on human flourishing.

11. Newbigin, *Household of God*, 67. Bishop Lesslie Newbigin was a British theologian, missiologist, and missionary.

12. Yoder, *Priestly Kingdom*, 92, 94. John Howard Yoder was an Anabaptist theologian, ethicist, and biblical scholar best known for his masterpiece, *The Politics of Jesus*.

13. Wolterstorff, *Until Justice and Peace Embrace*, 72.

14. Richards, *New International Encyclopedia*, 479.

Human Flourishing

For many of the world's poor, the beginning of well-being is simply staying alive. Food, shelter, and a livelihood that allows for school fees and access to health care are a good place to start. But there is more to life, even for the poor. Africans pray for "life, as well as the means to make life worth living."[15] Being poor and living life on the edge of death are clearly not all that God intends. What, then, does a more fully human life look like? This is both a biological question and a theological question.

Biologically, human flourishing is concerned with the well-being of the body, the mind, and the soul—each are inseparably part of being human. This is why a biblical view of human well-being has a transcendent dimension. We are not flourishing unless all our relationships are just and peaceful to the degree that they can be in a fallen world. This is the foundation of the commandment that we love God and love our neighbors as ourselves.

But our theology suggests something more. Human beings, made in the image of God, are to be creative and productive, nurturing God's creation for the well-being of all. This means two things. First, human beings are to be actors in God's world; human freedom and human agency matter. Second, we need to correct any actions or conditions that diminish human flourishing, and we must ensure that everything that enables human flourishing is available to all. This leads us to questions relating to politics, economics, and civil society. How do these domains promote human well-being and the flourishing of all? What conditions need to be in place to support human health, creativity, and innovation? How do these domains protect those who are too wounded or too excluded to flourish? For the biblical prophets, the test of Israel's social system—its politics, economics, and religion—was the well-being of widows, orphans, and aliens. If the "least of these" are doing well, the rest of society is probably doing well too.

Finally, and perhaps most importantly, because we are made in the image of God, our best life is with God—a life of worship, becoming more like Christ, and being Christlike in the world. So the vision of what God intends to recreate and restore is clear and unambiguous. It is God's intention that we—the world and the church—are to work for human flourishing in this fallen world, emulating what Jesus did during his ministry on earth.

I close this section on flourishing with two notes of caution. First, having too little could mean not having the means to live a life worth living, and thus more wealth and health are positive contributions. But we also need to remember that having too much is an uncertain road to human flourishing as

---

15. Musopole, "African Worldview."

well. While it is true that economic globalization has meant good news for the poor, globalization's twin globalisms—modernity and neoliberal capitalism— have not satisfactorily conveyed the purpose of this increased health and well-being. The answer seems to be simply "more." Yet increasing amounts of money, stuff, and experiences often fails to lead to human flourishing in either a secular or Christian sense. This crisis of meaning as we move toward a world of "more than enough" is something we will address in the final two chapters of this book. This failure to define the purpose of human life is one of the theological limitations of globalization.

Second, the outcomes of shalom and human flourishing are clear—peace, justice, enjoyment, and flourishing. However, the biblical account is less clear about how to create these conditions. Each of us can do our best to live up to these values and outcomes in our personal lives, and that is a good thing. But, as far as I can discern, there is no clear prescription in Scripture for how these good things are to be created by governments, social institutions, and what we now call the private sector.

In today's postmodern world, we seem to be faced with only two choices. On the one hand, some encourage us to distrust the state and place our trust in individual choice and the private sector; this is the path toward liberty and economic growth. On the other hand, others encourage us not to trust individuals, with their desires and their tendencies toward inequality and even violence, in favor of a strong state that reins us in through laws and regulation; this is the path to equality and justice. I believe we need to do more theological work on this question. It is not clear to me that relational human beings who love God and their neighbors will ever be produced by either the market or the state, but it is less clear in today's globalizing world that we have anywhere else to turn. We will come back to this in chapter 13.

Complex Adaptive Social Systems[16]

> Life is understood backwards, but must be lived forwards.
>
> —Sören Kierkegaard, cited in Bak, *How Nature Works*, 8.

I need to declare my understanding about how historical change takes place. First, as a Christian, I take it as a given that God is the God of history and that God is creating the future. The more difficult question is, how does God work in history to pursue God's ends? Whether your theology of

16. Some of this material was adapted from Myers, "How Did Britain Develop?"

creation argues for light out of darkness and the Holy Spirit hovering over the deep or for the idea of a Big Bang and evolution, everything that followed the beginning of the world is a story of adaptation, change, new directions, and unexpected turns and outcomes. History is a series of unforeseen discontinuities, as empires come and go, nations rise and fall, new ideas emerge and disappear. The singular characteristic of historical change is that it can only be described and analyzed by looking back in time; its future has always been unpredictable. Why?

One possible answer lies in the recent understanding of what are called complex or dynamical systems. These are systems of such complexity, with so many moving parts and feedback loops, that they are intrinsically unpredictable. By simplifying assumptions, we can create models that explain the past, but they do not enable us to make accurate predictions. Complex systems develop counterintuitively, and this means they cannot be managed or controlled.

It gets worse. Complex adaptive social systems made up of large numbers of human beings—cities, states, and the world—take this uncertainty and ambiguity to an even higher level.[17] Civilizations, societies, and cultures are made up of self-aware people who do not have to follow rules in the way that atoms and molecules must in mechanical systems. Everyone in a social system is an actor and gets to choose how they will behave. Sometimes the choices of individuals are rational and predictable, and sometimes they are not. People adjust, usefully or not, to what is going on around them. All of these largely unrestrained choices mean that social systems are more than dynamical or complex; they are also adaptive. Examples of adaptive social systems include economies, stock markets, political parties, geopolitical organizations, and terrorist networks. The only consistent feature of adaptive social systems is their unpredictability and the resulting failure of efforts to "manage" these kinds of systems toward predetermined goals.

As an example of an unmanageable social system, think of the challenge of feeding the people in New York City. Every day millions of people live and go to work with little or no knowledge about who is going to bring the tomatoes, flour, meat, milk, and thousands of other foodstuffs into the city that day. Yet somehow tens of thousands of other people inside and outside the city, working with no master plan or central coordination, solve this daily logistical nightmare. Some who are supposed to deliver food get sick. Farmers wake up to ruined crops, trucks break down, and restaurants close. Yet somehow this unmanaged system adapts to the challenges and opportunities of each day, and every restaurant and home has the food it prefers on

17. Gunderson and Holling, *Panarchy*.

its table for the most part. The result is neither perfect nor just. It fails too many people, and the system incurs a lot of waste. But the fact remains that this enormously complex logistical challenge is neither master-planned nor coordinated centrally, yet it happens every day. If we cannot manage the flow of food into New York, on what grounds do we assume we can "manage" or "direct" the economics and politics of the entire world?

High levels of complexity and continuous adaptation do not mean that systems involving large numbers of human beings are eternally chaotic. Structure can and does emerge. Imagine pouring sand on a sand pile. For a time, the sand pile *organizes itself* into a cone that grows higher and higher. The sand pile appears to be a stable structure. Then, unpredictably and without warning, the next grains of sand hit the cone and the cone collapses. But as you continue to pour more sand on the collapsed pile, it begins to self-organize into a cone once again.[18] Thus, structure in complex social systems emerges (and also goes away) unexpectedly. I will use the concept of emergence a great deal in this book and particularly in chapters 5 and 6 (on the First and Second Eras of Globalization) and in chapter 13 (on Christian engagement with globalization).

Niall Ferguson has applied the idea of adaptive social systems to the unfolding of history. Setting aside traditional explanations of historical change involving arbitrarily named epochs, the work of great men or the result of great ideas, Ferguson wonders "if history is not cyclical and slow-moving, but arrhythmic—sometimes almost stationary, but also capable of violent acceleration."[19] New historical directions (structure) do emerge, unexpectedly and unbidden, triggered by constellations of relatively small events. These seemingly stable new structures break down unpredictably as well. As we will see in chapter 5, Britain's economic and social transformation emerged from very little, coalesced and grew into a global empire, and then collapsed rather quickly at the end of World War II. Global economic growth seemed inevitable in the mid-2000s, only to collapse with the Great Recession of 2008–9. The Arab Spring emerged unexpectedly in 2010 and is now in the midst of a chaotic aftermath. The shape or timing of a future emergent order in the Muslim world is unknown, yet the international community aspires to "manage" the situation.

So how does the reality of complex adaptive social systems help us with our investigation of globalization? First, the history of globalization fits

18. Adapted from Bak, *How Nature Works*, 32.
19. Ferguson, *Civilization*, 299. Niall Ferguson is professor of history at Harvard University and a senior fellow at the Hoover Institution, Stanford University.

Ferguson's proposal for historical change as the unpredictable unfolding of a complex adaptive social system. David Held argues that "globalization as a historical process cannot be characterized by an evolutionary logic or an emergent telos. Historical patterns of globalization have been punctuated by great shifts and reversals."[20] The starts and stops, the successes and crashes, the comings and goings that seem typical of human history now have an explanation that will be useful as we examine the history of globalization and some of its characteristics.

Second, since structure emerges from within such systems, as opposed to being caused by external direction, we need to pay more attention to what is actually happening in a social system and spend less time and money trying to impose structure or change from the outside. Instead of trying to manage globalization, we might pursue a strategy of rewarding emerging structures we deem good with attention, affirmation, or increased allegiance while withholding these things if what is emerging does not appear to be helpful or lifegiving. However, pursuing a strategy of encouraging the good and starving the bad assumes that a common moral system or moral criteria could be used to make these value judgments. As we shall see later, especially in chapter 12 (on the theological limitations of globalization), this is not an easy question to answer in the postmodern world.

Third, our inability to control and direct globalization should not be a surprise to us as Christians. We do not believe that human beings can manage, redeem, or restore a creation that we did not make and whose condition is a result of our failures. We sometimes succumb to modernity's myth of human progress and hope for positive outcomes from efforts to make peace and increase social justice. But we have always known that only God, who created this world and is redeeming it, is in charge. The bottom line is that we Christians must be humble before the complexity of globalization. We lack the language, categories, and godlike perspective to make sense of it all. This is where faith comes into play. None of this ambiguity and seeming confusion is unintelligible to God. In fact, somehow God is at work in this bewildering, unpredictable world. From this perspective, faith can be seen an asset as well as the only adequate response.

Fourth, an understanding of history as discontinuous and unpredictable may help us to be more appreciative of the history of the church with its geographical, theological, and ecclesial wanderings over the centuries. The

20. Held et al., *Global Transformations*, 414. David Held is professor of politics and international relations and master of University College at Durham University; Held is a major globalization scholar.

history of the church should be understood as a story of Holy Spirit–directed adaptive change within the complex adaptive social systems of the world. This perspective should give us a sense of optimism that God and the church will continue to adapt creatively today and, with God's help, the church will continue to play its God-given missional role in the world even in a very ambiguous future.

Finally, I wonder if it might be the case that God chooses to work through the adjustments and adaptations of complex adaptive social systems. Might this be God's preferred method for guiding human history toward its ultimate goal? Such a process of change allows God to be God and yet provides an essential role for human beings. There is space for God to guide creation toward God's ultimate goal while we human beings contribute meaningfully through our creativity, imagination, reason, and observation, despite our sin. This is consistent with God's deep and abiding commitment to human freedom, to human agency, and to our being God's partners as cocreators.

Questions for Discussion

1. What elements of the theological affirmations in this chapter are most appealing to you? Why?
2. Which elements are most troubling? Why?
3. Are there other theological affirmations critical to assessing globalization that are missing?

Section 2

INTRODUCING GLOBALIZATION

3

Understanding Globalization

In this chapter I will explore the complicated and sometimes paradoxical world of globalization, including its processes and outcomes. What is it? What is it doing? I will introduce two metaphors that may help readers understand why globalization is so complex and hard to define. I will then examine how globalization is being perceived and changed "from below." The chapter closes with a brief examination of the dynamic domains of globalization—technology, economics, governance, culture, and human beings in large numbers.

The Problem of Definitions

> The debate about what to do about globalization is still very much a debate about what globalization is.
>
> —V. S. A. Kumar[1]

I begin with what is normally a straightforward preliminary—a definition. It would be helpful to have a simple and clear definition of *globalization*. Sadly, this is not possible; we are faced instead with complexity and ambiguity.

An Amazon search for books on globalization returns over 41,000 listings. Googling the phrase "definitions of globalization" is overwhelming with nearly

1. Kumar, "Critical Methodology of Globalization," 87.

300,000 results. One academic research effort to summarize definitions of globalization from historians, sociologists, economists, political scientists, and other scholars identified 114 different definitions.[2] Drawing from this study, I have selected some examples to highlight the varying perspectives as well as the multidimensional nature of the globalization conversation.

- "I define globalization as producing where it is most cost-effective, selling where it is most profitable, sourcing capital from where it is without worrying about national boundaries" (Narayama Murthy, cofounder and CEO of Infosys, India).[3]
- "The world is becoming a global shopping mall in which ideas and products are available everywhere at the same time" (Rosabeth Moss Kantor, Harvard Business School professor).
- "Globalization is the process of world shrinkage, of distances getting shorter, things moving closer. It pertains to the increasing ease with which somebody on one side of the world can interact to mutual benefit with somebody on the other side of the world" (Thomas Larsson, Swedish journalist).
- "Globalization is what we in the Third World have for several centuries called colonization" (Martin Khor, president of Third World Network).
- "'Globalization' is a myth suitable for a world without illusions, but it is also one that robs us of hope" (Paul Hirst and Grahame Thompson, globalization skeptics).
- "Globalization is the establishment of the global market free from sociopolitical control" (Pavel Nikitin and John Elliot, anti-globalizationists).
- "Globalization is the latest stage in a long accumulation of technological advances which have given human beings the ability to conduct their affairs across the world without reference to nationality, government authority, or time of day or physical environment" (Richard Langhorne, technologist).
- "Globalization is a historical process, underway for centuries, of increasing interconnectedness of economic and cultural life in distant parts of the world" (John Gray, historian of ideas).
- "Globalization is the widening, deepening and speeding up of worldwide interconnectedness in all aspects of contemporary social life, from

2. Al-Rodhan, *Definitions of Globalization*, 6.
3. "Interview: Narayana Murthy," *PBS: Commanding Heights* (blog), February 5, 2001, http://www.pbs.org/wgbh/commandingheights/shared/minitext/int_narayanamurthy.html.

the cultural to the criminal, the financial to the spiritual" (David Held, globalization scholar).[4]

This sampling of definitions shows that globalization is an enormously complex and multidimensional topic. Globalization is commonly connected to issues of economics, trade, finance, environment, culture, crime, disease, and religion. Sometimes globalization is a noun—something that is. Sometimes it is a verb—something that is acting upon us. Sometimes it is a verb personified—someone who is doing something to us.

For some, globalization is something suspect, even evil. It must be resisted, even stopped, because it is an imposition of processes and values by the powerful over the less fortunate, and it is a threat to the well-being of God's creation. Globalization means losing local cultures and increasing inequality. For others, globalization is the way to the promised land of material progress for the poor, democracy, human rights, and eventual peace. One's view of globalization tends to be shaped by what one cares most about—political ideology, cultural values, socioeconomic status, ethnicity, or religious perspective.

Globalization is on everyone's lips, a fad word fast turning into a shibboleth, a magic incantation, a passkey meant to unlock the gates to all mysteries. "For some, 'globalization' is what we are bound to do if we wish to be happy. For others, 'globalization' is the cause of our unhappiness. For everybody, though, 'globalization' is the intractable fate of the world, an irreversible process."[5] Yet definitions matter. One cannot discuss or assess something whose nature and dynamics are different for different people. Such is the case when exploring globalization today. So we must fully explore the idea of globalization; in doing so, the hope is that things will become somewhat clearer. The following two metaphors may help.

Metaphors for Globalization

First, we need to find a way to enlarge our perspective so that we can grasp the multidimensionality of globalization. One way to do this is to think about globalization as a gemstone with many facets. All the facets contribute to the beauty and integrity of the whole gem, but each is distinct. The many facets of globalization include economics, finance, politics and governance, religion, crime, disease, culture, technology, and the like. There is no comprehensive account of globalization without all these facets in view. Said

4. All definitions from Al-Rodhan, *Definitions of Globalization*, 9–20.
5. Bauman, *Globalization*, 1. Zygmunt Bauman is a retired professor of sociology at the University of Leeds.

another way, focusing on one facet to the exclusion of the others unhelpfully reduces the interactive, multifaceted nature of globalization and hence leads us astray.

We must also cultivate an awareness of the differing academic disciplines that are trying to make sense of globalization. Sadly, having many conversation partners seems to muddle the topic. "Scholars not only hold different views with regard to proper definitions of globalization, they also disagree on its scale, causation, chronology, impact, trajectories and policy outcomes."[6]

This leads us to our second metaphor for globalization. Some have turned to the Hindu parable of the blind men and the elephant for help.[7] Each blind man is busy announcing what he deduces the globalization elephant looks like on the basis of the part of the elephant he can touch. Sociologists, political scientists, cultural critics, theologians, economists, and anthropologists all focus narrowly on those social processes most central to their field of interest or their ideological concerns. Each develops a definition, description, or assessment from that part of the globalization elephant they can touch. Everyone speaks to that bit of globalization that they know best, and because they are scholars, they tend to argue endlessly past one another.

It is beyond the scope of this book to try to resolve these conflicting conversations. For our purposes, the lesson is simple. We must not assume that we know what someone is talking about when they refer to globalization in generic terms. We will have to read more deeply or ask further questions to figure out what discipline or theological/ideological perspective the author favors and make our assessment accordingly.

Charity demands one final observation. Most of the confusion around language and conceptualization is not the product of incompetence or poor scholarship. Most scholars and social commentators are doing their best to make sense of a worldwide process of increasingly rapid change whose ultimate future we simply do not know. We need to relax, take a deep breath, and be gracious as we explore this subject.

It may help to remember that the Industrial Revolution began in Britain in 1760, yet the term and concept "Industrial Revolution" did not show up in print until the mid-1800s, some eighty years later.[8] "Classical economists

6. Steger, *Globalization*, 11. Manfred Steger is professor of sociology at the University of Hawaii at Manoa and was formerly professor of global studies and director of the Globalism Research Centre at RMIT University in Australia.

7. Hanciles, *Beyond Christendom*, 65; Steger, *Globalization*, 12. Jehu Hanciles is associate professor of world Christianity at Candler School of Theology at Emory University and has done considerable research on contemporary migration. LCWE, "Globalization and the Gospel."

8. Hawke, "Reinterpretations of the Industial Revolution," 54.

were not merely unaware of changes going on around them. . . . They were in fact committed to a view that ruled out the possibility [of an Industrial Revolution]."[9] When social change is profound and deep, and has not worked itself out fully in history, scholars and experts may be forgiven if the results of their efforts are incoherent and contradictory at times. We will all be a lot clearer on globalization in twenty-five years or so.

The Outcomes and Processes of Globalization

It is helpful to think of globalization as both an outcome and a family of processes. The first outcome of globalization is that people, images, ideas, news, contagious diseases, crime, and pornography, as well as goods, services, and money, are all moving faster and more freely around the world. Economies, cultures, and politics are no longer embedded within national boundaries but are increasingly connected and global as a result of the rapid exchange of information, money, and ideas.[10] The second outcome of globalization is that our understanding of the world is changing in favor of what some call a new global imaginary.[11] This second outcome will be easier to understand if we first name the processes of globalization.

Manfred Steger, in his helpful and accessible book *Globalization: A Very Short Introduction*, suggests that globalization consists of three major processes that are changing our social condition. First, he talks of *expanding connections* across the traditional boundaries of nations, cultures, politics, and economics. Amazon and YouTube operate globally and digitally out of reach of national governance, while treating all cultures as if they were the same. Second, Steger points to the *stretching and expanding* of our social relations. Financial markets reach around the globe, and we can wire money to anyone, anywhere, at any time. Our computers and our T-shirts are assembled in a global supply chain that includes a number of nations. Tearfund, Compassion International, and World Vision International alert us to humanitarian emergencies and help us respond to victims anywhere in the world.

Third, Steger describes the *intensifying and accelerating* of our social relations. "The local and the global intermingle."[12] Communications technology means communicating with anyone, anywhere, anytime on Skype or announcing your personal news to anyone who is a Facebook friend or a

---

9. Anthony Wrigley quoted in McCloskey, *Bourgeois Dignity*, 89.
10. Summarized from Held, *Globalizing World?*, 6.
11. Steger, *Globalization*, 10.
12. Ibid., 15.

A Relief Worker in a Globalizing World

Ben Ramalingam, research fellow at the Institute
of Development Studies (UK)

[As I sit in this disaster setting, I] look at my notepad, my pen, my mobile
phone, which vibrates occasionally as SMS messages arrive, the bag contain-
ing my scratched and battered laptop slung across the back of my chair. The
laptop: Korea for manufactured components, China for the assembly, Japan
for the marketing, and India for the case. The phone is American, powered
by chips made from metals mined in the Democratic Republic of Congo. My
pen is from a German firm but was made in Taiwan. The notepad I picked
up at a small shop on my way through Denpasar, Bali's capital—it was made
in China. . . .

As I sketch, sip, chew, text, and reflect, I am actively participating in a
global network of trade relations and value chains, of purchases and legal
obligations, of brand identities and cultural symbols.

Ramalingam, *Aid on the Edge of Chaos*, x

Twitter follower. The internet and global media bring the news of refugees
fleeing their homelands to our phones and into our homes. Our local lives
are affected daily by events taking place a world away from us. Coming
online at a dizzying pace, technological and communications innovations
are reshaping the social world in which human beings live. In this sense we
need to remember that globalization is a relational phenomenon, not just
a technical one.[13]

The words *expanding, stretching, intensifying*, and *accelerating* describe
the change processes of globalization. But these dynamics of change also
create the second major outcome of globalization. Globalization is not just
changing the world; it is changing us and the way we view the world. While
we tend to remain rooted in our local and national identities, the "death of
distance" made possible by communications technology and the resulting
sense of global connectedness means that we cannot escape developing a
global way of viewing, thinking about, and experiencing the world. We are
learning new things, and we are learning in new ways. We are changing how
we consume and interact. We know more about more cultures, we interact with

13. Kalu and Low, *Interpreting Contemporary Christianity*, 6.

more people unlike ourselves, we are more globally aware. We are developing a new global imagination, and we like it.[14]

Having said all this, it is also true that the sheer speed of change today creates a set of new problems. A functioning society requires, among many other things, that its people, innovations, markets, and government can keep pace with each other at least well enough to create conditions and rules that make sense for the most part and that work tolerably well. Yet regulations regarding technology and markets often lag years behind a technological world that updates itself every few years. For example, the US Senate took four years to develop and pass a cybersecurity bill that was out of date by the time it was passed in 2015.[15] Technological change alone is making the world so small so quickly that it is not clear whether coherent societal processes can keep up. Robin Niblett, director of the Chatham House think tank in London, observes, "Globalization has helped raise hundreds of millions of people out of poverty, but it's moving faster than people and states can adapt to, politically, socially and institutionally. As a result, levels of trust between governments and citizens are fraying."[16] The political developments of 2016—the vote by Britain to leave the EU (Brexit) and Trump's election in the US—are clear evidence of this.

We have globalized trade and manufacturing, and we have introduced robots and artificial intelligence systems, far faster than we have designed the social safety nets, trade surge protectors and educational advancement options that would allow people caught in this transition to have the time, space and tools to thrive. It's left a lot of people dizzy and dislocated.[17]

Globalization from Below

Much of what has been summarized thus far reflects a perspective of globalization "from above"—global economics, global governance, globally connecting technology, and the like. We also need to pay attention to how globalization is experienced and understood "from below"[18] in terms of its impact on local economics, politics, and culture.

From the perspective of the location of decisions being made about their world, the rural poor and urban slum dwellers are seeing their local livelihoods

14. Steger, *Globalization*, 10, 15.
15. Sanger and Perlroth, "Senate Approves a Cybersecurity Bill."
16. Quoted in Fidler, "Globalization."
17. T. Friedman, "You Break It, You Own It," A6.
18. Mittelman, *Globalization Syndrome*. James Mittelman is professor emeritus of international affairs at American University.

Questions from Below

Olúf̣ẹmi Táíwò, professor at the Africana Studies and Research Center, Cornell University

If globalization is about anything at all, it is about movement, motion, and dynamism—the movement of peoples, ideas, services, kindness, vices, crimes and exploitation. . . . It is not a self-actuating activity. It is always something anchored on some actor or another, be it a person, a group of persons, an institution, a country, and so on. . . . Whenever we talk about globalization, we cannot escape some reference, direct or oblique, to the issue of *who* is doing the globalizing.

. . . The question of what the *object* of globalization is can be posed in at least two ways. The first refers to *what* is being globalized . . . what is being moved from one location to another. . . . Candidates range from cultural forms to economic institutions and ideologies. The second refers to purpose. . . . Here the reference turns on the *why* of globalization. . . . The desire to globalize, that is, the desire to cover the globe, to ensure the distribution of whatever the object is to all the nooks and crannies of the globe.

Táíwò, *Colonialism*, 238

---

change as countries in the Global South adjust to global markets and their demand for new skills and higher quality. Politically, confidence in one's local government and even national government is being undermined as more distant global decision makers influence local life.

From the perspective of what is shaping culture, local values often give way to those associated with the "successful" West. Internet access brings news and weather reports while making communication with distant relatives easier, but it also brings pornography and gambling within easy reach.

From the perspective of an emerging economic powerhouse like China, which is very sensitive to having lost its primacy on the world stage when Britain forced it to open its borders to trade in the Opium Wars in the mid-nineteenth century, today's globalization is seen as a *globalization by a minority*. Globalization as the West understands it is neither a gospel for the world nor inevitable in the eyes of the Chinese.[19]

19. Han, "Analytical Remarks of Anti-Economic Globalism."

Who Is Changing Whom?

Jehu Hanciles, professor of world Christianity, Candler School of Theology at Emory University

Recent decades have witnessed a dramatic rise in the spread and pervasiveness of the values associated with Western secular society. Much less attention has been paid to the impulses and initiatives in the reverse directions; impulses that, principally through massive immigration movements, significantly extend the reach and penetration of religious activities associated with non-Western societies. But such movements—conceived of as "alternative globalizations" or globalization from below—have received short shrift in the globalization discourse. . . .

The processes of globalization are collapsing distance and juxtaposing cultures in an unprecedented fashion and, for Western societies, posing profound questions related to cultural identity and managing religious plurality.

Hanciles, *Beyond Christendom*, 46–47, 377

The perspective "from below" also arises from the impact of what has been called "globalization across time." The world of the twenty-first century and the values of modern globalization are anathema to countries and cultures that passionately disagree that emulating the globalization of the contemporary West will result in a better human future. Boko Haram, the Taliban, and al-Qaeda look back to a pristine eighth-century vision of Islam as a desperately needed alternative to what they see as apostate Western modernization. Putin's Russia longs nostalgically for the great power era of the czars. Kim Jong Un of North Korea and Nicolás Maduro of Venezuela are struggling to recover the "successes" of totalitarianism and socialism.

An important irony exists in our understanding of globalization from below. Change brought on by globalization is not a one-way street from the West to the rest. The West is also being changed as a result of globalization from below. People are moving in all directions—from places of poverty and violence to the developed world. Some are refugees fleeing violence, and others are economic migrants trying to find a better future for their families. These refugees and migrants are often religious people with a religious outlook that shapes the way they live and, in the case of some Muslims, the way they wish to be governed. This leads Jehu Hanciles to argue that the combination of migration and religious expansion represents "the most fundamental cultural divide of the new global order."[20] The contemporary fear directed at Muslims in Europe and the United States is a case in point.

The Dark Side of Globalization

The processes and outcomes of globalization are tools that can be used for good or for ill. This has become an especially acute problem in Globalization II (from the late 1980s to today). On the economic side of globalization, unfettered trade, along with the easy movement of money in the global financial system, enabled the trade of automobiles and drugs. Globalization's technology—the internet, encryption, cell phones, digital copying—sped up and empowered both legitimate and illegal activity. The Washington Consensus of the late 1990s resulted in smaller governments, underpaid bureaucracies, less law enforcement, and more corruption.[21] The adversary of criminal behavior—the state—was starved for resources.[22]

The enabling power of today's globalization has increased the sales and reach of human activities that are not good for health or well-being. Five of the top global markets for Johnnie Walker Whisky now include Brazil, Mexico, Thailand, China, and global travel hubs in Asia and the Middle East.[23] Online gambling has globalized with over 150 million people—mostly in the United States, Europe, and East Asia—wagering in excess of $140 million in 2013.[24] Online pornography is considered by some to be the first consistently successful e-commerce product.[25] There were over forty-two thousand sex-related internet sites in 2010. The bad news is that global pornography sales were over $20 million (half in the United States) in 2010. Revenues for pornography were cut by half in the past five years, which would otherwise be good news except that this is only the result of increasing amounts of free pornography on the internet.[26]

---

20. Hanciles, *Beyond Christendom*, 46.
21. The Washington Consensus was a product of the neoliberal economic policies of the Thatcher-Reagan era. It was imposed by the World Bank and the International Monetary Fund as a condition for poor nations receiving loans. It called for reducing public expenditures, extensive privatization of government businesses and services, trade liberalization, floating exchange rates, and deregulation. We will explore this in more depth in chaps. 8 and 9.
22. This argument is a summary of that made in Naím, *Illicit*.
23. Molawi, "Straight Up."
24. Statista, "Size of the Online Gaming Market from 2003 to 2015."
25. Hughes, "Internet: Pornography and Predators."
26. Covenant Eyes, *Pornography Statistics*.

Then there is another major problem concerning globalization and criminal activity. In addition to secure communications, anonymous money transfers, and the "dark web," which promises drug dealers, gun runners, and pedophiles a safe, anonymous place to carry out their illegal work,[27] the absence of the globalization of law enforcement and border controls creates plenty of space for all manner of transnational organized crime to flourish. Gangs have globalized—Russian, Nigerian, American, Italian, Chinese, and Central American—and are now working across borders. Counterfeiting goods (fake pharmaceuticals and knockoff clothing, machines, and technology), along with piracy of web videos, software, video games, and books, was projected to be a $1.2–1.7 trillion underground economy in 2015. Drug trafficking, smuggling migrants, and trafficking in firearms, young girls, and body parts is a $950 billion business annually. All of this illegal activity is enabled by a $1.6 trillion global money laundering system that allows for anonymity in financial transactions.[28] Global corruption is estimated at $2.6 trillion, of which $1 trillion takes the form of bribery.[29] Corruption diverts funds from development, and bribes are often the price the poor have to pay for services that should be free. Taken together, this criminal activity accounts for more than 12 percent of the world's GDP.[30]

Terrorism is both a product and a driver of globalization. Although its message is a conservative anti-globalization call to an earlier, purer world, terrorism functions very much like most modern businesses.[31] Al-Qaeda and the Islamic State are highly decentralized network organizations operating through what look a lot like franchises. The key to creating terror is to be a media-savvy, strategic marketer of the terrorism brand. Terror networks are dependent on the technological side of globalization for their operations and recruitment—satellite phones, internet, encrypted communications, and social media. Their fundraising and the financing of their operations rely

27. *Economist*, "Amazons of the Dark Net"; McKim, "Privacy Software, Criminal Use."
28. UNODC, "Illicit Money."
29. OECD, "Rationale for Fighting Corruption."
30. Consolidated figures from the following sources:
     Fraud: Gee and Button, *Financial Cost of Fraud 2015*.
     Corruption and bribery: OECD, "Rationale for Fighting Corruption."
     Transnational organized crime: UNODC, "New UNODC Campaign."
     Counterfeit goods and piracy: Peasgood, "Counterfeiting Conundrum."
     Gambling: Singh, "Illegal Sports Betting."
     Cybercrime: Nakashima and Peterson, "Report."
     Drug trafficking: Ellyatt, "Global Drugs Trade."
     Prostitution: Havocscope, "Prostitution Statistics."
     Piracy: Raustiala and Sprigman, "Music and Movie Piracy."
31. Kepel, *War for the Muslim Mind*.

on globalization's anonymous international financial system and an ancient money-transfer system, *Hawala*, developed in the First Era of Globalization. Without the tools of Western globalization, it is hard to see how terrorism could sustain a global reach.

Intriguingly, terrorism has evolved into a driver for an alternative form of globalization standing over against the globalization I am describing in this book. Today's globalization is perceived by many Muslims to be impure and ungodly, and it is being resisted throughout the Muslim world. Al-Qaeda and the Islamic State are offering an alternative globalization, an eschatological vision of a reestablished Muslim global caliphate. I will say more about this "clash of globalizations" at the end of chapter 8.

At the end of the day, an argument can be made that one of the outcomes of globalization is that the world is less safe because globalization empowers those who reject good governance; creates economic shelter for rebels, crooks, and terrorists; stimulates corruption; contributes to global instability; and impairs development.[32] This is the dark side of globalization.

The Dynamic Domains of Globalization

There are five interacting and reinforcing domains of globalization: technology, economics, governance, culture, and human beings in large numbers. The first four are obvious, but human beings as a group seldom makes the list. I'll explain why this is a critical addition in subsequent discussion.

Technology

From developing metal tools and agriculture to digging canals to direct water flow and creating the tools to build large buildings, technological innovation has been a central, enabling factor in the long history of human material development. In the First Era of Globalization, an era of migration and empires (as we shall see in chap. 5), ships, steam engines, and railways were critical to immigrants and militaries moving across the globe. In the nineteenth century, technology made human work easier and more productive as machine labor replaced human physical labor. Machines like the grain table and sewing machine enabled us to be more productive, and internal combustion engines meant machines could deliver large loads over long distances. In addition to making human life easier, this wave of technological innovation also increased the connectedness between people and nations as ships, the

32. Naím, *Illicit*.

telephone, and the telegraph enabled easy and fast communication, thus allowing businesses to operate at a distance.

While technological change has always been part of the human story, it was the technological innovation in the last part of the twentieth century that boosted globalization into an entirely new gear with a far greater reach. Billions of individuals, all manner of civil society organizations and terrorist movements, as well as governments, financial institutions, and transnational corporations use wireless communication, digital and social media, and online social networking tools to create a world full of horizontal networks in numbers unimaginable even a quarter century ago.[33]

It is important to note that the period of Globalization II, which began in the late 1980s, coincided with the emergence of the neoliberal expression of capitalism as the only remaining viable economic system. When digital technology met global capitalism, the impact was complicated, uneven, and breathtaking. The domain of technology reinforced the domain of economics.

We need to remember that technology is not just a dynamic domain in the West. As aid agencies helped men replace their simple fishing boats in the aftermath of the 2004 Asia tsunami, South Indian women begged for cell phones so they could go to internet cafes to view satellite images of the ocean in order to call their husbands with directions to the best catch and to the ports with the best prices for their fish. Or consider these modern phenomena: A red-robed Masai tribesman, wearing flip-flops made out of recycled tire tread, has a cell phone tucked into his enlarged ear lobe so he can check the weather and the London price of tanzanite. Neo-Pentecostal pastors of poor urban churches in Ghana spend time on Saturdays downloading sermon ideas from Ghanaian churches in London and Los Angeles. New things are afoot, and the world is getting smaller before our eyes.

Economics

In human history, a central task of living required that people find ways to procure what their families needed to stay alive—food, shelter, and the like. For a long time, families did all these things for themselves, or they were done in small bands or tribes. But as people began to aggregate into villages and cities, the task of producing and distributing what people needed became more and more complicated. The ideas of markets and trading arose, although for most of human history this took place in relatively simple ways.

33. Steger, *Globalization*, 35.

One of the defining characteristics of the transition to the Second Era of Globalization at the beginning of the nineteenth century was the emergence of Britain and the world's first modern economy based on the principles proposed by Adam Smith for how a national economy might work. Things that people had made by hand were made by machines and then were mass produced. Markets moved from towns to cities to the nation and are now global. Most things you buy today are products of global supply chains and often come from far away, made by people you do not know.

Capitalism was the norm in the modernizing West in the nineteenth and twentieth centuries, creating wealth and thus new capital to invest in economic growth. However, as we will see in more detail in chapter 6, competing theories of political economies emerged in the aftermath of World War I. The Great Depression led to reversing free trade among nations, and capitalism was under siege. Then fascism fell away with the end of World War II, and communism with the end of the Cold War in 1989. For the last thirty years, a particular expression of capitalism— neoliberalism and its commitment to global free trade—has been the economic driver of today's globalization.

The economic dimension of globalization is characterized by the flow of capital from city bankers to national governments and now to global financial institutions working in cyberspace, largely unfettered by national governments. This in turn enables increasing global trade in goods and services. The institutions necessary for capitalism to function effectively followed suit, moving from family businesses to national firms to transnational corporations and regional trading systems. All of this was enabled by the development of global institutions, established after World War II, to encourage economic growth with loans for the reconstruction of Europe and eventually to help poor nations in the Global South to develop (World Bank), maintain a reliable system of currency exchange (International Monetary Fund), and develop and oversee rules governing global trade (eventually known as the World Trade Organization).[34] This economic dimension of today's globalization would not have been possible without the technological dimension of globalization with its global communications and the World Wide Web.

The result of all this is a global market system that allows for the global movement of things, people, and ideas. Underlying beliefs in free trade, unrestrained flow of capital, and easily convertible currencies make this possible. This is the heart of economic globalization.

34. Ibid., 38–39.

Governance

The governing of societies has necessarily evolved over time.[35] For most of the First Era of Globalization, the governance model was that of the tribe and then the empire. Empires were created and ruled by conquerors, and their power—military and economic—was centralized; the resources for keeping order and seeking new conquests came from taxes and tribute. But empires lacked an adequate political model and the administrative ability to extend and sustain military power, and thus empires came and went.

From the fifteenth to eighteenth centuries, governance in the West was provided by princes and kings who claimed that their positions and laws were ordained by God. The unintended consequence was a centralization of economics and financial arrangements and a monopolization of military power that resulted in the emergence of a sense of national identity defined by territory and culture. It was but a short step to the idea of the modern nation-state and even the idea of an emerging society of states. To claim autonomy for one's country meant having to concede the claims of autonomy of other countries. This led to a new conception of international law embodied in the Treaty of Westphalia in 1648.

The European nation-states were also empires that, as we will see, were the catalytic agents of the Second Era of Globalization. The emergence of modern technology—fast ships, telegraph, and telephone—allowed for the management of very large overseas territories and trade between colonies and their home countries. But just as the absolute claims of monarchies contained the seeds of their own destruction, these new forms of information and communications technology, along with the increasing power of international trade and a global market system, eventually began to undermine the sovereign claims of the nation-state. Globalization changed and is changing the governance structures of the world.

After two world wars between nation-states, confidence in the Westphalian nation-state model of governance alone began to erode, and over time a number of global institutions with limited governance responsibilities were created. The United Nations was established in 1945 to help avoid a return to war, promote human rights, safeguard international law, and promote social progress within nations. Humanitarian law and human rights conventions set common established standards for behavior of all nations who became signatories. The need to coordinate some economic, social, communication, and environmental matters led to narrowly defined global institutions such as

---

35. Much of the next four paragraphs is summarized from Held et al., *Global Transformations*, 35–49.

the International Telecommunication Union, the Civil Aviation Organization, the World Health Organization, the UN High Commission on Refugees (UNHCR), and the World Food Programme (WFP). Regional political and economic unions such as the European Union and ASEAN[36] also emerged, as did regional trade agreements such as NAFTA.[37]

With the emergence of Globalization II after the end of the Cold War, these formal structures were joined by a host of transnational networks relating to all areas of life—the flow of goods, capital, people, knowledge, crime, fashions, beliefs, and so on. As noted earlier, this included transnational corporations as the financial system globalized in response to the globalization of markets. But transnational networks also include over five thousand INGOs that implement about 15 percent of the world's development aid, including such organizations as World Vision International, Compassion International, Tearfund, and Opportunity International. Among these transnational networks, we also find Christian movements such as the Lausanne Committee for World Evangelization, the World Council of Churches, and the proudly decentralized Pentecostal movement. This proliferation of networks and global institutions together created a piecemeal expression of international order that is only periodically or sporadically under the control of the nation-states. Today we live in a world of multilayered governance, partly national and partly global, with a significant diffusion of political authority. Thus, we need to be clear about the answer to the question "What has globalized and what has not?" (see fig. 3.1).

FIGURE 3.1 What has globalized and what has not?

Yet, governments still imagine that they have a measure of control over the affairs of their nation. The European Union cannot make a decision until all

36. The Association of Southeast Asian Nations was formed in 1967.
37. The North American Free Trade Agreement was established in 1994.

of its twenty-plus members agree at the national level. The French government feels responsible for protecting French culture. We still talk about American or Chinese power. This is evidence of the failure of globalization to create an accepted and empowered political dimension of globalization—systems of global governance commensurate to the challenges resulting from the financial, economic, technological, and criminal dimensions of globalization. While it is hard to imagine what such a solution might look like, the inability to do so has consequences. Its absence makes fighting transnational crime or creating solutions to the global environmental crisis much harder, as both are global problems not susceptible to solutions at the level of the nation-state. Of greater consequence, without an accepted political dimension to globalization, there is no counterbalance to the militant nationalism that has been reemerging as a serious global threat. China and Russia are clear examples of this today, as are the nationalist parties in Europe and the strong popular support in the United States to the populist, nativist appeal, "Make America Great Again."

Culture

Cultural globalization refers to the increasing and intensifying cultural flows and exchanges between people and their cultural groups. The focus here is on the language, music, and images that communicate meaning and identity.

Cultural exchange is not new. Empires often imposed their culture on the people they conquered. All of the major world religions extended their reach by inviting or coercing conversion to their beliefs far beyond the place they were founded. National cultures were created in Europe as part of the nation-state process. Western culture traveled the seas with the European empires and was offered, sometimes coercively, as a replacement for the "inferior" culture of the colonized. The words *cultural* and *imperialism* are often linked.

Secular ideologies followed this path of cultural globalization as the twentieth century became known as a century of competing ideologies—fascism, communism, and capitalism. After World War II, the twentieth century became the American century. With the end of the Cold War, the dominant globalism—the neoliberal expression of capitalism—appeared to have won the day. With the advent of new information and communication technologies and the success of the American economic system, globalization became perceived as an American phenomenon. American transnational corporations and the media empires of television and film carried American culture—Coca-Cola, McDonald's, blue jeans, and Nike shoes—to the ends of the earth. In the late 1990s there were deep concerns about globalization creating cultural homogeneity, but things changed.

In the early part of the twenty-first century, economic growth in the West began to wane, and the economic rise of China and India meant the emergence of an Asian face to globalization. The world began to be described as multipolar and post-American.[38] The disintegration of the nation-states in the Middle East is a reaction to their colonial past. These countries view globalization as a cultural invasion of the West and its irreligious values. Thus far, the twenty-first century is becoming the century of competing cultural and religious identities.

In such a globalizing world, new questions arise. How does one feel at home in a global world? Who am I and who are we in a world in which everything and everyone is connected? Most of us are not yet prepared to yield our cultural or religious identity in favor of becoming a global citizen. Cultural identities matter and are passionately held. Russia feels humiliated in the aftermath of the Cold War and is seeking to reestablish Russian greatness. China, which mobilizes millions of its citizens whenever the nation feels it has been slighted internationally, is seeking to reestablish what it sees as its rightful place as the world's dominant power. Iran reacts violently against what it calls the "Great Satan" (the United States). This suggests that we need to bring emotions into the globalization conversation, particularly when it comes to the cultural dimension of globalization. Foreign policy is also going to have to pay attention to the key emotions of identity: fear, hope, and humiliation.[39]

At the same time, we need to affirm the value of being part of and engaged with cultures beyond our own. As anyone who has lived outside their own culture for some time knows, being part of other cultural expressions allows us to more critically engage our own culture, valuing those elements that enhance life and naming those that do not. We have similar opportunities for enrichment through the cultural exchanges mediated by receiving and caring for refugees and migrants. Engaging with other cultures enriches our lives and makes us more fully human.

Human Beings

When it comes to the dynamic domains of globalization, we must include human beings in large groups for two important reasons. The first is obvious, although it is not often named in globalization discussions. The drivers of globalization are reflections of how large numbers of human beings make decisions, take action, and demonstrate the capacity to adapt and learn.

38. Zakaria, *Post-American World*.
39. Moïsi, *Geopolitics of Emotion*.

Technological innovation does not occur if people in large enough numbers are not willing to learn new ways of doing things and so adopt and use new technology. Economic growth does not happen if people in sufficiently large numbers are not willing (or are unable) to work, save, innovate, and become more productive. The wishes and desires of large numbers of people contribute to the very slow process of cultural change. The importance of naming this reality is that it allows us to place the actions of human beings in the center of any conversation on globalization, a position critical to affirming human dignity, and it is also highly relevant to answering the question, "Who is in charge of globalization?" I will take up this question in the next chapter.

Second, it is increasingly normative in this globalizing world for people to understand themselves as actors who can and should do something about their futures and the world they live in.[40] This perspective allows them to be informed consumers, who understand that their choices matter, and aware citizens, who can and do change their political leadership. Most importantly, people are the innovators, migrants, activists, employees, business leaders, and politicians whose values, desires, and aspirations create the energy and momentum that ultimately drives globalization. People matter. Human freedom matters.

Summing Up

This chapter is titled "Understanding Globalization," and we end the chapter knowing that this is a problematic claim. The definition of globalization appears to be very much in the eyes of the beholder, and there are many differing perspectives from which to behold it. We used two metaphors for globalization—a gemstone and an elephant being studied by blind men—as a way of sorting through this confusion. We noted that the processes of globalization are expanding, stretching, intensifying, and accelerating our social relations across the world and that there are two outcomes: everything is moving faster and easier around the world, and globalization is changing us as much as we are changing it. We examined how globalization appears to others from different social, economic, and religious locations, and we looked at the dark, criminal side of globalization. Finally, we named five interacting and reinforcing domains of globalization: technology, economics, governance, culture, and human beings in large groups. All of this leads us to conclude that the values, promises, processes, and outcomes of globalization are ambiguous. The next chapter further explores this ambiguity.

40. Rosenau, *Turbulence in World Politics*, 13.

Questions for Discussion

Discussion 1: Watch the latest version of the YouTube video "Shift Happens."[41]

1. What intrigues you about globalization? What gives you cause for concern?
2. Do you think God was surprised by this rapidly globalizing world?

Discussion 2: Watch the two-and-a-half-minute YouTube video "Trade Matters to Me."[42]

1. Where do your clothes, television, and food come from? How did the folks that made them know that you needed them? What route did these items take to come to your door?
2. What else in your life reminds you that you are living in a globalized, rapidly changing world of many cultures?
3. How does the foregoing make you feel?

41. See "Shift happens 2015," YouTube video, 3:31, posted by "TheMusicGuru22," September 14, 2015, https://youtu.be/wMB77eJPYs8. Newer renditions of this video may be available.
42. Created by the WTO, YouTube video, 2:32, October 1, 2014, https://youtu.be/Crby5 WYko0g.

4

The Ambiguities of Globalization

[handwritten: exponential time]

[handwritten: Summary]

In the previous chapter, I called our attention to the impact of globalization on large numbers of human beings. Human beings as a social system are both a contributor to the processes of globalization and also one of its outcomes. This brings us back to the idea of complex adaptive social systems, which I introduced in chapter 2. This concept will help us understand another dimension of the ambiguity of globalization: no one is in charge of globalization, nor can anyone foresee its eventual outcomes. But globalization can be shaped by a widely held ideological or theological set of beliefs, or what some call "globalisms." Understanding globalisms is essential to understanding the potential role of the church which we will explore in chapter 13.

This chapter turns to a family of issues that arise from the processes of globalization and that are deeply concerning to many. The issues include asymmetries of power, income inequality, economic disruption, the health of our planet, and a concern for human identity and purpose. In yet another example of ambiguity, we simply do not know enough today to predict how each of these issues will be resolved. We can only do what we can to keep a light shining on these issues and to continue working to create an ethical discourse that allows us to reach a satisfactory resolution. Finally, I close the chapter with a brief note about the challenge to the church in mission, a topic taken up in depth in the final two chapters of this book.

The Emergent Nature of Globalization

When we examine globalization, whether in its political or economic or cultural forms, we need to remember that we are talking about a world of over seven billion people living in over two hundred countries. Thus, globalization is by definition a complex adaptive social system of stunning proportions and complexity. Recalling my brief description of the nature of such social systems in chapter 2, we now turn to globalization as an emergent phenomenon rather than a planned and executed one.

Who's in Charge of Globalization?

The question of who's in charge goes to the heart of much of the confusion and anxiety about globalization. We in the West, deeply influenced by the modern worldview, have for two centuries assumed—with not a little hubris—that *we* were improving the human condition and bringing order to a disorderly world. Whether we assumed that this was or is being done by an empire, American hegemony, or the United Nations and the international community, the underlying assumption is that someone or some group has enough information and brains to know what needs doing and the power to do it. Today we hear a never-ending series of calls for the international community to take action to make peace, eliminate chronic poverty, demand human rights for all, or sort out some other social ill. We have internalized a belief that the right group of people with enough intelligence, money, and technology can and will refine and recreate our world for the better.

But this faith commitment that globalization can be managed is called into question by the inescapable fact that the phenomenon of contemporary globalization is a result not of top-down direction but of the actions of billions of consumers, investors, global activists, corporations, academics, governments, Christian charities, and ordinary individuals. The reality is that all the actions of all these people take place every day without coordination or even common intention. The complexity of globalization is exponentially larger than the challenge of getting food into New York City each day, as I described in chapter 2. The bottom line is that globalization is the ultimate complex adaptive social system. "*No one seems now to be in control. . . .* Globalization refers primarily to global *effects*, notoriously unintended and unanticipated, rather than global *initiatives* and *undertakings.*"[1]

1. Bauman, *Globalization*, 57–60 (emphasis original).

Furthermore, one wonders if this spontaneous and emergent nature of globalization is not in fact a key to its rapid development and spread.[2] The bottom line is simple: no human being or human institution is in charge of globalization. Much of the fear and anxiety about globalization has its roots in this uncomfortable reality. The important consequence of this is that to "fix" or "control" globalization with experts, money, technology, and global strategies is simply unworkable.

What Shapes Globalization?

To say that globalization is an emergent phenomenon of a complex social system that cannot be directed or managed is not to say that it cannot be shaped or influenced. Major historical shifts are always accompanied by shifts in values, ideas, beliefs, or worldviews on the part of large numbers of individuals. The role of Christianity in the emergence of the modern West, with its commitment to human dignity, reason, liberty, and the rule of law, is unarguable. The secular ideology of Marxism and its promise of a just, more equitable human future was compelling in terms of motivating the allegiance of large numbers of people, even though it failed as an economic system and was brutally totalitarian as a political system. Ideology, culture, and religion, believed by a sufficiently large number of people and institutions, can influence social change.

Some use the word *globalisms* to describe these influential economic, political, or religious value systems that reflect a family of generally accepted assumptions about the way the world works and, most importantly, how it ought to be ordered.[3] These globalisms attract large, enthusiastic, and often powerful groups of people who use them to try to guide economic and political life.

This sets the stage to introduce a third metaphor for globalization, one that clarifies the difference between globalization and globalisms. We might imagine globalization as an ocean, its drivers as ocean winds, and globalisms as the ocean tides.[4] The metaphor of an ocean reminds us that globalization is an immutable historical process that is beyond management or direction by human beings, markets, and governments. It crashes on human shores, and we simply have to adjust and make do. The drivers of globalization are like the winds that rush across the globalization sea. Winds such as advanced communications and information technology, the global integration of markets, and

2. Griffiths, *Globalization*, 54.
3. Steger, *Globalization*; LCWE, "Globalization and the Gospel."
4. This metaphor and the following paragraph are adapted from LCWE, "Globalization and the Gospel," 12.

the flow of people, ideas, and capital across borders can result in a globalization that is storm-tossed and threatening in some places yet useful for travel, leisure, or securing a livelihood in others. Finally, globalisms are like the ocean tides, powerful currents, and undertows that push people, ideas, and money in certain directions judged to be more favorable than others. Some currents are concerning as they seem to push the "least of these" toward uncharted and possibly unsafe waters or into back eddies of poverty or exclusion. For others, these globalisms appear benign or even useful because they enable trade and new discoveries and offer the promise of a better life.

Since globalisms are human constructs of explanation and meaning, they tend to come and go as the world changes. The dominant globalism of the nineteenth century was colonialism with its dynamics of conquest, commerce, and sometimes civilization (mission). The twentieth century was a battleground between competing utopian globalisms—fascism, communism, and capitalism—all of which promised a better human future.

In the twenty-first century, there is one dominant globalism with some serious competitors. The dominant globalism is the neoliberal expression of capitalism, in a democratic political form in the West and in a totalitarian form in China and more recently in Russia. Competing against this globalism is an anti-globalization movement that is deeply suspicious of and often antagonistic to capitalism as an economic system.[5] It sees this system as the incarnation of greed and domination, harmful to the poor, indigenous peoples and their cultures, and the environment. An alternative to capitalism must be found, its adherents argue. Nationalism is a globalism that some thought was going away under the impact of globalization and two world wars, yet it persists as a powerful force in China, India, and Russia, and has surprised many by resurfacing as a serious threat to the future of the European Union and in the powerful nativist, anti-globalization slogan, "Make America Great Again" in the United States. Islamism, a theopolitical globalism, is a powerful force in the Muslim world and is deeply antagonistic to what is perceived as Western and Christian globalization in all its forms. Given the missionary calling of the church and our global truth claims, it should not surprise us if others see Christianity as yet another competing, and even dangerous, globalism in this century.

We need to explore the dominant globalism of our current age—the neoliberal expression of capitalism—because its values and conceptual framework influence every part of the globalization conversation and because we in

5. The LCWE's 2005 Occasional Paper on globalization correctly points out that this is really an anti-globalism movement with its rejection of neoliberal capitalism (LCWE, "Globalization and the Gospel," 13).

the West remain only vaguely aware of this globalism in which we so deeply believe and are so deeply invested. Sadly, this includes many Christians and much of our theology.

Capitalism in all its forms is the child of Western modernity and the European Enlightenment, which elevated human reason over faith, facts over values, and championed a belief that understanding how things work could be usefully divorced from issues of purpose or meaning. The aftermath of the Enlightenment was a time when God and religion were relegated to the spiritual realm of faith, church, and theology, while empirical science and human reason took over the "real" or material world of politics, economics, and social concerns. Thus did secular humanism become the unstated faith commitment of modernity and consequently capitalism.

In the West, we came to understand human beings as emancipated, autonomous individuals who could act in their world. This in turn gave rise to a Promethean belief in our ability and responsibility to remake the world into a better place. Our abiding confidence in human progress is based on the idea that observation and reason lead us to more knowledge, which in turn causes us to believe we can create better people through education and laws, better organizations through rational business processes, and a better natural world by using science to remake nature to suit our purposes. "Progress has long since replaced God as the icon of our age. . . . All the modern advances of science, technology, democracy, values, ethics and social organization fuse into the single humanitarian project of producing a far better world."[6]

Capitalism, in its laissez-faire form of the late nineteenth century and the neoliberal expression dominant today, is one central feature in the ideological framework undergirding modern globalization. Modernity, with its secular humanism, is another. Together these two globalisms animate the Second Era of Globalization and retain the power to shape political and economic strategies today. The developed nations still operate within these globalisms, as does the international community—the UN, World Bank, IMF, and WTO. Most overseas development-assistance funding and implementing agencies, including international development NGOs, do the same. We will return to a theological critique of these two globalisms in chapters 11 and 13.

Is Globalization Inevitable?

Many argue that globalization is an immovable force in history and is here to stay. Yet we have already noted that the structures of complex adaptive

6. Peet and Hartwick, *Theories of Development*, 1.

social systems emerge and then go away, as was the case with the British Empire. And remember that globalization itself nearly disappeared in World War II. Regarding the inevitability of the economic dimension of globalization, it is not clear what the long-term impact will be of occurrences like the increasing nationalism and anti-EU sentiment in southern Europe, Britain's vote to exit from the European Union (Brexit), and the anti-globalization sentiment that accompanied the 2016 Trump election in the United States. James Mittelman reasonably observes that "as with slavery, feudalism, and mercantile capitalism, there is no reason to believe that neoliberal globalization is eternal."[7]

The weakness of my description of globalization thus far is that I have largely focused on those elements of a globalizing world that support the understanding of globalization as expanding, stretching, intensifying, and accelerating our global connectedness. As a corrective, we also need to take note of forces for disintegration that are pushing back or working against the idea of a globalized world (see fig. 4.1).

First, large groups of people resist moving forward into globalization's future on religious and cultural grounds. Growing fundamentalist movements— Muslim, Christian, Jewish, Hindu, and Buddhist—reject both the processes and the outcomes of globalization as they understand them. They want to go back to a purer, more righteous way of living in the world. Adherents to these movements are deeply passionate, self-righteous, and already a source of violence in some places.

Second, national governments, losing power and sway over processes and institutions that have always been theirs to control, are between a rock and a hard place. The economic benefits of globalization for their citizens are clear, but the erosion of their power, authority, and even national identity invites protective reactions. Countries like Iran, Saudi Arabia, North Korea, and Venezuela come to mind as resisting the Second Era of Globalization. Even China, seemingly committed to economic globalization, may face a difficult future choice, as its economic and political systems are at odds in the long term.

Finally, many tribal, ethnic, or religious groups, finding themselves inside someone else's country because of maps drawn by their colonizers, are working to become their own nations—Kurds in Turkey, Syria, Iraq, and Iran, or Basques or Catalans in Spain, for example. These groups are a potential source of festering violence and threaten to cause a flood of very small, economically challenged new nations that will make the governance of globalization even more difficult than it is today.

7. Mittelman, *Contesting Global Order*, 231.

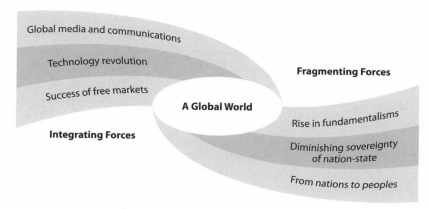

Global media and communications

Technology revolution

Success of free markets

Integrating Forces

A Global World

Fragmenting Forces

Rise in fundamentalisms

Diminishing sovereignty
of nation-state

From nations to peoples

FIGURE 4.1 Forces for integration and disintegration

Globalization's Unresolved Issues of Concern

Many are concerned about globalization as it is being experienced today. In the paragraphs that follow, I will briefly examine issues of asymmetries of power, income inequality, economic disruption from technological advances, the threat to the environment, and the impact on our understanding of human beings and their purpose in this world.

The challenge in understanding and addressing these concerns is that we are still in the middle of the rapidly changing processes of Globalization II, and we cannot see the future. The final trajectory and importance of each of these areas of concern is unclear, yet doing nothing seems deeply problematic. Bottom line: these are issues that will need to be carefully tracked and studied over time, and as always in dealing with complex adaptive social systems, it is best to follow a strategy of nudges and small corrections—no grand plans or one-size-fits-all global strategies. Small steps with continuing evaluation allow emerging successes to be rewarded with more resources while allowing failures to fall away. With complex adaptive social systems, we must learn our way into the future.

Asymmetries of Power

Some people think that within globalization, the economic and political rules of the game are biased in favor of the rich and powerful at the expense of the poor and those on the margins. Others observe that globalization results in winners and losers in both developed and underdeveloped nations as elites form new centers of power creating inequality within nations. Some are concerned that globalization is undermining democracy and local decision making as national and local sovereignty is eroded by global rules and decisions made elsewhere. Others complain, rightfully, that in the name of globalization and neoliberal capitalism, governments were coerced into macroeconomic policies that reduced their sovereignty and often harmed their citizens in the near term. Some argue that free trade means opening up the markets of developing nations while markets in developed nations remain protected by subsidies and tariffs.[8]

All of this adds up to a series of political and regulatory gaps.[9] A jurisdictional gap exists between the nation-state and global policy-making institutions. A participation gap exists because the international system is only partially open to the views of non-state actors such as the environmental movement, indigenous people's movements, INGOs, and other civil society institutions. An incentive gap exists in that no global body or set of institutions are responsible to ensure the supply and use of global public goods or to hold countries accountable who are enjoying these goods but not contributing to them. The solutions to these gaps are not yet in sight.

Income Inequality

There is considerable concern about the issue of globalization's impact on inequality in income and wealth, as well as considerable confusion as to what to do about it. Three kinds of inequality need to be examined separately: inequality among the people of the world, inequality among the nations of the world, and inequality within nations.[10]

Economist Branko Milanović has created estimates of the changes in inequality between the people of the world and between nations over the last two hundred years. The resulting inequality curves are different (see fig. 4.2).

The inequality among the people of the world is high but has not changed much over the last two hundred years. It increased a bit between the end of the nineteenth and beginning of the twentieth centuries, largely because the West's economic development took off over a century before that of most of the countries in the Global South.[11] But this increase in inequality slowed

8. Griffiths, *Globalization*, 10.

9. The following is summarized from Kaul, Grunberg, and Stern, *Global Public Goods*, xix.

10. Inequality is measured by an index called the Gini Coefficient, created by Italian sociologist Corrado Gini. The index represents distribution of income. A Gini of 1 is maximum inequality—all income goes to a single person. A Gini of 0 means absolute equality of incomes—everyone gets the same.

11. Milanović, "Short History of Global Inequality." Branko Milanović was a senior researcher at the World Bank and is now a senior scholar at the Luxembourg Income Study Center at the City University of New York.

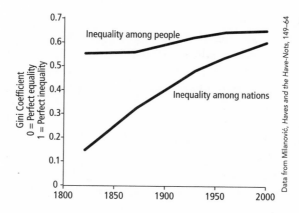

FIGURE 4.2 Income inequality among people of the world and among nations

in the second half of the twentieth century and has begun to decline in the first decades of this century, reflecting the high levels of economic growth in China, India, and Brazil in the last fifteen years.[12] (This latest information is not shown in fig. 4.2.)

What we do know is that in the first twenty years after the start of Globalization II in 1989, a substantial rearrangement of individual incomes around the world took place.[13] There were two significant shifts. The groups of people with the greatest increase in income were the top 1 percent and those between the 40th and 70th percentile of the world's global income distribution. The latter have increased their real incomes by 60 percent during this period, with the greatest change taking place in China and other parts of Asia. Over the same twenty-year period, the lower and middle classes of the mature economies of the United States, Europe, Latin America, and post-communist countries saw their incomes increase only marginally. While causality has not been established, the fact is that middle-class incomes in the Global South are rising, while they are stagnating in developed nations. This is good news in China and not so good news in the United States or Europe. All this makes for contested politics, especially in the developed West.

Those who find this level of inequality among the people of the world troubling and unacceptable face a seemingly insurmountable problem: In a world of autonomous nation-states, there are no institutions to which an

12. Bourguignon, "Inequality and Globalization," 11.
13. Milanović, "Winners of Globalization."

appeal can be made nor one with the authority to create and impose a solution. There is no global governance mechanism in place where inequality among the people of the world can be addressed. Yet the daily television and other media make the income gap clear to everyone in the world, and this creates a powerful force for what could prove to be unmanageable migrations, legal or otherwise.[14] Not having a way to address this part of the inequality problem does not mean there are no consequences.

The second measure—inequality between nations—shows a sharp upward trajectory since 1800, although it began to slow down in the middle of the twentieth century (see fig. 4.2). This rapid increase in inequality in the first 150 years is a result of two things. First, some nations and regions moved to the market system and free trade as strategies for economic growth in the nineteenth century, while other countries did not make the shift until the twentieth century. At the same time, many of those who did not make these adjustments were colonies that were not permitted to participate in the Industrial Revolution of the nineteenth century.[15] This divergence between nations could ease (and some argue even reverse) as developing countries and regions begin to experience faster economic growth while the growth rates of the developed nations and their mature economies slow.[16] At this point in time, however, there is no sign of a reversal.

The third measure—inequality within nations—is different still. Of the twenty-one nations with the highest index of inequality, ten are in Africa, nine in Latin America, and two in Asia. Of the twenty with the lowest level of inequality, almost all are in Europe.[17] The good news about this kind of inequality is that it can be addressed through citizen action, at least where a functioning democracy and the rule of law exist.

Unending Economic Disruption

With each wave of technological change over the last two hundred years, serious disruptions occurred within the economic system. Some businesses failed in the face of innovation, and their workers were displaced as their skills were no longer needed. The invention of the horseless carriage was not good news for the makers of buggy whips or carriages. At the same time, the larger society experiences increased economic growth and an improvement in general quality of life. The first two waves of technological change, late in the

14. Milanović, *Haves and the Have-Nots*, 161.
15. Milanović, "Two Faces of Globalization."
16. Milanović, *Haves and the Have-Nots*, 100–101.
17. Central Intelligence Agency, "Country Comparison."

eighteenth century and then late in the nineteenth century, led to increasingly effective manufacturing, which in turn provided better quality and cheaper goods, more manufacturing jobs, and decent middle-class incomes. Yet many other businesses and jobs fell away in the process. There was a lot of short-term pain for some, but longer term gain for many others.

The third wave of technological invention and economic disruption was the digital revolution with its gig economy, robotics, and increasing machine intelligence.[18] However, this wave is showing little evidence of increased productivity or new, better-paying jobs, both associated with the past two technological revolutions. Jobs that once belonged to knowledge workers are now outsourced to lower-cost countries or done by sophisticated computers.

It gets worse. Uber, the world's largest taxi company, owns no taxis. Alibaba, the world's most valuable retailer, has no inventory. Facebook, the world's largest media owner, creates no content. The internet allows a perfect match between those who need something and those who have something to offer.

The net result is that, at the writing of this book, increasing company value is not being accompanied by increasing middle-class employment opportunities as was true of our manufacturing past. A large gap is opening up between technically skilled and college-educated workers and everyone else who is seemingly migrating toward lower-paying, less-satisfying jobs with no prospect of upward mobility. Some argue this may be irreversible as "global employment in manufacturing is going down because productivity increases are exceeding increases in demand for manufactured products by a significant amount."[19] The political consequences of failing to create an adequate response that cushions the impact on the middle class in the democratic societies of the West could end up threatening globalization itself.

The Health of Our Planet

It is no secret that there is growing concern for the natural environment of our planet. The rapid and sustained increase in economic growth enabled by machine production fueled by oil and coal, which began in the 1800s, causes one to wonder if this form of growth can be sustained indefinitely. This concern becomes more urgent as more than 2.5 billion people in China and India are now on the same trajectory requiring the same oil and coal dependency, and other developing nations are in line to do the same. The result will be increased carbon dioxide emissions, thus increasing climate change. A second

18. The following material is drawn from Avent, "Third Great Wave."
19. Stiglitz, "Future of Europe."

environmental limit is water supply. China, India, and the United States are the world's largest consumers of water, while forecasts suggest that water may become so scarce that countries will fight over it.[20]

Some argue with passion that the end of the planet is in sight if we do not make radical changes now, and they look to governments and international institutions to take the lead. The United Nations Convention on Climate Change was developed in 1992 to assist nations in responding to climate change. After a series of over twenty international meetings—some a step forward, others a step backward—187 nations signed the 2015 Paris Agreement, consenting to meet "intended nationally determined contributions" to keep the global average temperature to less than 2 percent above preindustrial levels.[21]

Others argue that human creativity in the form of technological innovation has historically overcome what appeared to be environmental limits and that the doomsayers have a long history of getting it wrong. Free people up to innovate and create an environment conducive to sustainable businesses, and solutions will emerge, they reason. But we cannot see the future, and so it is hard to make a choice. The cost of waiting to see if innovation will once again deliver us has the potential to be catastrophic. We seem caught in modernity's polar choice between trusting markets or trusting governments and their regulations.

There is one final challenge to the environmental problem: it is a global problem that ignores the boundaries of nations. Smoke from the annual burning of Indonesia's palm oil plantations poisons the air in Singapore, Malaysia, and much of Southeast Asia. Climate change is a truly global problem with all nations contributing to its severity, and yet its global nature makes it hard to solve. Politics—the making of public policy—is the one area of our human activity that has not globalized. The international struggle with a long series of climate change conferences witnesses to this.

The Reduction of Human Identity and Purpose

Finally, there is concern for the damage done as globalization's faith commitment to secular humanism reduces our understanding of the identity and purpose of human beings. Markets alone reduce human beings to rational actors seeking what they value and whose purpose is to consume. No common good or solidarity here. Government alone reduces human beings to socialized role players or human resources whose purpose is to line up with

---

20. Chang, "Blue Gold."
21. *Economist*, "Paris Agreement on Climate Change," 89.

The Missiological Challenge of Globalization

Samuel Escobar, retired professor and missiologist,
Palmer Theological Seminary

A great challenge to [Christians in mission] in the coming years will be how to remain first and foremost messengers of Jesus Christ and not just harbingers of the new globalization process. They will have to use the facilities of the [globalization] system without being caught by the spirit of the system. This is a question not only for [Christians in mission] in affluent societies but also for those from poorer countries who are tempted sometimes to rely mainly on the economic facilities and the technical instruments available to them.

Escobar, *New Global Mission*, 63

the policies of the state. No human dignity or liberty here. Economic growth alone reduces human beings to our personal and national income levels. While the Human Development Index provides a modest corrective by adding health and education to income, there is more to life than just staying alive. Our understanding of human flourishing has been reduced to very thin gruel. Yet, for most of us, the identity and value of human beings and what makes for human flourishing is important, and this is a place where Christian theology has something significant to contribute. We will come back to this topic a number of times in this book.

The Challenge to the Church in Mission

Christians reflect all of the differing views of globalization just described. For some, globalization is metaphorically equivalent to humankind trying to build a Tower of Babel. For others, it is like the sign of the rainbow in the days of Noah,[22] God's faithfulness to God's covenant to redeem and restore the world. Regardless of our theological inclinations, globalization simply is, and we need to learn to engage with it.

The missional question is, what is the church to do? The Lausanne Forum in Thailand in 2004 reminded us that the church is to be an actor in the great story of humankind, a story "written by the good and saving Author whom

22. LCWE, "Globalization and the Gospel," 8.

we know."[23] Sitting on the sidelines is not an option for a faithful church. God is at work in today's globalizing world and is pursuing God's mission of restoring and redeeming the creation, and we need to play our part. At the end of the day, we need to pray and think hard about how to follow Christ on the global road. We will explore this more deeply in later chapters.

What's Next?

In the next chapter, I will begin to place globalization in historical perspective. I will describe the First Era of Globalization, which began at creation and continues today. This era of globalization is characterized by the migration of people, plants and animals, ideas, and empires across God's world. I will also describe the radical redirections of history that launched the Second Era of Globalization. The hinge between these two eras of globalization lies in the story of nineteenth-century Britain as a range of new things coalesced into the discovery that wealth could be created and people—all people—could become actors in changing the world.

Questions for Discussion

1. Which of globalization's unresolved concerns listed in this chapter is most important to you? Why?
2. Are there other concerns that you think should be added to the list?

23. LCWE, "Globalization and the Gospel," 33.

THE TWO ERAS
OF GLOBALIZATION

5

The First Era of Globalization

Going Global by Migration, Conquest, and Mission

By way of summary, I find it useful to think of the history of globalization as having two broad eras with the Second Era being an expansion and acceleration of the first. The First Era of Globalization began at the beginning of time and has been characterized by the migration of people, animals, plants, disease, empires, and religions across God's world.

Three kinds of people were the primary agents of the First Era of Globalization. Nomads and eventually farmers migrated in search of food and safety. Warriors and emperors went on the move to conquer and extend their territories. Finally, missionaries, warriors, and traders carried three religions—Buddhism, Christianity, and Islam—to the ends of the earth, with each religion eventually becoming global, though not universal.[1]

The First Era

In the Beginning—Migration

From our beginning in a garden to a world of seven billion people—half of whom live in cities—the basic story line seems clear. Everything began in one place, but it did not stay this way.

1. Held et al., *Global Transformations*, 415.

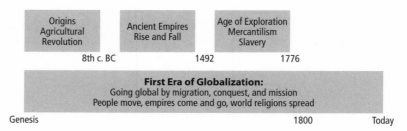

FIGURE 5.1 The First Era of Globalization

Nature began as one ocean and one landmass, and over a very long period of time, the landmass broke into parts, each part developing its own climate and environmental uniqueness. Plants and animals migrated across the forming continents and adapted to their new contexts. This global migration of nature led to all the diversity and uniqueness of plants and animals on the earth. The diversity and intricacy of nature is evidence of God's creative glory.

For human beings, the story is similar. Migration seems to be part of what God built into the creation and also into us. *Homo sapiens* were the first mammal species to voluntarily spread across the globe—the first truly globalized species.[2] Human freedom, creativity, and agency were at play from the beginning, it seems.

The first human beings walked out of Africa following the Nile and Jordan River valleys and journeyed south to the coast of Yemen and to the western part of the Mediterranean.[3] From there, some wandered north and east into what is now Europe, and others went east into central Asia. From central Asia, some went south to the islands of the Pacific and Australia or further east across a land bridge to finally settle in North America and South America.[4]

While these migrations eventually covered the world, this was not an expression of globalization, as these disparate groups were not connected in any way. They lived in very different climates, they began to look different, and their languages became mutually incomprehensible. While they began to organize into distinct communities and eventually cultures, they were essentially disconnected from other communities and cultures.[5] The outcome of the story of the Tower of Babel actualized, if you will.

We need to take note of the fact that God's creation was not equal everywhere. Some places had animals that could be domesticated; others did not.

2. Chanda, *Bound Together*, 3.
3. Tucci and Akey, "Population Genetics," 179–80.
4. Chanda, *Bound Together*, 12.
5. Ibid., 20.

As plants adapted to new ecological systems, some did well and others did not. Some places had plants that human beings could eat, and these plants became domesticated; other areas of the world were less fortunate.

Somewhere around ten thousand years ago, an important transformation took place.[6] The emergence of what has been called the agricultural revolution meant that people could settle down and societies could develop beyond simple hunting and gathering groups. Human beings began to replace stone tools with metal ones, and then domesticate animals and develop agriculture. More importantly, this transformation represented a major shift in how human beings understood themselves as actors in God's world. People moved beyond the passive view that food was provided by the gods or benevolent spirits and discovered that they could use what God put in nature to supply their own food.[7] Theologically, this shift is evidence of the impact of being made in the image of a rational, creative, and innovative God.

With the agricultural revolution, the long period of global divergence began to reverse and globalization as human interconnectedness began. With enough food, population centers could become larger. Migration became less a means of survival and more a way of extending the social and geographical reach of one's group or culture—new lands could be developed with new skills and better tools. As different cultures and peoples expanded their geographical reach and encountered other groups, they began to communicate and exchange ideas and goods. This drive to seek a better and more developed material and social life "prompted traders to brave the waves, . . . warriors to occupy foreign lands, preachers to set out to convert others to their ideas of the good, . . . and adventurers to seek new lands and opportunities."[8]

The merit of the idea of migration as a strategy for survival and conquest is unarguable, but it does not tell the whole story. Although the traditional interpretation of the Tower of Babel in Genesis posits God's judgment on human pride and our desire to be like God, another perspective is worth naming. When human beings decided to try to remain in one place and become a single people with a common language, God blocked the effort and "scattered them over the face of the whole earth" (Gen. 11:1–9). In a sense, this was an act of grace as well as an act of judgment. The cause and the result of this globalization (migration and cultural diversity) was a gift from a loving God who knows what is best for us.

6. The following was taken from Wootton, *Invention of Science*, 3. The theological interpretation is mine.

7. According to Harvard archaeologist Ofer Bar-Yosef, quoted in Chanda, *Bound Together*, 23.

8. Chanda, *Bound Together*, xiii.

Another theological comment on migration. While fleeing insecurity and following food and water were clear drivers for migration, human beings were also curious about what was just over the hill and across the sea. This curiosity and the desire to explore God's world was built into us by God from the beginning. Nature declares God's glory, which creates a sense of wonder and curiosity in us that combines with our God-given ability to figure out how God's world works and how to organize it (Gen. 2:19–20). This creative and order-making quality of human nature enabled us to invent tools that made us more productive and to build musical instruments for culture and worship (Gen. 4:21–22). Learning to farm, domesticate animals, and build cities all reflects the natural outcome of our being made in the image of God. We acted as cocreators, creating out of what God had made, thus fulfilling our vocation, our mission, to be productive and to migrate to fill the earth (Gen. 1:28).

Migration and Conquest

The next period of human migration saw the emergence of ancient empires, with warriors and emperors as the agents of globalization. As some states or cities overcame others, "the resulting territorial accumulation formed the basis for the Egyptian Kingdoms, the Persian Empire, the Macedonian Empire, the Empires of the Aztecs and Incas, the Roman Empire and the Indian Empires."[9] The creation of these empires was a form of militarized migration. While this extension of power fostered the development of simple forms of long-distance communications, nonetheless these empires expressed a limited form of globalization. Most were relatively local, lacked global ambitions, and seldom interacted with other empires.[10]

The motivation for the formation of these first empires was mixed.[11] For some it was simply looking for a better life. For others it was a religious mission of conversion, by force if necessary. More frequently the motivation for building an empire was shaped by ethnocentrism, where *our* people and *our* culture are superior, and *those* people are barbarians, unbelievers, pagans, and thus not fully human. For others it was curiosity—new peoples, new cultures, and new foods. For still others it was greed and visions of glory and power over others. History again reflecting both original good and original sin.

Because economics is a critical piece of understanding globalization, we must remember that household economics dominated this period—families carefully managed their scarce resources in an attempt to survive in an inhospitable

9. Steger, *Globalization*, 24.
10. Held et al., *Global Transformations*, 415–16.
11. Chanda, *Bound Together*, 178–79.

world. This economy of the household existed in the context of cities and then empires. Though wealthy, these empires did not have economies as we understand the term today.[12] There were only three ways to increase wealth: sell resources such as timber or gold, extract wealth in the form of taxes and duties from your people, or take wealth from a neighboring country or empire.[13] This zero-sum understanding of economics was normative for most of human history. It was not until the nineteenth century that human beings and nations figured out how to create wealth—how to make the economic pie bigger.

Migration and Mission

Three of the world's major religions, Buddhism, Christianity, and Islam, emerged during the First Era of Globalization and spread over large parts of the world through migration.

Buddhism was founded in the fourth century BCE by Siddhārtha Gautama in ancient India. By the third century BCE, Buddhist missionaries, in the form of teachers and traders, had spread across India, and Emperor Aśoka had dispatched missionaries to Sri Lanka, central Asia, Egypt, the Hellenistic world, and along the Silk Road to Southeast Asia. By the second century after Christ, missionaries had taken Buddhism to China, and by the fourth century, most of northwestern China was Buddhist and the religion spread to Korea and then to Japan. Buddhist missionaries created vernacular versions of Buddhist texts in most of the Asian languages,[14] anticipating the Bible translation efforts of nineteenth-century Christian mission.

Migration was the method of Christian mission from the very beginning. Believers in the Jerusalem church became missionaries as a result of becoming refugees fleeing persecution. Some scattered to Syria, where a church emerged that kept moving east, reaching as far as China in the seventh century. Tradition names the apostle Thomas as founder of the church in India, Mark in Egypt, and Matthew in Ethiopia. Paul and others went to Greece, Asia Minor, and eventually to Rome. The link between migration and mission "proves to be decisive for the survival of the Christian faith."[15] We will explore the history of Christian mission in more depth in chapter 11.

The third major religious migration resulting in a global faith began with the revelation of Allah to Muhammad in the Arabian Desert in the seventh century.[16]

---

12. Finley, *Ancient Economy.*
13. Heilbroner and Thurow, *Economics Explained*, 13.
14. Mair, "Buddhism."
15. The following is summarized from Hanciles, *Beyond Christendom*, 151.
16. The following two paragraphs are summarized from Chanda, *Bound Together*, 128–33.

By the time of the prophet's death, the tribes of Arabia were united behind this new faith. A century later, Muslim warriors had conquered territory from Spain to Armenia and Persia and were only just stopped from overwhelming Christian Europe by force. For the first several centuries, the expansion of Islam was done by the sword. With no tradition of missionaries, the faith was shared by ordinary Muslims who accompanied the armies. Later, as Muslim traders followed trade routes across the Sahara, on the Silk Road to India, and eventually to China and East Asia, Islam took root and a global Muslim empire emerged.

With a one-line creed and five easy-to-remember duties, Islam was a faith that traders and warriors could carry wherever they went. Islam provided both a faith in a global God and a social system for traders as they traveled. For those following traditional religions of spirits, angry ancestors, and threats of the demonic, the traders' one God, visible devotion, and Qur'an seemed a more powerful option. There was a lot to commend Islam as its traders and soldiers spread across the world.

We cannot speak of the missionary eras of three of the world's largest religions without noting that the motivations for their missions and migrations were ambiguous to say the least. The motivations for missions were varied—sometimes spiritual, sometimes linked to trade or education, sometimes linked to empire and the sword. There was often confusion between the faith and the culture that birthed it. At times it was hard to separate missions from the extension of empire or commerce. Cultures were changed for better and for worse.[17]

The Age of Exploration: 1400–1700

To provide some context for understanding the age of exploration, fifteenth-century Europe was a global backwater recovering from the impact of the Black Death and seemingly endless wars while Beijing was building the Forbidden City. At the beginning of the sixteenth century, Beijing was the largest city in the world—estimated to be four times the size of London at that time. Only Paris made the list of the world's ten largest cities.[18] The Muslim Ottoman Empire was multinational and multilingual, controlling much of southeastern Europe, North Africa, the Horn of Africa, Western Asia, and the Caucasus. At this time, "Chinese technology, Indian mathematics and Arab astronomy" were far ahead of those in Europe.[19] The economic and intellectual center of the world was outside Europe.

17. Ibid., 113.
18. Ferguson, *Civilization*, 4–5.
19. Ibid., 5.

Center and Periphery

Roberto S. Goizueta, professor of Catholic theology, Boston College

Globalization thus begins, not with the relativization of borders, but, on the contrary, with the creation of a frontier that will separate "civilization" from "barbarism"; the frontier is central not only to the U.S. identity but to the Western identity beginning with Columbus. From its very origins and of its essence, modernity needs and demands a center and a periphery, separated by a border [frontier]; conquest is not the consequence but the origin of modernity.

Goizueta, *Christ Our Companion*, 147

The age of exploration saw the rise of European maritime empires, which led to increasing international trade and cultural exchange made possible by the development of better sailing ships, compasses, and crude instruments for estimating speed and latitude.[20] The Portuguese and Spanish Empires were followed by the Dutch and British Empires in the sixteenth and seventeenth centuries. By the seventeenth century, chartered companies were a new innovation in world trade. The British East India Company, the Massachusetts Bay Company, and the Dutch East India Company were among the world's first transnational corporations.

The Portuguese and Spanish Empires followed the historical pattern of extracting gold and silver from the colonies to enrich the coffers of the king.[21] For the British and Dutch Empires later in this era, the plantation economies of coffee, sugar, tobacco, and cotton were the economic driver. This expression of zero-sum economics—empires taking from their colonies or from other empires—was normative across the world until the nineteenth century. People who wanted more wealth had to take it from someone else. Human beings had not yet discovered how to create wealth.

Another form of economic exchange was more tragic and immoral—the slave trade. Its creation was a direct result of Portuguese, Spanish, Dutch, and

20. Crosby, *Ecological Imperialism*, 106.
21. Australian economist Brett Parris argues that by amassing gold and silver, Spain and Portugal created a disincentive for themselves to invest in developing industrial economies in contrast to the Dutch and British Empires that followed them. Parris, *Development and Wealth Creation*, 8.

English merchants desiring low-cost sources of labor.[22] While a number of systems of slavery emerged in different parts of the world between 1440 and 1850, the largest and most profitable was the transatlantic slave trade. In this first phase of modern migration, "some ten to twelve million Africans—typically men and women in their prime—were brutally enslaved and transferred to the Americas in a period lasting more than three centuries."[23] The long-term impact of slavery is equally distressing. The slave trade undermined Africa's economic potential, created a breach in African-Western race relations that persists to this day, and changed the cultural and economic complexion of the Americas.[24]

The age of exploration was also the period of the Roman Catholic missionary movement. Priests such as the Dominican Bartolomé de las Casas, a missionary to the New World, returned to Spain to report on the horrible treatment of the indigenous peoples of the Americas by Spanish Christians and eventually came to believe that all forms of slavery were wrong. In 1537 Pope Paul III imposed the penalty of excommunication on anyone who subjected the indigenous peoples to slavery or took their goods. This policy was reaffirmed in the seventeenth century by Pope Urban VIII at the request of the Jesuits of Paraguay. Sadly, these papal policies of the Catholic Church held little sway over the "Catholic" empires of Portugal and Spain.[25]

Finally, it is important to note a third form of global exchange during this era.[26] The ships that sustained the age of exploration also carried plants, animals, and diseases. Horses and apples went to North America and tomatoes went to Europe and Africa. Maize went to Africa and sweet potatoes to East Asia. Unseen and unintended, a host of insects, grasses, viruses (small pox, influenza, measles), and bacteria (tuberculosis, cholera, typhus) hitched a ride. This globalization of nature has been called the Columbian Exchange and represents a kind of ecological dimension to imperialism.[27]

It is also instructive to note that as the European nations began the process of going global, China turned inward. At the beginning of the fifteenth century, a Chinese general, Zheng He, commanded an exploration fleet of over three hundred ships and nearly twenty-eight thousand men.[28] Each of the sixty treasure ships in his fleet was three times larger than the Portuguese

---

22. Manning, *Migration in World History*, 137. Patrick Manning is professor of world history at the University of Pittsburgh.
23. Hanciles, *Beyond Christendom*, 160.
24. Ibid.
25. Stark, "Catholic Church and Slavery."
26. Summary from Mann, *1493*, xxiii, 14.
27. Crosby, *Ecological Imperialism*.
28. Gronewald, "Ming Voyages."

and Spanish ships that sailed to the Americas. Zheng explored the waters of Southeast Asia as well as the Indian Ocean as far as the west coast of Africa. Then, for unclear reasons, the leaders of the Ming dynasty recalled Zheng He and burned the ships. China then turned inward, cutting itself off from the rest of the world.[29] With the exception of being forced to trade with Britain because of the Opium Wars, China did not reengage with the economic dimension of globalization and reemerge as an economic power until after the end of the Cultural Revolution in the late 1970s.

Setting the Stage for the Second Era of Globalization

Shortly, I will introduce the economic and technological transformation that took place in Britain at the beginning of the nineteenth century. This transformation represented a fundamental reimagining of the economics at the level of the nation-state, and resulted in a radical transition point in the world's economic history. But before moving to this part of our story, it is important to point out that Britain's transformation did not emerge in a vacuum.

First, the British took full advantage of the accomplishments of other European nations during the age of exploration: "They had robbed the Spaniards, copied the Dutch, beaten the French and plundered the Indians."[30] Furthermore, the age of exploration had developed a foundation for the expansion of globalization in the form of a skeleton of worldwide connections and exchanges that the British ultimately used to their advantage.

Second, a lot of other critical bits and pieces that enabled the economic transformation of Britain had emerged elsewhere over the preceding four hundred years while remaining dispersed and disconnected. It just happened to be in Britain that these innovations from elsewhere and the British innovations in political economics, modern science, technology, and governance coalesced into something radically new. So what kinds of bits and pieces am I talking about?

In Europe during the Middle Ages, there emerged a family of new ideas and institutions that, taken together, were necessary for the takeoff in Britain in the 1800s.[31] In the thirteenth century, monasteries emerged as proto-economic centers, while city-states arose in Italy and trade between them began to develop. In the fourteenth and fifteenth centuries, secondary institutional arrangements began to develop between city-states: *commendas* and *societas* (early forms of business partnerships) linked investors and agricultural producers as food

---

29. Chanda, *Bound Together*, 152.
30. Ferguson, *Empire*, 51.
31. The following is summarized from North and Thomas, *Rise of the Western World*.

moved to distant markets. The idea of a deposit bank, probably existent since Roman times, was revived. Insurance had its beginnings, thus enabling the market to manage risks. A variety of methods for extending credit were developed. A body of commercial law emerged.

Also in the fifteenth century, nation-states were emerging in the form of absolute monarchies with a related new economic theory and practice—mercantilism.[32] Mercantilism became the dominant economic practice in Europe from the sixteenth to the nineteenth century, when it gradually gave way to Adam Smith's new idea of a political economy based on human liberty, free markets, and competition. During the mercantilist period, military conflict between nation-states became more frequent and extensive. European armies and navies became full-time professional forces to deter attacks from other countries and to aid their own colonial expansion.[33]

It has been argued that the mastery of financial risk is the defining boundary between modern economic times and earlier eras: "By showing the world how to understand risk, measure it, and weigh its consequences, they converted risk-taking into one of the prime catalysts that drives modern Western society."[34] A number of discoveries in mathematics provided the tools necessary to manage risk—probability theory, the law of large numbers, and regression analysis. These were discovered by mathematicians in France, Switzerland, and Germany in the seventeenth century. Setting aside the notion that the future is determined by the whim of the gods and that men and women need to be passive before nature was a major liberating step forward.

The Transformation of Britain

In nineteenth-century Britain, the understanding of economics began an enduring change. For the first time, human beings figured out how to create wealth by increasing the production of the nation's goods and services, thus increasing the size of the nation's economic pie. The result was a radical new direction in the economic history of the world that continues to this day. The discovery that wealth could be created, not just accumulated or redistributed,

32. Mercantilism is a system of political economy that dominated European economic thought from the sixteenth to the late eighteenth centuries. A form of economic nationalism, it encouraged exports and discouraged imports. Mercantilism was an economic bargain between the merchants and producers such as the British East India Company, whose activities were protected by the state in return for their support for the state and its empire. Summarized from LaHaye, "Mercantilism."

33. LaHaye, "Mercantilism".

34. Bernstein, *Against the Gods*, 1.

connected with a wave of technological innovations. The result was a broad economic, technological, and social transformation that reordered the British economy, its intellectual landscape, and ultimately the way people viewed themselves. In time this transformation spread to Europe and ultimately to the rest of the world. We need to understand this change to make sense of the idea of globalization as a phenomenon of migration. Empire—going global—was evolving into an augmented form of globalization.

What Changed?

From the beginning of time, almost everyone, save the powerful few, lived in a world of material scarcity and insecurity (see fig. 5.2). For the first thousand years after Christ, most people in the world lived on the equivalent of $1.25 a day.[35] From 1000 to 1820, this only grew to $1.80 a day, today's average poverty line for low-income countries. During this same period, the world's average life expectancy never rose above thirty-five to forty years.[36] The baseline at the beginning of the nineteenth century was simple: while there were always a few with relative wealth, almost everyone was as poor as most of the rural poor in the Global South today. It was a Malthusian world in which competition between economic growth, disease, and population growth allowed for only limited change in material well-being.

Until the British transformation in economics took place, work was not something one did for a wage but rather something the family did to stay alive. The idea that wealth could be created, the concept of a market system, the idea of selling one's labor, and the concept of using capital to invest in businesses whose profits would generate more capital simply didn't exist.[37] Then, at the dawn of the nineteenth century, there was a stunning historical shift that saw a radically new trajectory in global wealth and health (fig. 5.2).

Over the last two hundred years, the world's wealth increased over sixty times. During this same period, the world's population increased sixfold as child mortality dropped rapidly[38] and life expectancy in Europe almost doubled.[39] The per capita wealth of the world increased an incredible nine times in this brief period.[40] More people, better health, more wealth per person. What on earth happened?

35. In 2008, the World Bank established $1.25 per day in 2005 international prices as the definition for extreme or absolute poverty. The Bank updated this to $1.90 in 2015.
36. Maddison, *Contours of the World Economy*, 69.
37. Heilbroner, *Worldly Philosophers*, 18–20.
38. Griffin, "Changing Life Expectancy."
39. Maddison, *Contours of the World Economy*, 68.
40. Heilbroner, *Worldly Philosophers*, 256, 259.

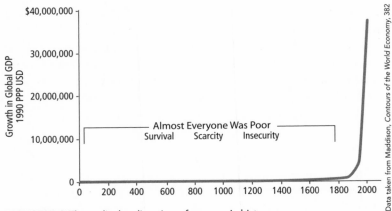

FIGURE 5.2 The radical redirection of economic history

As the eighteenth century closed, Britain was wealthy compared to its neighbors. It had the world's largest navy and an empire. An agricultural revolution meant more food production, and the first stage of the Industrial Revolution was under way. Yet Britain's economic growth was sharply limited by population growth, a mercantile economy with few limitations on those who preferred to steal the work of others, a preponderance of uneducated rural and urban poor, and low human productivity in the absence of widespread technological innovation.[41] From within this context of contradictions and limitations, the radical redirection of the history of economic growth unexpectedly emerged. This change, which eventually spread to Europe, the United States, and Japan, marked the turbocharging of the First Era of Globalization by adding the Second Era of Globalization, which we will explore in the next chapter. This radical reinvention of economics and its accompanying technological innovation and social change was something new that God created over the last two hundred years. What made all of this change possible?

Tectonic Shifts

What happened in nineteenth-century Britain is the story of a remarkable convergence of the idea and practice of political freedom and the rule of law, coupled with the emergence of technological innovation and a fundamental change in Christian theology. These coalesced into a new family of conceptual formulations that led to Adam Smith's proposal for a political economy and the market system.

41. Summarized from Mokyr, *Enlightened Economy*, 8–11.

The first part of the story entails the emergence of the rule of law and political freedom. While some claim its importance is overstated, the Magna Carta was nonetheless the start of a process by which the idea that no one, not even the king, is above the law. Over the centuries, this idea led to an understanding of political freedom, which included both democracy as a way to govern a nation and the negative freedom that one's property cannot be arbitrarily taken away. This evolution of thinking found expression in a series of legal and economic institutions that created an environment conducive to the creation of wealth—an independent judiciary, a fair and just legal system, a sound banking system, a free press, and systems for mass education and public health.[42]

Second, this was a time of rising scientific curiosity and an emerging realization that even common people could invent useful things.[43] Scientists, working largely on their own with simple equipment they made themselves, began to study God's other book—nature—and slowly pieced together knowledge about how God's creation works. New agricultural methods were developed by trial and error in the fields. Investigations into the working of the human body led to the study of disease, which in turn led to new health interventions and healthier people. Farmers and family businesses, applying the new technical knowledge and making simple mechanical innovations, became more productive. Transportation and communications were transformed. All of this joined the new understandings about economic growth.

Finally, a profound shift in theological thinking began in Europe. As religious explanations for natural events were losing sway in the face of the new sciences, the Protestant Reformation reimagined the role of human beings in society and provided a re-visioning of the previously dubious view of merchants.[44] Every human being was to be individually valued, and individual behavior became more important than church membership. A new ethic about work, thrift, and honesty emerged in Geneva and then slowly spread across Protestant Europe. Being productive and successful was an indication of one's standing before God.

While all of these value changes fit nicely with the behaviors necessary to be successful in a market system, the impact of Christian theology on Britain's transformation was far deeper and extensive than just instrumentally useful values. We will come to how human beings changed their view of themselves and their social role soon. More surprising, however, is that the economic

42. Parris, *Development and Wealth Creation*, 16.
43. Heilbroner, *Worldly Philosophers*, 36.
44. Ibid., 35.

and social transformations in nineteenth-century Britain were accompanied by what has been called the "globalization of compassion," which resulted in the humanitarian movement and eventually the idea of development to reduce poverty. We will come back to this in some depth in the chapter 9.

The Economic Transformation

It was into this evolving context with its emergent structures that Scotsman Adam Smith created a new vision for the economy of a nation. To understand Smith we have to remember that he was a moral philosopher before he began to write about economics. He was concerned with moral choices. In his *Theory of Moral Sentiments* (written before *The Wealth of Nations*), Smith, a Deist, wondered how a human being, who is so clearly a creature of self-interest, can make moral judgments that appear to set aside self-interest in favor of others. He concluded that human beings have the ability to put themselves in the position of another person, which creates the ability to be sympathetic to the objective merits of a situation in contrast to solely a selfish assessment.[45] Self-interest and the common good need not be at odds, according to Smith.[46] This thinking set the stage for Smith's major insights on political economy—the economy of a nation and the market system.

Seventeen years later, trying to understand the nature and cause of a nation's prosperity and arguing against mercantilism, Smith wrote *The Wealth of Nations*. His vision of a market economy took it for granted that it would be located in a society governed by broader moral sentiments (remember this when we come to chapters 11 and 12 and the absence of such moral sentiments in today's globalization).[47] Smith's insights included the critical idea that labor, not nature, was the source of economic value.[48] Human ingenuity and productive effort, under the right conditions, can increase the wealth of nations (as evidenced by the last two hundred years; see fig. 5.2). Smith argued that in a climate of freedom or natural liberty, an individual's pursuit of self-interest—exchanging goods and services with others—leads to competition, which, when combined with specialization (division) of labor, significantly increases production and the economic well-being of the nation. Finally, Smith argued that increased economic activity, income, and wealth

45. Ibid., 47.
46. It is interesting to note that the basis for Smith's observation is generally consistent with Christian anthropology and today has a solid foundation in recent science. Zak, *Moral Molecule*; Haidt, "New Synthesis in Moral Psychology."
47. Groody, *Globalization, Spirituality, and Justice*, 16.
48. Heilbroner and Thurow, *Economics Explained*, 49.

are morally beneficial to the nation: "A market system is not just a means of exchanging goods; it is a mechanism for sustaining and maintaining an entire society."[49] For Smith, the primary threats to economic growth were monopolies in any form, whether on the part of businesses or a mercantile state.[50] We need to look more deeply at three important ideas from Smith and then correct a common misrepresentation.

First, the economy of the nation is no longer a zero-sum game. Wealth, the annual production of the land and labor of a society, can be created (increased) through innovation and investment in a market system guided by the choices of free individuals. This was a new and important shift in perspective. "After *The Wealth of Nations*, men began to see the world about themselves with new eyes; they saw how the tasks they did fitted into the whole of society, and they saw that society as a whole was proceeding at a majestic pace toward a distant but clearly visible goal. In a word, a new vision had come into being."[51]

Second, economic life no longer needed to be organized around cultural tradition or authoritarian command. "The great chariot of society, which for so long had run down the gentle slope of tradition, now found itself powered by an internal combustion system,"[52] namely, the market system and Adam Smith's "hidden hand." Without this paradigmatic shift in how we understand economics, the idea of development—that is, of improving the material dimensions of the human condition—is unintelligible.

Finally, adding to the existing idea of political freedom, Adam Smith argued that individuals must also have freedom in the economic realm. For the most part in precapitalist societies, peasants were not free to move and artisans were bound to their trades. The institution of private property did not exist.[53] Smith called for an economic liberty that would allow every person—not just the privileged and powerful—to take initiative, innovate, and create without fear of losing the value of what they created. This new freedom in the economic realm doomed the old social order: "The freedom of economic contract was a chance to rise from a station in life from which, in earlier times, there had been almost no exit."[54]

Theologically, this call to increase human freedom is consistent with God's highest value for human beings. Freedom is so important to God's intention for human well-being that God gives us the freedom to turn our backs on God

49. Heilbroner, *Worldly Philosophers*, 27.
50. This paragraph summarizes ibid., 49–69.
51. Ibid., 41.
52. Ibid., 33.
53. Heilbroner and Thurow, *Economics Explained*, 12.
54. Ibid., 17.

and walk away. The emergence of political and economic freedom created a context that allowed human beings to be more of who they were always intended by God to be.

Adam Smith is frequently misrepresented in one area by both those who dislike his ideas and those who support free markets and smaller governments. The common good, along with the role of government in providing and protecting it, mattered to Smith. He was "very clear about the important role of government in providing resources the market could not provide and yet without it could not prosper."[55] Promoting the peace and security of the nation, protecting the rule of law and justice, providing effective tax systems including honest and competent bureaucrats, and providing public goods such as education are among the nonmarket goods that only a competent and honest government can provide.[56] "Importantly, these limits of the market, which politics and government supply, require a contribution of values and norms like trust, truth-telling and reciprocity."[57]

Increased Human Agency

Deirdre McCloskey argues compellingly that the rapid takeoff of innovation and economic growth in early nineteenth-century Britain was accompanied by a shift in ordinary people's self-understanding of their personal and social lives. A new middle class began to emerge and was treated with increasing respect and given the freedom to innovate and enjoy the rewards of their efforts.[58] Ordinary people began to act as if they could change their conditions and make choices about their lives, actions that had been unimaginable not much earlier in Britain.

The combination of increased human freedom and human agency released human creativity and a corresponding hope that a better future was possible—all of which have their roots in Christian theology. This idea of social progress was radically new. For most of human history, change was feared; it was seen as a threat to the survival of communities in climates of scarcity and insecurity, the natural climate of the world since time immemorial. The idea that human beings can choose to shape creation by using reason, experimentation, and innovation turned change into a good thing.[59] Thus,

55. Atherton, *Transfiguring Capitalism*, 20.
56. Summarized from Butler, *Adam Smith—A Primer*.
57. Atherton, *Transfiguring Capitalism*, 20.
58. McCloskey, *Bourgeois Dignity*, 11. Deirdre McCloskey is professor of economics, history, and English at the University of Illinois at Chicago.
59. Gillespie, *Theological Origins of Modernity*, 36.

"the idea of progress through bourgeois dignity and liberty took hold in the social imaginary of the West."[60]

The result of this widespread release of human agency was a stunning wave of creativity that led to inventions and, more importantly, to new conceptualizations and ideas. Taken together, this new role of human beings as rational and creative actors in history, the possibility of economic growth through a market system of exchange, and the enabling contributions of science and technology changed the trajectory of the world. A world of scarcity began to undergo a profound transition into a world of surplus and, some would say about the West, ultimately into a world of indulgence and overconsumption. These changes in Britain, which spread rapidly to Europe, the United States, and Japan, transformed the First Era of Globalization into an enhanced or augmented form of globalization as the world, its people, and its social systems became connected at an increasing pace.

Before describing the emergence of the Second Era of Globalization, I need to make two cautionary statements so that I am not misunderstood. First, I reject the argument that the development of Britain was because the British had a superior culture or superior leaders or anything else that supports a claim of superiority. There is no evidence that Britain developed as a result of a grand British vision of a better future, a brilliant strategy for economic growth systematically pursued as a nation, or the discovery of the will and resources necessary to gather up the innovations of the fourteenth to seventeenth centuries and make them work for the transformation of Britain. A better argument is that the radical change in Britain is an example of Niall Ferguson's dynamical understanding of history—a major new structure emerging unbidden and unplanned in bits and pieces, with fits and starts, with good news and not so good news.[61] Uneven, erratic, and often unfair, the understanding of how to create wealth and share that wealth among the many simply emerged. This new trajectory in history had to emerge for the first time somewhere and, without merit or favor, Britain just happened to be that place.

Second, my brief and highly simplified summary of what happened in nineteenth-century Britain focused on the key elements relevant to the intensification of the economic and technological dimensions of globalization. I have not addressed the fact that this transition was very hard on a lot of people; it was neither fair nor just. While the change I described ultimately benefited Britain's poor and, in time, the poor around the world, the process

60. McCloskey, *Bourgeois Dignity*, 25.
61. This emergent understanding of historical change was introduced in chap. 2.

was uneven, painful, and often tragic. This new kind of economics and the new kinds of politics and technology that followed it reflect the human story and its tragic mixture of original good and original sin working within human beings and their social structures.

Questions for Discussion

1. Migration is a central feature and driver of the First Era of Globalization. How do you react to this statement? Does this shift your view of migration today in any way?
2. What lessons or questions do you draw from the fact that three major religions all grew as a result of migration?

6

The Second Era of Globalization

Globally Connected and Closer Together

The First Era of Globalization continues as people, animals, plants, diseases, food, and music continue to spread across the world and nations continue to try to improve their lot, often at the expense of their neighbors. Migration is increasing, though in different ways, with new effects, and at a faster pace.

In the previous chapter, I described how the emergent transformation of nineteenth-century Britain became the hinge between the First and Second Eras of Globalization. Elements of Britain's transformation began to spread to Europe, resulting in the rapid economic growth of the British and European empires. Later in the nineteenth century, the United States and Japan joined in. Global trade took off, and the world was materially transformed. The Second Era also developed a new dynamic. The world's people and their social systems were becoming globally connected in an increasingly rapid and complete way.[1] Thus, the First Era of Globalization was extended and turbocharged by the Second Era of Globalization (see fig. 6.1).

The Second Era

The impact of the combination of the First and Second Eras of Globalization is stunning. As we have noted, Europe was a relative backwater on the world

1. Steger, *Globalization*, 15.

87

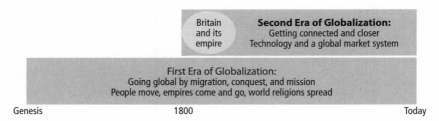

FIGURE 6.1 The Second Era of Globalization: connected and closer

stage in the fifteenth century. Yet, by the start of the First World War, eleven
European empires exercised control over almost 60 percent of the world's land
surface and close to 75 percent of the world's economic activity.[2]

As we trace the outline of the Second Era of Globalization, we are reminded
that this historical change was an emergent phenomenon: "One of the strik-
ing features of the 19th-century economic system—if it can be termed a
'system'—is that it evolved piecemeal and autonomously, not by international
design and agreements."[3] The Second Era had no master plan. No superior
culture was at work; no visionary leaders understood what was coming.

The Second Era of Globalization consisted of three phases (see fig. 6.2).
Globalization I frames the period between the story of Britain's economic and
social transformation in 1800 to the beginning of the First World War. The
period of the two world wars up to the end of the Cold War can be called the
Great Disruption—a time when globalization was on the brink of extinction
in a world of competing economic visions. At the end of the Cold War, in
the late 1980s, a new consensus emerged among Western nations around a
neoliberal expression of capitalism that coincided with an unfolding digital
revolution. The result was that globalization, gravely wounded by the Great
Disruption, began to reassert itself in what we will call Globalization II. This
is the phase of globalization we are living in today.

Globalization I: 1800–1914

> Globalization has two faces: a benign one, based on voluntary exchanges and
> free circulation of people, capital, goods and ideas; and the other face, based
> on coercion and brute force.
>
> —Branko Milanović[4]

2. Ferguson, *Civilization*, 4–5, 11.
3. WTO, *World Trade Report 2013*, 50.
4. Milanović, "Two Faces of Globalization," 668.

FIGURE 6.2 The three phases of the Second Era of Globalization: Globalization I, the Great Disruption, and Globalization II

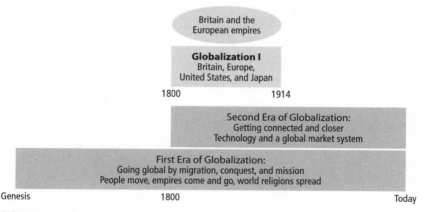

FIGURE 6.3 Globalization I

Globalization I was the story of how the economic and technological innovations of Britain spread to European nations, which then raced to create their own modern empires (see fig. 6.3). Later in the nineteenth century, the United States and Japan followed suit. By the beginning of World War I, there were a plethora of European empires, and the United States was the world's largest economy. How did this happen?

Technological and Economic Change

The first quarter of the nineteenth century saw new manufacturing processes emerge that became a major element of this change. What was once made by hand was now being made with machines with ever-increasing efficiency. Water power, steam power, and the development of machine tools led to the development of a factory system of manufacturing. The textile industry in Britain was the first to use this modern production system.

By the 1840s, two major technological innovations matured and created new opportunities for trade and investment in ways not possible before. In communications, the rapid spread of the telegraph and then undersea cables made global communications increasingly instantaneous. In the transportation arena, larger and larger steamships replaced sailing ships, and railroads replaced roads in large swaths of the world. The cost of shipping commodities in bulk and the cost of finished goods dropped dramatically, enabling them to become available in world markets. By mid-century, refrigeration technology was widely available for trucks and ships, making food transport possible and affordable. Global food markets emerged.

Thus, the world saw a very large expansion in trade and greatly increased flows of capital and technology. We've already noted that since 1820 the world's population has grown sixfold and world income sixtyfold, but even more stunning is the fact that global trade—although unevenly shared and often unfair—has grown 140-fold.[5] Economic globalization as we understand it today was gathering steam.

Between 1800 and 1870, the story of economic growth was predominantly a British story. But Germany, France, and other European nations also experienced economic growth as they emulated Britain and innovated on their own (see fig. 6.4). A former British colony on the other side of the Atlantic began to catch up and eventually overtook Britain as the century closed. Japan was the only non-European country to make the change.

This economic and technological transformation enabled the European empires to grow robustly, if unfairly and unjustly. The European "Scramble for Africa" and the expansion of European territory in Asia meant that European domination extended to most of the world, with the exception of Japan and the Ottoman Empire of the Middle East and Persia. By the end of Globalization I, the Ottoman Empire was no more and the European nations had divided up the Middle East.

The account of increasing global trade in the nineteenth century had two dark sides. The first was that being connected to global markets was often involuntary. If a country was another country's colony, it had no choice but to adopt the economic system of its colonizer. If a country wished to avoid the impact of this new globalization and tried to close access to its nation,

5. Summarized from Held et al., *Global Transformations*, 155.

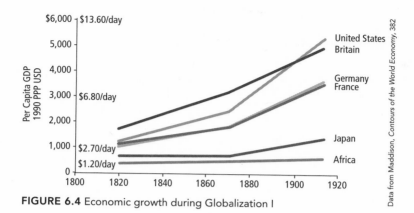

FIGURE 6.4 Economic growth during Globalization I

stronger countries could and did insist on its acceptance. Japan, China, and the Philippines were forced by gunboats to open their economies. Once these nations were forcibly opened to "free trade," Western capital built the infrastructure of trade: railroads and telegraph lines linked places with raw materials or farm commodities to the nearest harbor that could handle Europe's steamships. Western technology was at the service of the empire, not local populations or neighboring countries.

The second dark side of Globalization I was how the West developed and the rest did not. To understand this dark side, we need to qualify a common criticism of this phase of globalization. Unlike the Spanish and Portuguese Empires, Globalization I and the resulting increase in wealth in the West were not the result of extracting wealth from the Global South. Recent research in economic history reveals that it was other way around: economic growth and the creation of wealth in the West fueled the growth of the British and European empires.[6] This provocative finding is good news. If economic development had depended on exploiting or extracting wealth from a nation's neighbors or colonies, then the less developed countries of today could not develop.[7] The economic growth of the Asian Tigers (Hong Kong, Singapore, South Korea, and Taiwan) and then China, India, Brazil, and Indonesia was a result of creating wealth, not taking it from elsewhere.

This should not be read as an argument that the Global South does not have a legitimate complaint regarding questions of fairness and justice. It is a historical fact that colonial administrators created a series of roadblocks that prevented the Global South from participating in the Industrial Revolution. "Free trade"

6. Bairoch, *Economics and World History*, 85. Paul Bairoch was professor emeritus of history at the University of Geneva where he did his research at its Centre for International Economic History.
7. Ibid., 97.

The Dark Side of Empire

Branko Milanović, former World Bank researcher, senior scholar at the City University of New York

Globalization was brought to the many at the "point of a gun," and many were "globalized" literally kicking and screaming, from Commodore Perry's ultimatum which opened Japan, to British and French gunboat diplomacy in Tunisia, Egypt and Zanzibar, to the Opium wars and gunboats that patrolled Chinese *internal* waterways. Worst of all, for the millions who were sold in slavery or who toiled 16 h[ours] a day on plantations from Malaya to Brazil that too was globalization. Globalization was not merely *accompanied* by the worst excesses of colonialism; colonialism was not an accident. On the contrary, globalization *was* colonialism because it is through being colonies that most of the non-European countries were brought to the global world.

Milanović, "Two Faces of Globalization," 669 (emphasis original)

enabled raw materials to be sent to Europe. Then Britain and Europe produced finished goods that "free trade" exported back to their colonies. The result was a large-scale deindustrialization of the colonies. The disappearance of the textile industries of India and China are cases in point.[8] The net result was that the Industrial Revolution was largely reserved for the nations of the West. The residual effect of this and the other echoes of their colonial experience play a role in undermining economic development in the former colonies to this day.

Globalization I also saw two very different forms of migration, one internal and the other international. Internal migration took the form of a massive movement of people from farms to cities looking for work in the new factories. From 1800 to 1890, the proportion of the population living in Britain's cities jumped from 17 to 72 percent.[9] A similar but slower rural-to-urban shift eventually took place in Europe and the United States.

The second form has been called the second period of modern migration.[10] It was migration primarily at the service of the European empires and their increasing demands for labor. With the abolishment of the slave trade within the British Empire in 1807 and of slavery itself in 1834, slaves were replaced

8. Ibid., 88.
9. Long, "Rural-Urban Migration."
10. This paragraph summarizes Hanciles, *Beyond Christendom*, 162–63.

by tens of millions of indentured workers from China, India, and East Africa. This was also a period of growing migration out of Europe into the rest of the world. The European empires needed people to serve as administrators of their companies and colonies. One in five Europeans—over 50 million people—boarded steamships to flee crowded European cities, seeking a better life in the Americas, Africa, and Asia. Thirty-three million ended up in the United States.

The significance and contributions of Britain in the early half of Globalization I cannot be ignored. We've already noted the radical increase in economic growth and the social changes that began in Britain and spread throughout its empire. The British drove the establishment of global free trade. Their empire exported capital to "emerging markets" such as the United States, and the British pound served as the global currency.[11] The British imposed free markets, the rule of law, protection of investors, generally incorruptible government officials, and English language and culture on a quarter of the world.[12] The British demonstrated that capitalism was a superior form of economic organization and promoted democratic institutions as a better form of political organization. The British Empire spread Protestant Christianity to much of the world, where it endures to this day. The bottom line is that the British Empire was a powerful force for change, but it was an uneven affair with contributions that were positive and many that were not—a mixture of original good and original sin once again.

The Contribution of the Church

One mitigating bit of news about the British Empire comes in the form of Victorian evangelicals. Many Victorian evangelicals shared a vision for redeeming the world in contrast to the desire of the British government to rule it.[13] Exploiting other nations gave way to an evangelical desire to improve them, although with a heavy dose of ethnocentrism little different from that of British colonial administrators and company directors. *Mission* meant telling the people the good news and improving agriculture, education, and health. In addition to these, the list of positive social contributions of some elements of Protestant missions included the promotion of religious liberty, development of written forms of spoken vernacular languages, newspapers, voluntary organizations, many colonial reforms, and the rule of law, including legal protections for nonwhites.[14]

11. Yergin and Stanislaw, *Commanding Heights*, 385.
12. Ferguson, *Empire*, xxi.
13. Ibid., 113.
14. Woodberry, "Missionary Roots of Liberal Democracy."

Victorian evangelicals were an odd mix of Christians. Some had roots in the Wesleyan revival of the seventeenth century. The Clapham Sect was an informal group of Anglican social reformers that included evangelical politician William Wilberforce, who added a keen understanding of British politics, and a few Quakers, who were connected to Quakers in the United States. Separately and together, they managed to develop what amounted to a campaign of moral reform directed at the British Empire.

At home, Victorian evangelicals were a force behind the campaign to abolish the slave trade. The result was the birth of a new kind of politics of mass mobilization with "zealous activists armed with pens, paper and moral indignation."[15] The antislavery movement was the world's first transnational movement upholding the notion that all human beings are created equal, in many ways foreshadowing the human rights movement of today.[16] Modern-day advocacy campaigns have their roots here as well.

Abroad, the Clapham Sect organized a campaign to get the British government to open India to missionaries who would challenge the strongly business-only stance of the British Empire. The campaign had twin motivations. First was the predictable claim that the gospel must be preached everywhere. Second, they challenged the "live and let live" religious toleration policies of the East India Company that ignored the ethical challenges of exporting opium and inhuman cultural practices such as child labor, thuggee (cult of assassin priests), and suttee (self-immolation of widows).[17] This missionary concern for human dignity and rights has been called the "globalization of values."[18]

Victorian missions was largely a voluntary movement. Its missionary societies were in many ways like the aid agencies of today, practicing what we now call holistic mission (spiritual and material assistance combined) while nonetheless supporting the British colonial project. David Livingstone was an iconic example. While participating in the colonial endeavor, he also united in himself the two major intellectual currents of the day: reverence for science and passion for Christian mission. His was a vision "not only of commerce, civilization and Christianity, but of free trade and free labor [no slavery]."[19]

The result was an unanticipated convergence between Christian mission and its desire to convert and improve the "heathen," on the one hand, and the liberal, democratic desire to spread capitalism and democracy, on the other.[20]

15. Ferguson, *Empire*, 118.
16. Chanda, *Bound Together*, 139.
17. The forgoing is summarized from Ferguson, *Empire*, 116–33.
18. Chanda, *Bound Together*, 137.
19. Ferguson, *Empire*, 131.
20. Ibid., 139.

Evangelicalism in Britain produced large numbers of evangelical Christians and Christian mission agencies deeply committed to changing the policies of the British government at a time when a private sector was emerging that was narrowly committed to free trade, capitalism, and the creation of wealth. In a sense, the Victorian evangelicals created what we today might call a moral ecology that was compelling and popular enough to shape and correct the globalization of its day. Please keep this in mind when we come to chapters 12 and 13, which explore the need for such a moral ecology today.

Globalization of Mission

We need to take note of one other change that occurred toward the end of Globalization I. While Globalization I was an era of empires, it was also an era when the global missions movement emerged. In addition to the mission societies of Britain, the Paris Mission was established in 1820 with the intention to spread the gospel and to take "a position against the colonial power in order to defend indigenous societies."[21] By the latter part of Globalization I, America had over ninety mission societies. The first World Missionary Conference was held in 1910 and formalized the emergence of a global mission imaginary—the globalization of missions, if you will.

At the same time, the American mission movement became enmeshed in the modernist-fundamentalist controversy of the late nineteenth and early twentieth centuries. Reacting to attempts by liberal Protestants to find ways to reimagine traditional Christian theology in light of developments in the modern sciences, especially Darwin's theory of evolution, the fundamentalists (as they called themselves) circled the wagons and devoted themselves to protecting the fundamentals of the Christian faith—the historical accuracy of the Bible, the mission to take the good news to the ends of the earth, the efficacy of Christ's death and resurrection for salvation, and so on. Thus, evangelicalism, particularly its American form, separated evangelism from social action. Sadly, while trying to protect the faith from modernity, evangelicals allowed themselves to be co-opted by modernity's argument that religion, mission, and God belong to a private and personal spiritual realm that is separate from and has nothing to offer to the real world of politics, economics, and social change. Salvation seemed to have nothing to do with the material world.

By the end of Globalization I, the world had invented time zones, and the electrification of the West was widespread. Global trading networks were established (mostly linked through London), an international monetary system (the

21. Blocher and Blandenier, *Evangelization of the World*, 696.

The End of Globalization I

John Maynard Keynes, father of macroeconomics

The inhabitant of London could order by telephone, sipping his morning tea in bed, the various products of the whole earth, in such quantity as he might see fit, and reasonably expect their early delivery upon his doorstep. . . . What an extraordinary episode in the economic progress of man that age was which came to an end in August 1914!

Keynes, Economic Consequences of the Peace, 9

gold standard) had been created, and capital markets were becoming globally integrated. Technological innovations in manufacturing and production enabled widespread adoption of preexisting technology to gas and water supplies, electrification, and sewage systems. Per capita incomes had risen dramatically, and innovations in public health were extending life expectancy. But this period has also been called the Gilded Age of laissez-faire capitalism, characterized by business monopolies, increased urbanization and slums, governments protecting businesses against unruly workers, and extreme inequality of wealth.

The Great Disruption: 1914–89

Globalization I came to an abrupt end as the world witnessed the globalization of war in the tragedy of World War I (see fig. 6.5). Ironically, Globalization I contributed to its own demise. Technological innovations, such as the machine gun, military aircraft, and the mass production of weapons and poison gas, made war horribly more efficient. Rapid economic growth and competition between empires created an infectious form of nationalism that undermined any sense of a global order. "The struggle for empire turned into the life and death struggle of empire builders that we know as the First World War."[22]

Between the Wars

The war shattered the global capitalist system that was based on European imperialism and left the European powers in crisis economically and politically.

22. Wolf, *Why Globalization Works*, 125.

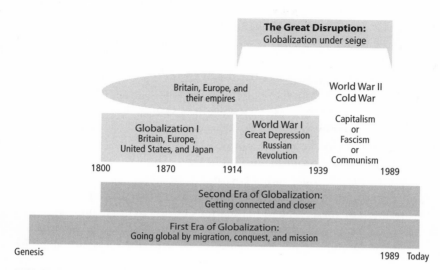

FIGURE 6.5 The Great Disruption: globalization under siege

Political leaders, scholars, and artists experienced a profound crisis of confidence in the liberal democratic ideal. After all, the promises of Globalization I had not prevented a global conflict and the death of millions. Surely there had to be other options. Marxism and the Russian Revolution seductively promised an alternative path to social justice and economic equality. In time fascism and National Socialism provided a second option.

The period between the two world wars was marked by a continuing suspicion of unfettered capitalism and a belief that business cycles were evidence of the inherent instability of market systems. Then the world experienced the Great Depression of the 1930s. As countries struggled with the debts of World War I and stagnant economies, the gold standard was abandoned and free trade was largely dismantled. Then a second global conflict left much of the world in ruins. At the end of World War II, the only liberal democratic countries with capitalist economies were the United States and Great Britain, and Britain was broke. Globalization nearly disappeared from history.

Post–World War II

In the immediate aftermath of the Second World War, two things happened that contributed to the resurgence of the economic dimension of globalization. First, while the economies of Europe, Russia, and Japan lay in ruins and millions of soldiers began returning home, the Marshall Plan was launched to rebuild Europe. New global financial institutions—the World Bank, the International Monetary Fund, and the General Agreement on Tariffs and Trade (which became the World Trade Organization in 1995)—were created to fund economic recovery, ensure that a global great depression could not recur, and recreate free trade among the nations. These three institutions formed the major building blocks of today's globalized economy. At the same time, the technological innovation that emerged during World War II in the West spilled over into the peacetime economy.

Second, the era of European empires began to draw to a close. European colonies received their independence with little or no preparation on the part of their former imperial rulers. The number of nation-states grew from 74 to 192 by 1995: of these, 58 had populations of less than 2.5 million.[23] The continuing challenges of creating economic growth and effective governance in the Global South are considerable especially since the residual impact of the colonial era has proved hard to remove.

The Cold War

At the end of the Second World War, the Soviet Union and communism were the sole remaining challenge to liberal democracy and capitalism. This became a cold war between the totalitarianism and state-directed economies of the Soviet Union and the democracies and capitalism of the West. During this time, two factors in particular sped up the processes of globalization. First, continuing technological innovation in the West was a critical component in ensuring military security, and the spillover from this research into the private sector contributed to economic growth. Second, the newly independent nations of the Global South became pawns in the Cold War game. To entice them to lean in favor of capitalism and democracy, the West sought ways to help poor nations in the Global South develop economically. The idea of development, and the possibility of doing something about poverty, became a normative element of Western foreign policy. We will explore the consequences of this development and its current manifestations in depth in chapter 9.

In the West, many felt that state-directed economies had won World War II by following a macro theory of economics developed by John Maynard Keynes. Perhaps state-directed economies could win the peace. Rejecting Winston Churchill and his call to return to laissez-faire capitalism, Britain voted in favor of a socialist government and moved toward a form of social welfare

23. Ferguson, *Empire*, 372.

democracy in which the state was to manage or direct its economy. Most of Europe and eventually the United States followed suit.

By the early 1980s, the limits of this form of mixed economy became hard to ignore. The economies of the West slowed dramatically, unemployment soared, and inflation increased to intolerable levels, all exacerbated by the first-ever oil embargo by Middle Eastern oil producers. Britain's political leaders proved unable to break this downward cycle, and the limitations of the government setting the price of haircuts and the rates of plumbers became clearer. In the United States, the regulations designed to protect Pan American Airways actually increased prices by undermining competition and innovation.[24]

The response to this has been called the Thatcher-Reagan Revolution. Margaret Thatcher, as prime minister of Britain, adopted a robust free-market/ free-trade position and faced down militant union opposition in Britain. Ronald Reagan followed suit with a massive bout of deregulation in the United States. After tough transitions, both economies began to grow rapidly, and the neoliberal expression of capitalism was born.

This "tough love" reorientation of state-directed economies was then pushed on the emerging economies of the Global South in the form of what came to be known as the Washington Consensus. Loans from the World Bank and the International Monetary Fund required that borrowing nations reduce public expenditures, privatize government businesses and services, enable free trade, and reduce government regulation of the economy. This formula for a better economy made things a lot worse before they started to get better. The poor paid a high price. We will come back to this in more depth in chapter 9.

The Great Disruption ended when the Soviet Union collapsed from within and the Berlin Wall came down. Communism joined fascism as an ineffectual approach to running the economy of a nation, much less an empire. A period of euphoria and triumphalism in the West followed. Some even announced the "end of history."[25] Neoliberal capitalism was the last economic system left standing, it seemed.

Globalization II: 1989 to Today

In the aftermath of the Great Disruption, three things came together to create a new expression of globalization. First, the adoption of the key elements of the neoliberal model of capitalism and the market system began to spread

24. The last two paragraphs are summarized from Yergin and Stanislaw, *Commanding Heights*, 47–48.
25. See Fukuyama, *End of History*.

rapidly over much of the world. The modern economies of Europe, the United States, and Japan were joined by the Asian Tigers,[26] China, India, Indonesia, Brazil, and South Africa. Second, the digital revolution in technology exploded onto the scene. Third, the international economic institutions created after World War II—the World Bank, International Monetary Fund, and eventually the World Trade Organization—were reinvented to support the spread of neoliberal economic orthodoxy (the Washington Consensus) and thus to help eradicate poverty. The current period of very fast economic growth and a more closely connected world is called Globalization II (see fig. 6.6).

Rapid and Uneven Change

The map of global economic growth began to undergo significant change during Globalization II. In the twenty-five years leading up to 2015, the emerging economies of the world grew faster than the developed economies, in spite of the 2008 global financial crisis. The bulk of this economic growth took place in China, India, and a small number of other Asian countries. Latin America and Africa also resumed growth after lagging in the 1970s and 1980s.[27] Over a billion new customers entered the global market place, with another two billion forecast by 2030.[28] The global workforce has roughly doubled to three billion people as emerging economies have become middle-income countries.

The unfortunate downside of the economic dimension of Globalization II was a series of financial crises, beginning with the Mexican currency crisis in 1994. Asia, Russia, and Brazil experienced financial crises in the late 1990s. The twenty-first century opened with one financial crisis every year as Turkey, Argentina, and Venezuela took turns. It was argued that this was a transitional problem of countries that came late to the globalization game, that is until the United States and the West experienced a financial crisis in 2008–9 that created a global recession that came perilously close to another Great Depression. It is not clear that this era of economic instability is over.

Globalization II has two contradictory tendencies that are very much in play today.[29] On the one hand, most of the world is connecting in varying degrees

26. Hong Kong, Singapore, South Korea, and Taiwan. These countries found their own paths to joining the global market system apart from the neoliberal Washington Consensus that was followed or imposed elsewhere.
27. The foregoing is summarized from Rodrik, "Past, Present, and Future," 2.
28. Kharas, "Emerging Middle Class."
29. Ferguson, *Empire*, 373.

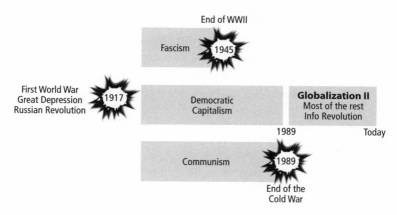

FIGURE 6.6 Globalization II: 1989 to today

to the global economy, resulting in increased economic growth. On the other hand, there has been a growing tendency toward political fragmentation. Not only are nations seeing their sovereignty erode in the face of economic globalization, but an increasing number of civil wars have broken out in countries with multiple ethnic or religious groups. Many of these minority groups want a country of their own. This tension between the two is a second source of instability in the world of Globalization II.[30]

On a more positive note, the last twenty-five years have seen a dramatic decrease in global poverty. Poverty eradication became part of the global political agenda with the adoption of the Millennium Development Goals in 2000. This United Nations initiative was the first time that the nations of the world addressed poverty as a shared issue and set out measurable targets for change. The good news is that a lot of progress was made, especially in the areas of chronic poverty, child mortality, and universal primary education.[31] There is disagreement as to what caused this progress—free markets or international aid—and both sides have a point. Government policy and aid appear to have been helpful in the areas of health and education. Free markets and economic growth are more likely responsible for moving large numbers of the poor out of extreme poverty.

The Relegation of the Church to the Spiritual Realm

Finally, an observation about Globalization II and the church in mission. As we've seen, the role of the church and its mission began to shift its social location in the last half of Globalization I. This shift continued during the

30. Kaplan, *Coming Anarchy*, 36.
31. UN, *Millennium Development Goals Report 2015*.

The Consequences of Relegation

Emmanuel Katongole, associate professor of theology
and peace studies, University of Notre Dame

One major reason why such a socially active Christianity has yet to make a dent in the social history of Africa is . . . the premise that Christianity is a religion—and therefore distinct from the realm of politics. . . . Christianity in Africa, in spite of its outward appearance to the contrary, still operates under the burden of a Western legacy, both in its social outlook and self-understanding. . . . [This] self-understanding of "religion" not only places Christianity, at least imaginatively, outside the boundaries of the historical, material, and political processes that shape the social history of Africa; it obscures the full import of the gospel as a social vision. . . . In the end, the self-understanding of Christianity as a religious domain contributes to the gradual disappearance of Christianity as a social and political body. The disappearance takes many forms, ranging from reticence to frantic activism.

Katongole, *Sacrifice of Africa*, 41–42

Great Disruption, and the push-pull relegation of the church and its mission to the private realm of spiritual matters has become largely complete. The push has come from the activists and academics of development economics, technology innovation, and the secular mission movement around human rights, all of whom view religion as either part of the problem or irrelevant to improving the human condition. Sadly, the pull has come from parts of the church that retreated, with little protest, from the world of secular humanism and globalization, and settled comfortably into a Christian subculture.[32]

In Europe, the church declined in numbers and wallowed in its guilt over the sins of its colonial past. The guilt became so debilitating that Lamin Sanneh wrote a stinging public letter begging the church in Europe to get over its "Western guilt complex" and get back in the mission game.[33] In the United States, liberal Protestants and parts of the Catholic Church doubled down on an understanding of mission that was largely about social justice and material development, with evangelism receding into the background.

32. Crouch, "How Not to Change the World."
33. Sanneh, "Christian Missions." Lamin Sanneh is a Gambian Christian who converted from Islam. He is professor of mission and world Christianity at Yale Divinity School.

The evangelical church focused only on evangelism until the late twentieth century, when it began to recover the holistic gospel of its Victorian forebears.[34] Yet, even with its growing commitment to holistic mission, the evangelical church has not lived up to its early nineteenth-century history. Two hundred years ago, evangelicals had been at the center of the newly emerging process of globalization—spreading the faith; improving agriculture, health, and education; and providing a compelling moral framework that challenged a number of the ethical failures of their nation. Now, for the most part, we have abandoned any missional engagement that seeks to shape the processes, values, and outcomes of globalization. Any effort to shape contemporary globalization is now a largely secular affair.

Summing Up

We have seen that globalization is a deeply embedded historical process that began at creation. Globalization has adapted and changed as the human story developed over time. We have shaped and participated in globalization as we have learned new things about God's world and how it works. Poverty has declined in many places, and yet today's world is full of fragile states that have not found the economic growth or experienced the peace that the proponents of globalization promise. Justice is often hard to find. The powerful have used their power, and while the poor have materially improved, their voices are hard to hear. Materially, it is a good story; morally and theologically, not so much. The church is also part of this ambiguous story. Sometimes the church has been a clear witness to the goodness of the gospel, sometimes not. We will examine the impact of the last two hundred years of globalization in more depth in the next chapter.

Questions for Discussion

1. What lessons might we draw from the story of the church in nineteenth-century Britain?
2. Should evangelical churches aspire to a similar role today? What holds them back?

34. Largely as a result of the Lausanne Movement, which began under the leadership of Billy Graham in the 1970s.

THE IMPACT
OF GLOBALIZATION

7

The Impact of Two Hundred Years of Globalization

The Second Era of Globalization began with the economic and social transformation that emerged in Britain and spread to much of Europe and finally the United States and Japan. I called this phase Globalization I. After globalization's near death during the Great Disruption, the phenomenon reasserted itself during Globalization II with the extension of economic and technological innovations to the Asian Tigers, China, India, Indonesia, and Brazil. Other parts of the world are now following suit. This chapter presents a summary of the impact of this two-hundred-year process of change.

Economic Growth

Toward a Global Economy

The major outcome of this two-hundred-year period is that much of the rest of the world has opted in varying degrees for the neoliberal expression of capitalism. For some, it was simply a question of emulating ideas and practices that had worked elsewhere. For others, such as the Asian Tigers, it was a matter of following their own path to connect to the global economy. For still others, the adoption and adaptation was hard in light of memories of gunboats, colonialism, and slavery; to move in this direction felt like a kind of defeat or re-colonialization. Thus, the change was easy for some and hard, imperfect, and even incomplete for others.

In fact, it makes a big difference when a country transitions to the global market system and the new economic growth curve. Britain, much of the rest of Europe, and the United States enjoyed the cumulative impact of economic growth throughout the nineteenth century (recall fig. 6.4). Japan made the shift in a most unusual way. Forced to open itself to trade with Britain in 1853, the country decided to make a radical break with its feudal and agricultural past. The Meiji Restoration (1868–1912) was a Japanese-driven and Japanese-conceived movement of rapid industrialization. Their efforts at modernization required Western science and technology, and, under the banner of *bunmei kaika* (civilization and enlightenment), Japan adopted much of Western culture, from intellectual trends to clothing and architecture. By the early twentieth century, this self-imposed revolution had turned Japan into a modern industrial nation, and although it went in reverse during the Great Disruption, the foundation was set for a dramatic economic recovery after the end of the Second World War. For any nation, getting on the new economic growth curve earlier created a significant economic head start over the rest of the world. The impact can be seen in figure 7.1.

Africa, Asia, and Latin America began their movements toward neoliberal strategies of economic growth in the second half of the twentieth century. For much of Africa, the delay resulted from their struggle to emerge from colonial experiences that did little to prepare them for a market system as well as an understandable concern that the capitalism of the West had been an author of both economic exploitation and slavery. For China and Vietnam,

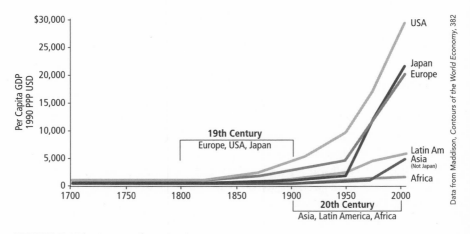

FIGURE 7.1 The impact of starting late

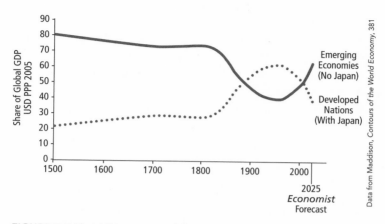

FIGURE 7.2 The shifting center of the economic world

the delay resulted from an excursion into Maoist communism. Then, in the 1970s, both nations opted for an unexpected marriage between a communist political system and a modern economic system. In Latin America, there was a late move away from the residual mercantilism of its colonial past and a deep suspicion that the neoliberal market system was a cover for continuing Western economic hegemony. By joining the economic globalization process over a century after the West, this group of nations has had a lot less time to enjoy the benefits of compounding economic growth. This is a second explanation for the inequality between the West and the rest in addition to the impact of the deindustrialization strategies of the European empires that I described in the previous chapter.

While being late to adopt market-based strategies for economic growth had an impact, the effects do not appear to be permanent. As the world's emerging or developing economies have begun to experience rapid economic growth, an interesting reversal is taking place. A comparison of emerging economies to developed economies in terms of their respective share of the world's GDP since 1500 illustrates the point (see fig. 7.2).

For most of human history, more people meant more wealth. The result was that the emerging economies of today, which have always had larger populations, dominated the world's wealth up until the beginning of Globalization I. With the advantages of globalization, today's developed economies then inverted the comparison. But today we are seeing the roles reverse yet again. In the last quarter century, the world's economic center of gravity moved steadily eastward from the mid-Atlantic (the United States and Europe) to the longitude of Eastern Europe, and it is forecast to be between

India and China by 2050.[1] One of the unexpected outcomes of Globalization II is the reversal of the Western economic dominance of the last two hundred years. China interprets this reversal as reclaiming its rightful place in history after a century of mistreatment by the West. In contrast, people and politicians in the West are struggling to regain their footing in this post-American world.[2]

Because most of the world today is on a trajectory of economic growth, we need to take note of some research that links growing household income with a fundamental shift in values. Ronald Inglehart has demonstrated that groups of people living in scarcity and insecurity tend to have traditional religious values that resist change and innovation, which are perceived as threats to survival. As household income increases above $5,000 a year, life begins to feel more secure and a sense of well-being emerges. The result is a gradual shift in cultural values in favor of individual initiative and achievement, wealth accumulation, and quality of life.[3]

A second finding from the same research is equally interesting. When a nation reaches an average annual income per capita of around $15,000, additional income growth no longer increases people's perception of well-being to anywhere near the degree that it did when they were much poorer.[4] Perhaps the biblical position on wealth is relevant today:

> . . . give me neither poverty nor riches,
>   but give me only my daily bread.
> Otherwise, I may have too much and disown you
>   and say, "Who is the LORD?"
> Or I may become poor and steal,
>   and so dishonor the name of my God. (Prov. 30:8–9)

Benjamin Friedman extends Inglehart's findings by arguing that economic growth and the concomitant increase in household incomes can lead to positive value changes in a society. "Economic growth—meaning a rising standard of living for the clear majority of citizens—more often than not fosters greater opportunity, tolerance of diversity, social mobility, commitment to fairness, and dedication to democracy."[5] On the other hand, wealth also induces greed,

---

1. Quah, "Shifting Centre of Gravity."

2. Zakaria, *Post-American World*.

3. Inglehart, *Modernization and Postmodernization*, 62, 71. Ronald Inglehart is research professor of political studies at the University of Michigan and the founding president of the World Values Survey.

4. Ibid., 65.

5. B. Friedman, *Moral Consequences of Economic Growth*, 4.

hedonism, and other undesirable behaviors. Original good and original sin coexist again.

Economic Centers Are Moving

In the last two hundred years, the world's economic center has moved in three ways. First, if we were to look at a map of the world with the size of countries made proportional to the value of the goods and services they produce (GDP), we would no longer see a mainly Western world. Today's world has two economic centers—China and India form one, and the United States and Europe form the other. While this is one view of the decentralization of the world's economic centers, this oversimplification focuses only on the size of the economy and may cause us to miss a second piece of important news.

The world's GDP was $30 trillion in 1995, 84 percent of which was located in the developed world. Twenty years later, the world's GDP had more than doubled to $73 trillion, while the share located in developed nations had dropped to 64 percent. The bottom line is that the share of the world's GDP in emerging economies more than doubled, while the share for the developed world decreased by almost 25 percent.[6] As long as the global economic pie gets bigger, poor countries can catch up even as rich countries still grow. It is not a zero-sum game.

Finally, it used to be true that the foreign direct investment (FDI) of the West was mostly invested in the West (that is, Western investors were investing mostly in businesses in other Western countries). But since the late 1990s, the economic growth of countries in the developing world outstripped those in the developed world, and so FDI followed suit. Today, more than half of FDI is going into the developing world.[7] While most is going into middle-income countries like China, India, and Brazil, it is now beginning to flow into Africa as well.[8]

Goods and Services Are Moving

Growth in international trade is one of the major features and causes of global economic growth in the Second Era of Globalization, particularly in the last fifty years. The total value of world trade in the aftermath of World War II was $57 billion. By 2010 it was $15 trillion, over a 260-fold increase.

6. Calculated using the World Bank's World Development Indicators database (July 22, 2016), http://databank.worldbank.org/data/download/GDP.pdf.
7. UNCTAD, *World Investment Report 2014*.
8. *Economist*, "Investment in Africa."

China was responsible for 11 percent of global exports, and the United States accounted for 13 percent of global imports.[9]

Increasing international trade has been enabled by the technological and economic dimensions of globalization. Because trade links distant markets, the "death of distance" made possible by technological innovations makes global trade faster, easier, and cheaper. Furthermore, global trade is empowered by the globalization of the world's financial systems and capital markets. As noted previously, the challenge of regulating both with responsible rules and regulations is considerable.

The fact that financial trading and capital flows are now globalized may be good for economic growth, but it also means that financial risk is globalized as well. The world experienced the consequence of this in the 2008 global financial crisis. We have noted in chapter 3 that unregulated financial markets operating in a digital global economy are a benefit to car manufacturers and flower importers as well as to criminals and terrorists. Human trafficking and the drug trade benefit too.

Opening up local markets to free trade is not always easy. Three factors contribute to countries being far from world markets, only the first of which is self-imposed: government policy, having a small population, or being a long distance from global economic centers. Combined, these three factors contribute to substantive barriers to trade in much of South America, sub-Saharan Africa, Central Asia, South Asia, and East Asia.[10]

Technological Change

The Emergence of Modern Sciences

Human beings do not do well in a world they do not understand. We seek meaning and an understanding of how things work because this is the way God made us. This God-given curiosity led to the emergence of physics, chemistry, and biology in the 1800s as people began to study what they could see and count and then create theories and formulations that were consistent with those observations. The test of a theory's validity was the accuracy of its predictions regarding future tests. Things seemed certain. These new ways of understanding how God's world works led to a broad array of technological innovations and new inventions in agriculture, health, and machines.

9. Statistics taken from Steger, *Globalization*, 41–42.
10. World Bank, *World Development Report 2009*, 222.

It is hard to overstate the degree to which the emergence of modern science changed Britain and Europe.[11] In the seventeenth century, well-educated Europeans believed in witchcraft and that mice were spontaneously generated by piles of dirty straw. They believed that it was possible to turn a base metal into gold. Their understanding of astronomy had the earth standing still while the sun and moon revolved around it, and they believed in astrology as well. Just over a century later, educated Europeans no longer believed in witches, had seen the world through a telescope and a microscope, and believed that ideas were tested by the scientific method. By the nineteenth century, the printing press enabled a proto-globalization of knowledge creation as scientists published their theories and results, which were then examined with skepticism and replicated (or not).

Technology Is Connecting Us

Human beings have always communicated, but for most of human history there were limitations on the reach and timeliness of their communications. At the beginning of the nineteenth century, communication was limited to a personal visit or writing a letter. Then a series of technological innovations changed that. The first commercial telegraph was created in 1837, and in 1866 the first transatlantic telegraph created the promise of global communications.

While the telephone has been around since the late 1890s, the current pace of its evolution is stunning. The first commercial mobile phone was made available in 1983, and the first smartphone only nine years later. In 2002 the BlackBerry combined phone service with email, and the first iPhone became available in 2007.

There is also good news from the Global South. The percentage of adults who own a cell phone in East Africa is almost the same as in the United States. Texting and taking photos are the most popular features for Africans, but there has been a rapid increase in internet searches and mobile banking as well.[12]

Internet technology became publically available in the 1990s. As I write this chapter, over 3.5 billion human beings are internet users and the internet has also taken over the global storage and transfer of information. In 1993 only 1 percent of the information flowing through two-way telecommunications networks went through the internet. The percentage increased to 50 percent by 2000 and to more than 97 percent by 2007.[13]

11. Summarized from Wootton, *Invention of Science*, 6. David Wootton is professor of history at the University of York.
12. Pew Research Center, "Cell Phones in Africa."
13. This is summarized from Hilbert and López, "World's Technological Capacity," 60.

The so-called digital divide is closely related to a country's potential to develop economically. Internet availability is highest in North America, Europe, and Latin America, with Asia and Africa at less than the world average of 42 percent. Sweden, Denmark, Iceland, and South Korea are the furthest along with over 80 percent internet penetration. In terms of the total number of people using the internet, Asia is in front with over 1.4 billion users. It is also significant that the top twelve internet-using countries include a group of middle-income countries known as "the BRICs" (Brazil, Russia, India, and China).[14] Even better news comes from the "2013 Human Development Report"; there are now more internet users in the Global South than in the developed nations.[15]

New Forms of Energy

For most of human history, the power to move things was limited by the strength of one's back and arms. The only alternative sources of energy were domesticated animals and water power. This severely limited the development of machines and thus economic growth. During the nineteenth century, coal as a source of energy was discovered. In the twentieth century, oil and then natural gas were added to the mix, enabling the very large increase in industrial production that took place over the last two hundred years. New forms of energy enabled new and better machines and ships, powered railroads, and also enabled the electrification of homes, cities, and nations.

Today we have become aware of the dangers of carbon dioxide released by burning these energy sources, especially as large nations such as China and India are in the process of industrializing. Thus, two hundred years of good news is now creating a new energy challenge as the world seeks renewable sources.

A New Technological Era Is Emerging

Listing some of the most recent technological changes runs the risk of making this book seem dated in just a few years because the pace of innovation gets faster and faster while the costs continue to lower. For example, the Human Genome Project, begun in 1990, took thirteen years to map the human genome and cost $3 billion. Today you can mail your DNA to a laboratory and have it sequenced in a few weeks for just over $1,000.[16] Various

14. The foregoing statistics come from Internet World Stats, "Internet Users of the World—2016."
15. UNDP, *Human Development Report 2013*, 15.
16. National Human Genome Research Institute, "DNA Sequencing Costs."

emerging technologies are in their infancy in terms of their impact on daily life; nanotechnology, genetic engineering, green technologies that promise to take us beyond the era of fossil fuels, wearable technology, the internet of things (everyday objects that are connected to the internet, allowing them to send and receive data), 3-D printing, and artificial intelligence come to mind.

The trend is clear. The rate of technological innovation and adoption is rapidly increasing and diversifying. These technological advances are changing how we relate to one another, reducing costs, boosting economic growth, eroding privacy, and wearing us out. Things we always thought we needed— like hard drives—are giving way to the cloud. Phones ask you what you want and carry out simple tasks. Phone calls and emails are giving way to instant messaging, and you can change the temperature of your home with a downloadable app. Thomas Friedman argues that the technological changes from 1990 to 2005 are the single biggest driver of globalization.[17] I wonder what will be said about technology and economic growth fifteen years from now.

People Are Moving

I have already described migration as a central driver of the First Era of Globalization. In a sense, the one consistent thread in globalization from creation to today is migration. But the modern period of migration has a number of new features that we need to take into consideration as we investigate globalization.

Modern Migration

I described the first two phases of modern migration in chapter 5. First, there was the slave trade and its horrible consequences. Second, there was its replacement in the form of indentured workers from China, India, and East Africa and the fifty million Europeans moving to the European colonies. For the most part, the direction of migration in this second phase was largely from the West to the rest.

The third phase of modern migration, according to Jehu Hanciles, was characterized by a disruption and then a reversal in the migration flow. With the outbreak of the First World War, European migration slowed dramatically as Europeans began to return home, and many fought in one or both world wars. Then in the 1960s the flow of migrants began to reverse; migration began to increase from the rest to the West.[18]

17. T. Friedman, *World Is Flat*.
18. Hanciles, *Beyond Christendom*, 167, 172.

Open Borders

Olúfẹ́mi Táíwò, professor of Africana Studies and Research
Center, Cornell University

Open borders cannot remain at the level of rhetorical commitment: They
must be truly open in both spatial and intellectual terms. Seen thus, the
movement of peoples becomes not the occasion for circling the *laager* but
the occasion for opening up to new experiences; endeavoring to learn new
tongues; cultivating new tastes in food, fashion, and loving; and generally
absorbing fresh productive energies while discovering the essential oneness
of humanity in its infinite presentations.

Táíwò, *Colonialism*, 272

A word before we look at the features of today's migration. There are
two important findings from migration studies. First, migration needs to
be understood as more than just people moving from one place to another.
Migration also drives social change, since as people move, their culture
moves with them. Second, we now know that migration results in a short-
term form of social development. Migrants and their families do benefit, but
so do their receiving cultures. There is a two-way exchange of languages,
customs, arts, rituals, and technology, all of which leads to innovation in
both cultures.[19]

New Features of Migration Today

There is a profound irony in contemporary migration. On the one hand,
the number of migrants has increased significantly over the last twenty
years, with a record 250 million people who left home, place, and culture
in 2015.[20] This is more than four times the number of people uprooted by
war and famine worldwide, which itself is at an all-time high.[21] On the
other hand, this number could have been much higher if it were not for the
fact that the post–World War II expression of economic globalization was
the first in which the free global flow in goods, services, and capital was

19. Manning, *Migration in World History*, 2.
20. World Bank, "Migration and Remittances," 1.
21. Forcibly displaced people include refugees, internally displaced people, and asylum
seekers. UNHCR, "Worldwide Displacement."

not accompanied by a free flow of labor. Migration became restricted in Globalization II.[22]

Contemporary migration offers two ways by which poverty eradication is or could be helped. One is in play today, and the other is not. First, many are unaware that, while most migrants begin their new lives in limited circumstances and with low-paying work, the amount of money they send home to members of their extended families is simply astounding. In 2014 over $430 billion in remittances was sent to developing countries, with India, China, the Philippines, Mexico, and Nigeria at the top of the list of receiving countries.[23] This is over three times the amount of global development aid and also exceeds global foreign direct investment (excluding China).[24] Migrants are seeking to improve not just their own lives but also the lives of their family members back home. Remittances are a very efficient way to get money directly into the hands of poor families, and the evidence suggests that the money is often used for improving homes, paying school fees, and accessing health services.

The second potential contribution has to do with a gap in migration economics. There is a single-minded focus on emigration and its impact on countries that receive migrants. However, the economic impact of emigration on the poor countries of origin has been largely unexplored and ignored. Contemporary migration and development research suggests that relaxing the restrictions on the free movement of labor could be a major contributor to poverty eradication. "The globalization of labor—greater mobility for workers across borders—quickly and massively raises migrants' living standards toward those of rich countries."[25]

Another feature of contemporary migration that is not always recognized is that for most of the twenty-first century, migration was not simply a case of the poor in the Global South migrating to the rich North as many North Americans believe. South-to-South migration within Africa, Asia, and Europe exceeded South-to-North migration in 2013.[26] The only exception was the movement of Latin Americans to the United States. The trend of South-to-South migration exceeding South-to-North may change as violence and economic hardship drove more than one million refugees and economic migrants

---

22. Clemens, "Economics and Emigration," 83. Michael Clemens is a senior fellow at the Center for Global Development, Washington, DC, and a visiting scholar in the Department of Economics and the Wagner School of Public Policy at New York University.

23. World Bank, "Migration and Remittances," 1.

24. Ibid., 5.

25. Clemens, "Labor Mobility Agenda for Development," 260.

26. World Bank, "Migration and Remittances," 1.

from North Africa, Eritrea, Syria, and Afghanistan into Europe in 2015. This is a humanitarian crisis of unprecedented magnitude and has stretched the capacity of the West to respond.

Another shift in contemporary migration is the result of the technological dimension of globalization. The many new communication technologies are reducing the pressure for acculturation, resulting in what has been called a "globalization of ethnicities."[27] Communications technology, such as Skype, Google Talk, and FaceTime, allows Nigerians, Indians, South Koreans, and other ethnic or religious groups to remain connected with their families and friends back home in real time and at reasonable cost. One of the interesting effects is that news about churches in the Global South is also being communicated to sister churches in Western cities.

Most of today's migrants are affiliated with one of the world's major religions. Just under half of the world's migrants are Christians; they are our brothers and sisters. Another 27 percent are from Muslim countries.[28] Muslims also make up over 70 percent of the world's refugees.[29] The challenge for Muslim migrants is to find ways to adjust to Western multiculturalism and its separation of church and state. Another challenge, particularly for Europeans, is to find ways to accommodate and welcome the presence of deeply religious Muslims in the context of Europe's fiercely held commitment to secularism.[30] All of this suggests that finding ways for Christians and Muslims to better understand each other and learn to live peacefully together is an urgent missiological challenge. (More on this in chapter 11.)

Another feature of contemporary migration is critically important to the church and to Christians. At roughly the same time that the center of gravity of the Christian world moved to the Global South, a wave of Southern Christians are migrating to the formerly Christian West. This expression of "globalization from below" has not received as much attention as it requires.[31] Many of these Christian migrants understand themselves to be missionaries to Western countries whose Christian identity is either fading or lost altogether. Some of the fastest growing churches in London are Ghanaian and Nigerian. African pastors lead the four largest megachurches in Britain.[32] The largest church in Europe is African-founded and led. Among the fastest growing churches in American cities

27. Smilde, *Reason to Believe*, 222. David Smilde is professor of social relations at Tulane University.
28. Both percentages are from Pew Research Center, "Faith on the Move."
29. Islamic Human Rights Commission, "UNHCR Statistics."
30. Hanciles, *Beyond Christendom*, 46–47, 254, 377, 381.
31. Ibid., 178.
32. Jenkins, "Believers Arrive First," 28.

are those of African migrants, and Hispanic, Korean, and Chinese congregations are also making the church landscape less and less European.[33]

There is a final feature of contemporary migration whose impact is not yet clear. Seeking a better economic future is not the sole factor driving migration. Demographics matter too. Some nations with aging populations—Japan, China, and much of Europe—are seeing sharp declines in the numbers of working-age citizens. The only solution to keeping their economies growing is inward migration of younger workers.[34] It is beyond the scope of this book to explore the complexities of migration further, but this often controversial topic needs a more nuanced and evidence-based exploration.[35]

Better Human Lives

Better Health

The last two hundred years have seen a radical improvement in the health of the world as measured by life expectancy. In addition to the widespread provision of clean water and better sanitation, the invention of vaccines, anesthetics, and antibiotics has changed the public health landscape. The Green Revolution in agriculture in the mid-twentieth century is estimated to have saved over a billion people from starvation.

Improving public health has been the single most successful part of the development aid portfolio in the last half century. Vaccination campaigns have greatly reduced polio and measles. Oral rehydration campaigns have greatly reduced deaths from diarrhea.[36] Globally, deaths of children under the age of five decreased by 49 percent between 1990 and 2013.[37] The bottom line is simple: economic growth and people being more connected lead to improved health and well-being.

Hans Rosling has put together a fascinating and revealing video account that tracks the changes in income and life expectancy of the world's nations from 1800 to 2013.[38] In 1800, Europe along with all the world's nations were poor—per person income was less than $4,000 a year (present-day equivalent), and life expectancy was short, less than forty years. Two hundred years later,

33. Hanciles, *Beyond Christendom*, 378.
34. International Organization for Migration, "South-South Migration," 2.
35. See, e.g., Collier, *Exodus*.
36. Easterly, *White Man's Burden*, 241.
37. WHO, "Under-Five Mortality."
38. Rosling, "Wealth and Health of Nations." Hans Rosling is professor of international health at the Karolinska Institutet in Sweden.

life expectancy is over sixty-five years for people in all nations, excepting some nations in Africa, which are experiencing the impact of the HIV/AIDS pandemic. There is an interesting wrinkle: the West had to get wealthier in order to get healthier. But because the West figured out so much about public health and developed vaccines and other medical interventions, the rest of the world has been able to get healthier before increasing in wealth.

Education and Literacy

The nineteenth century in Europe was accompanied by the first mass education movement in the world. Such movements were characterized by a focus on educational achievement, widespread access to schools, and the growing capacity to function in a rapidly changing, urbanizing, and industrializing world. For most of the nineteenth century, mass education was a shared responsibility between governments and religious institutions.[39] Two hundred years later, while quite uneven in terms of quality, mass education is largely compulsory and universal across the world. The connections between education and both the exercise of liberty and human agency seem clear.

Mass literacy means little without the widespread availability of things to read. The printing press was invented by Johannes Gutenberg around 1440. This led to the availability of newspapers, pamphlets, and magazines. But it was not until the nineteenth century—when the hand-operated press was replaced by a steam-powered rotary press—that the production of books took off. By 1800 the number of books in English printed per decade reached seven thousand, up from less than half that in 1700.[40]

A change in the reading habits of ordinary people was as important as having more books available. Even with the arrival of the printing press, most people owned only a few books and read them over and over. Rolf Engelsing, a German book historian, argues that the mass production of books created a "reading revolution."[41] Ordinary people read more and more books, which, he argues, had a liberating effect as it increased the ability of people to see the world from the perspective of others. Steven Pinker argues that the explosion of reading may have contributed to an increase in empathy for others outside their village or town "by getting people into the habit of straying from their parochial vantage points."[42] Reading enables people to connect in wider and wider circles.

39. Soysal and Strong, "Mass Educational Systems," 279.
40. Pinker, *Better Angels of Our Nature*, 173.
41. Darnton, *Kiss of Lamourette*, 154–87.
42. Pinker, *Better Angels of Our Nature*, 177. Steven Pinker is a cognitive psychologist and professor of psychology at Harvard University.

The Social Sciences Emerge

While the natural (mechanical) world seemed orderly and relatively easy to investigate using the scientific method, there were few conceptual tools to make sense of the large social changes that were gathering steam. As people moved from the country to the city, from working in their homes to working in factories and shops, people began to see the world as no longer fixed and immutable but as something that they could influence. In the face of the tidal wave of change that began in the early 1800s, the social sciences emerged as people struggled to understand and make sense of the change.

Primarily as a reaction to mercantilism, political economics—the relationship between markets and the state—emerged as a distinct field of study in the mid-eighteenth century as the Scottish moral philosophers Adam Smith and David Hume and the French economist François Quesnay began to study political economy in a systematic rather than piecemeal way.

The second half of the nineteenth century saw the creation of the social sciences of anthropology, sociology, and psychology. The modern understanding of anthropology—the science of humanity or human beings—emerged at the same time as Darwin's *Origin of the Species* and the discoveries in prehistoric archaeology in the 1860s. Also in the mid-1800s, Auguste Comte, the father of sociology, proposed to unify all studies of humankind through the scientific understanding of the social realm. In 1879 Wilhelm Wundt founded the first formal laboratory of psychology at the University of Leipzig, marking the formal beginning of the academic study of human emotions, behaviors, and cognition. Seven years later Sigmund Freud began practicing therapy in Vienna, marking the beginning of personality theory.

For a long time the social sciences longed for the certainty associated with the discoveries in physics, chemistry, and biology, including the ability to predict results of experiments as the proof of a theory. This hope for general theories that could be used to understand and shape people and societies proved unattainable. As I explained in chapter 2, complex adaptive social systems—made up of the actions of large numbers of unpredictable human beings—are by definition unpredictable. While it is possible to describe and even make sense of what happened looking backward into the past, the social sciences have never proved a reliable guide to the future. This is not to say that social sciences are fundamentally flawed; rather, it is an important reminder that the systems they study are not mechanical in nature and thus are not subject to linear logic and repeatable cause and effect.

Culture and People Change

The most fundamental shift in the Second Era of Globalization, however, was not in economics or technology but in the Western worldview and a concomitant change in how individual human beings came to view themselves and their roles in society. While these changes were generally quite beneficial, the change in society's view of religion and the role of the church was less so.

Changes in Human Self-Understanding

Sometimes we forget that for much of its history the West was home to a mixture of traditional cultures—featuring magic, spirits, and demons—that slowly mixed or coexisted with Christianity. During the Second Era of Globalization, this traditional and medieval worldview gradually gave way to the one we now label as modern and secular.

This shift in worldview was a combination of good news and not so good news. I have already described some of the bad news in the introduction and also its impact on the church in mission in chapter 6. The spiritual realm was separated from the material realm with the result that the evangelical church opted for witnessing to Jesus Christ and evangelism, thus losing sight of the "on earth as it is in heaven" aspect of our witness to the kingdom of God (more on this failure in chap. 11). There is another negative impact of this two-tiered worldview. When God and religion are relegated to the spiritual realm, they are treated as having nothing to contribute to the real world of politics, economics, and science. The consequences of this are a recurring theme in this book.

The good news has to do with a shift in how humans viewed themselves and their world. In the premodern or traditional moral order in the West, human identity was understood in tribal or social terms. *We are*, not *I am*. In the modern era, human beings began to understand themselves as individual, rational social agents—*I am* and *I can act*. In the traditional worldview of the West, the clan or extended family defined one's role and function within a hierarchical and often patriarchal social system that was understood as being ordained by God. Change for the individual was neither possible nor desirable. The modern worldview takes it for granted that, while family and social ties are important, the final decision on one's role is up to the individual. The idea that ordinary people were to serve the king gave way to the radically new idea that the purpose of the political system is to serve the people by respecting the rule of law as well as their rights and agency. Finally, in the world of traditional culture, there was no public sphere and thus no such thing as public opinion. In the modern worldview, the public sphere or civil society is the place where human beings act to shape their political and social order through voluntary associations, including mission agencies and churches. Public opinion matters in the modern world.

The major social changes in the Second Era of Globalization that I described earlier in this chapter were undergirded by and reflective of these changes in worldview. The discovery that wealth could be created, the importance of human liberty, the idea that individuals are entitled to protection by the rule of law, and the hunger for the orderly study of the inner and cultural life of human beings and their societies all emerged as a result of this change in worldview. From a traditional sense of resignation in the face of an inhospitable world of scarcity and oppression, human beings began to develop a new sense of personal agency, thinking of new ideas and taking actions to improve their circumstances. Everyone, even the poor, began to discover that they could change themselves and their world.

Over the last two hundred years, this new human self-understanding has meant that more and more ordinary people all over the world have developed a set of analytical tools that help them to understand why things are happening to them and to develop an orientation toward authority that is more critically self-conscious.[43] "Today's persons-in-the-street are no longer as uninvolved, ignorant, and manipulable with respect to world affairs as were their forebears."[44]

This change in worldview has been spreading across the world among indigenous peoples, minorities, and the socially excluded. Liberation theology, the "color" revolutions of Eastern Europe, and the Arab Spring are all examples. Globalization, in the sense of getting connected, enables this. Human beings who are self-confident enough and educated enough can use technology to find others with whom to act. Communications technology allows everyone's voice to be heard.

Globalization of Compassion

For most of human history, charity as a practice was limited to *our family* or *our village* because the horizon of our compassion was limited to those we knew and those we could see. It was not until the nineteenth century that charity was extended to *our people* and *our nation*. But it did not stop there. By the end of the twentieth century, the moral horizon of compassion became global.

43. Freire, *Education for Critical Consciousness.*
44. Rosenau, *Turbulence in World Politics*, 13.

Like so many other changes we have examined, this new understanding of compassion takes us back to nineteenth-century Britain. In addition to the changes in the people and society, a major shift took place in the moral imagination of the British people. For the first time in human history, the idea of charity (*caritas*)—feeling and acting with compassion for those who are suffering—took on two new dimensions. The first was the idea that human suffering was wrong and should be addressed by individuals and society, and the second was that human suffering should be prevented or ended, if possible.[45]

As to origins, Gertrude Himmelfarb points to a three-way intersection between the philosophy of compassion arising from Scottish moral philosophers, the Wesleyan revival and its gospel of good works, and Adam Smith's political economy of natural liberty. In spite of considerable philosophical and theological differences, these three converged when it came to practical and ethical matters, which included the idea of compassion for the less fortunate.[46]

The result was that Britain was the first country to have a public, secular, and national system of poverty relief.[47] Institutions whose sole function was compassionate caring, such as the National Society for the Prevention of Cruelty to Children, emerged for the first time in human history.[48] Other organizations were established to abolish the slave trade and prevent cruelty to prisoners and animals. As voluntary societies, clubs, trusts, and projects became instruments of charitable relief and religious renewal, civil society became an arena of moral action, and a moral entrepreneurialism became the norm.[49]

In Europe this new understanding of compassion led to the founding of the International Committee of the Red Cross (ICRC) by (mostly) Protestant Genevans in 1863 and the Catholic relief organization Caritas Germany in 1897. In time the ICRC became the global caretaker for what was eventually called humanitarian law and the humanitarian imperative—the obligation of the world's nations to respond to people suffering as a result of war and disasters.

With the end of World War II, this new understanding of compassion became even more robust as it converged with two other elements of the emerging global compassion imaginary.[50] The first was the expansion of our

45. Sznaider, "Sociology of Compassion," 122. Natan Sznaider is an Israeli sociologist at the Academic College of Tel Aviv-Yaffo.
46. Himmelfarb, "Idea of Compassion," 7, 9, 13.
47. Ibid., 13.
48. Sznaider was well aware of the charitable work of the Catholic mendicant orders, but charitable work was not their sole or central mission.
49. Sirota, "First Big Society."
50. Barnett, *Empire of Humanity*, 21.

understanding of human identity to include our being rights bearers; this idea evolved into the global human rights movement.[51] The second was a result of Raphael Lemkin's invention of the word *genocide* for the "crime without a name," as he termed the Armenian genocide.[52] Reinforced by the Holocaust, the idea of a crime against humanity has become part of international law.

This shift in the moral horizons of compassion was enabled by the communications dimension of globalization.[53] Television and eventually international media coverage meant that we could see the faces and hear the stories of actual refugees as well as victims of famine and war. Media brought the distant stranger into our homes. The barriers of citizenship, religion, and race were eroded by this visual reframing of "Who is my neighbor?" Jet travel, INGOs, and good logistics meant that something could be done to help. The media reminds us daily of the sheer amount of financial resources in the West. The combined impact of all this changed the modern moral imagination. Helping our distant neighbor became politically inescapable as domestic pressures to help increased, which in turn changed foreign policy.[54] In his encyclical *Deus Caritas Est*, Pope Benedict XVI enshrined this new understanding in theological terms: "Anyone who needs me, and whom I can help, is my neighbor. The concept of 'neighbor' is now universalized, yet it remains concrete."[55]

Church and Compassion

The worldview change in the West was both good and bad news for the church. On the positive side, the church has always been in the charity business and has a two-thousand-year history of compassion. Even with the church's relegation to the spiritual realm, it continued its mission of charity as it created institutions of compassion. Baptist World Aid was founded in 1905, along with the Quaker organization American Friends Service Committee in 1917. In the 1940s, Church World Service, World Relief, the United Methodist Committee on Relief, and Catholic Relief Services were founded in the United States. In 1950 the plight of Korean orphans led to the founding of World Vision. Most of these organizations draw their funding from within their denominations or by fund-raising directed at Christians. The larger secular society is mostly untouched, which leads me to a point of concern.

51. Some argue that the idea of human rights is a modern and secular concept at odds with Christian theology. This argument has been successfully refuted, and the Christian foundations for human rights and responsibilities can be found in Wolterstorff, *Justice*.

52. "What Is Genocide?," *History*, 2009, http://www.history.com/topics/what-is-genocide.

53. Summarized from Ignatieff, *Warrior's Honor*, 9–33.

54. Smillie and Minear, *Charity of Nations*, 177.

55. Benedict XVI, *Deus Caritas Est*, §15.

On the negative side, the relegation of the church left the "real" world of politics, economics, and social change to the secular world. Liberal Protestants and Catholics insisted on remaining active in the name of justice, but they slowly lost the plot when it came to conversion and personal faith. Evangelicals went the other way by accepting their relegation and refocusing their energies on protecting the fundamentals of the faith and evangelism. Consequently, evangelicals went silent on issues of social justice and social change for most of the twentieth century. In today's world, only the neo-Pentecostals seem committed theologically and in practice to resisting this material-spiritual dichotomy. (More on this is chapter 11.)

There was one other unintended outcome of the church accepting its place on the sidelines of politics, economics, and social change. The new global compassion imaginary needed to rest on a moral or ethical foundation. Where were the ethical foundations undergirding this compassion going to come from, if not from the communities of faith? In time, the answer emerged in the form of what Nayan Chanda calls "globalization of values," which transcended any religion. Moral leadership, working largely from a secular script, moved to civil society in the form of the human rights and the environmental movements. Organizations such as Amnesty International, Human Rights Watch, Greenpeace, and Oxfam emerged as ethical leaders in the public realm. A new order of secular missionaries were fighting for human rights, radical inclusion of minorities and the voiceless, and safeguarding the environment.[56]

Today Christian churches and organizations involved in advocacy as part of Christian mission are sometimes culturally captive to the secular assumptions of civil society advocacy movements. Those who avoid this captivity tend to focus on narrow issues important to Christians on the Christian-secular cultural fault line, another expression of relegation. When it comes to social ethics and advocacy, the tools of the church and secular agencies are largely identical. A deep and nuanced Christian understanding of what advocacy for social change is and how it ought to be done remains to be seen.[57]

It is a sad irony that the largely secular global advocacy movement looks back to William Wilberforce and his fellow Christians as the birthplace of the first national campaign for changing public policy. The church has gone from being an actor in the public square in Britain and its empire, speaking a critical moral voice to the centerpiece of the economic system of its day (based on slavery) and the mistreatment of children and prisoners, to effectively leaving

56. Summarized from Chanda, *Bound Together*, 137.
57. Offutt et al., *Advocating for Justice*, is an exception: it has recently been published and is a nuanced and generally useful evangelical examination of advocacy.

the stage by the end of the last century. The absence of a moral ecology to shape globalization and its processes is partly a result of the relegation of the church and our acquiescence to this relegation. More on this in the last two chapters of this book. Having outlined the impact of two hundred years of globalization, we turn to an assessment of it.

Questions for Discussion

1. Which of the impacts of globalization described in this chapter are most real to you? Why?
2. In the section on migrations, what was news to you? What was not?

8

Assessing the Second Era of Globalization

We need a baseline against which to judge the depth and breadth of the changes of the last two hundred years. In 1800, Europe and the United States were as poor as rural Africa is today. Most people lived in simple homes with no sanitation or clean drinking water. They lived by subsistence agriculture or making things by hand for barter or local sale. There was no electricity, and little was known about disease and how to prevent or treat it. It was a small world whose boundary was the village or the estate or the tenement. It was a world of scarcity and insecurity. People had little freedom and few options for changing the circumstances of their lives.

What Happened to the Poor?

So how are the poor doing in God's world today? In comparison to the baseline I just described, it is obvious that the poor all over the world have seen rather remarkable material improvement. I have already described how, over the last two hundred years, the world's per capita wealth increased over seven times, life expectancy has almost doubled, vaccinations have sharply reduced communicable disease, child mortality has dropped, availability of clean water and better sanitation has increased, and mass education is largely compulsory and universal across the world. More and more people are moving from chronic poverty to the middle class.

But what about the last twenty-five years of Globalization II? Is there still good news for the poor? The answer depends largely on the decade for which the question is asked. In the era of the Washington Consensus in the 1990s,[1] the poor were not doing well and poverty appeared to be increasing. While things were improving in East Asia (China) and to a lesser extent in South Asia (India), the percentage of people living in extreme poverty (less than $1.25 a day) was increasing in Africa and Central Asia and was largely unchanged in Latin America. The assessments of the economic dimension of globalization written in the 1990s and early 2000s were correspondingly negative. Globalization seemed to be hurting the poor. Liberation theology continued its call for some form of socialism, and many, including mainline Protestants, were calling for alternatives to capitalism.

By the first decade of the twenty-first century, the picture became significantly more positive. The percentage of people living on less than $1.25 a day began to drop in all regions, including Africa, and this continued into the next decade.[2] The percentage of people living in chronic poverty was down to 22 percent in 2015. The most dramatic reduction in extreme poverty took place in East Asia, where the percentage of people living on less than $1.25 a day dropped from 80 percent to 7 percent over thirty years. China alone accounted for most of the decline, with over three-quarters of a billion people moving above the extreme poverty threshold. The second largest regional decline took place in South Asia, where the share of the population living in extreme poverty dropped to 19 percent from 58 percent in 1981. In contrast, poverty in sub-Saharan Africa, which experienced some reduction, nonetheless stood at 43 percent in 2012.[3]

Regarding other dimensions of material poverty, there is also a lot of good news. During Globalization II, the rate of child mortality was cut in half and the global maternal mortality rate dropped 45 percent. The percentage of people without access to enough food to be active and healthy was reduced by half. Access to improved drinking water was extended to 2.6 billion people, and almost 2.1 billion people gained access to improved sanitation.[4]

1. Introduced in chapter 3, the Washington Consensus was a product of the neoliberal economic policies of the Thatcher-Reagan era. It was imposed by the World Bank and the International Monetary Fund as a condition for poor nations receiving loans. It called for reducing public expenditures, extensive privatization of government businesses and services, trade liberalization, floating exchange rates, and deregulation.

2. World Bank, *World Development Indicators 2015*.

3. Statistics from World Bank, "Poverty: Overview."

4. Ibid.

By any measure, this is a stunning transformation in the lives of the poor all over the world. But it is also true that this change was uneven and often unfair. The poor in some parts of the world are seeing better lives and more opportunities. This is less true elsewhere. There are valid concerns regarding issues of inequality, gender, and environmental impact. Furthermore, there is still a lot more to do in terms of poverty eradication (as we will explore in depth in chapter 9). A lot of work lies before us if everyone on the planet is to have enough to live and have a life worth living. But we need to celebrate the fact that the Second Era of Globalization, and particularly Globalization II, has provided good news for many of the poor, at least in material terms.

Differing Perspectives on Globalization

Commentators who argue for modern wealth creation as essential to reducing poverty invariably do not argue from the perspective of those who have suffered unimaginable damage historically and contemporarily. The continuing pursuit of material goods does not produce full prosperity or well-being for all. Yet to make the excuse to condemn wealth creation wholesale is quite misleading, if not fatuous.

—John Atherton and Hannah Skinner[5]

So how do scholars assess two hundred years of globalization and its radical redirection of human economic history? Where do they think it is taking us? I posed the question about the inevitability of globalization briefly in chapter 4, and now I will summarize some varying contemporary perspectives as a way of taking us deeper into the subject. As one might expect, the reactions run the gamut—from optimists who are confident globalization will take us to the best possible future, to skeptics who see a lot of competing cultural and ideological issues that make this rosy prognosis less certain, and finally to some extreme skeptics, who believe that globalization will take us toward a very bad place where things fall apart (see fig. 8.1). I do not intend to explore these varying perspectives in depth, nor will I endorse a single view, but I believe that a brief overview might be helpful as you formulate your own views.

5. Atherton and Skinner, *Through the Eye of a Needle*, 2. John Atherton is an Anglican theologian, director of the William Temple Foundation, and visiting research professor at the University of Chester. Hannah Skinner is the economic affairs advisor to the William Temple Foundation.

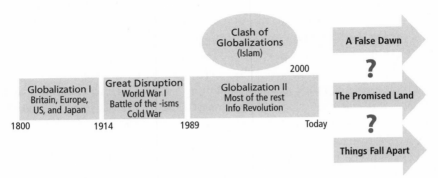

FIGURE 8.1 Whither globalization?

Toward the Promised Land

Martin Wolf is one of the optimists.[6] Having lived through the Great Disruption and the first part of Globalization II in Britain, Wolf insists that the lessons of history are unambiguous: human freedom is essential to a workable economic system, markets allow people to express their personal choices, and liberal democracies are the best—if messy—way to manage a society. This view is combined with an abiding skepticism about the wisdom and capacity of government to manage a nation's economy. On globalization Wolf is unambiguous: "The problem today is not that there is too much globalization, but not enough."[7] His message to those still reluctant to become part of the global market system is to take a hard look at figure 7.1 and see that the longer nations wait to connect to the global market system, the longer it will take them to catch up.

Wolf is a classic neoliberal economist, but not a blindly supportive one. His response to the critics of globalization is to agree that economic globalization has hard edges, even unjust ones, which need attention. But these shortcomings must be solved within the rubric of capitalism; there simply are no economic alternatives that work, in Wolf's view. He acknowledges that markets need states and states need markets, and he defines the challenge as one of finding ways of connecting free markets and cooperative global governance without one dominating the other. While a global market economy is a given in his mind, Wolf also affirms that the central unanswered question of our time is how best to govern and regulate it.

The weakness in Wolf's assessment is its narrow focus on economic globalization alone. Culture is treated as part of the background for Wolf and

6. Wolf, *Why Globalization Works*. Martin Wolf graduated from Oxford as an economist and a social democrat, although militantly anti-Marxist. Wolf worked in Africa for the World Bank and is widely respected as the associate editor and chief economics commentator at the *Financial Times*.
7. Ibid., xvii.

The Past Leaves Us No Choice

Martin Wolf, chief economics editor, *Financial Times*

The ruin of the first liberal order [with the advent of World War I] led to thirty years of catastrophe from which my parents' generation suffered so much. The lives of billions of people were blighted by those mistakes. Now we all—or almost all—know better. The ideas that undermined faith in the liberal order were wrong. Socialism does not work. Communism and fascism were crimes, as well as blunders. Imperialism was a blind alley. Militarism and national-ism destroyed European civilization. Now we have, by luck as much as by judgement, recreated a better liberal international order—one that extends opportunities to the world as a whole. It is our duty to our descendants not to throw away this golden opportunity once again.

Wolf, *Why Globalization Works*, xviii

is thus without significant influence. In a global world with so many differing cultures and histories, this assumption seems unwarranted. A second weakness is that the cooperative global governance Wolf says is needed seems a distant hope in light of the reluctance of today's nation-states to surrender sovereignty in favor of some form of global governance. Finally, the idea of governance implies a moral vision of some kind. Wolf is unclear as to where such a moral vision would come from, as it surely will not emerge from either the free market or the global political arena.

Several Christian voices affirm the good that economic globalization has done and what it promises for the poor, while nonetheless arguing that Christian theology, as well as that of other world religions, has something critically important to offer. For example, they call our attention to the fact that globalization ignores the transcendent, has a sharply reduced view of who human beings are, and ignores the purpose of human beings in the world. There is also a common concern about the absence of a moral ecology with the power and reach to shape the processes of globalization. We will return to this in chapters 12 and 13.

Anglican layperson Brian Griffiths, working from John Paul II's encyclical *Centesimus Annus*,[8] affirms the good that economic globalization has done

8. John Paul II's encyclical was written one hundred years after the first encyclical (*Rerum Novarum*) that launched what is now called Catholic social teaching. This tradition provides a

The Limits of Economic Freedom

Pope John Paul II

Economic freedom is only one element of human freedom. When it becomes autonomous, when man is seen more as a producer or consumer of goods than as a subject who produces and consumes in order to live, then economic freedom loses its necessary relationship to the human person and ends up alienating and oppressing him.

John Paul II, *Centesimus Annus*, §30

for the poor and argues that the biblical ideas of human liberty and human creativity are best suited to the practices of capitalism. But he notes that "[the secular] liberal market philosophy is an inadequate basis for globalization because it fails to provide a moral and cultural foundation that respects the dignity of the human person." With Wolf, Griffith's suspicion of governments (socialism) results in an ambiguous proposal for how this respect for the human person might be achieved: "It is important to distinguish global governance [world government] from the governance of globalization."⁹ Fair enough, but what might this mean in practical terms? Griffith's proposal is thin and unconvincing. The reform of global governance, he goes on to say, must be based on certain core values and principles. So we face the issue of the missing moral vision once again.

John Atherton takes us a step further by suggesting that economic capital and social capital need to be engaged by "religious capital" in order to provide a full account of human well-being. "Religion has a necessary if not essential place in our world, historically, contemporarily and in the future, in contributing to the necessary maintenance and transformation of our world."¹⁰ Atherton affirms what some won't say out loud: religion is the source of moral vision, and the world needs a moral vision to speak into globalization. This topic will be addressed in some depth in chapter 13 as I examine the work of Max Stackhouse, Daniel Groody, and others.

---

critical Catholic commentary on modern society and is critical of both socialism and capitalism primarily because both violate a Christian understanding of who human beings are and why they are here.

9. Griffiths, *Globalization*, 18. Brian Griffiths (Lord Griffiths of Fforestfach) was an advisor to Margaret Thatcher and is serving as vice chairman of Goldman Sachs.

10. Atherton, *Transfiguring Capitalism*, 1.

Thomas Friedman is a globalization optimist and a technological determinist who argues that the digital revolution in technology has made the world "flat"—information accessible to all.[11] Friedman argues that globalization's technological innovation is the primary driver of the economic growth that occurred in the last twenty-five years of Globalization II. The role of free markets was simply to allow this innovation to happen faster and to be disseminated more effectively. In Friedman's theory of change, technological change drives economic change, which in turn drives social or cultural change. Culture moves to the background once again.

Friedman observes that technology empowered nations to globalize in the nineteenth century, and companies in the last half of the twentieth century. Today it is empowering individuals and groups. Anyone, anywhere can innovate and offer a product or a service to anyone else in the world. Anyone or any group can find and mobilize like-minded people all over the world. For Friedman, concerns for the environment are the only limitation to globalization's future.[12]

Friedman acknowledges a downside to all this. "The playing field is not being leveled only in ways that draw in and superempower a whole new group of innovators. It's being leveled in a way that draws in and superempowers a whole new group of angry, frustrated, and humiliated men and women."[13] This new globalized technological world has enabled innovation and mobilization on the part of the frustrated young people of the Arab Spring and angry African Americans who see little justice in their justice system. Negatively, it has also enabled terrorists and criminals.

There are soft spots in Friedman's view of globalization. First, China, countries in the Middle East, and Russia are contemporary examples of the limits state power can place on the freedom of information to move and be used; in some places things are intentionally being made not so flat. Second, Friedman does not attribute much influence to culture and religion, which in his view are molded by technology and markets. But as we will see in a minute, Islam is doing a very good job of saying no to globalization. Third, while the world's technological playing field may be flat, its economic and political playing fields are not. It is unclear if Friedman's belief in the power of technology can overcome the resistance coming from these other playing fields.

11. T. Friedman, *World Is Flat*. Thomas Friedman is a three-time Pulitzer Prize winner and writes a weekly column for the *New York Times*.
12. T. Friedman, *Hot, Flat, and Crowded*.
13. T. Friedman, *World Is Flat*, 8.

A False Dawn?

Some skeptics argue that globalization is simply a myth, an ideological construction used to obscure the unchanging global expansion of capitalism; power and wealth remain in the West as they have for the last two hundred years.[14] The globalization myth, they argue, is a useful yet unjust tool: "The first and most hideous injustice of globalization is that [we] are told over and over that [we] have no choice but to accept it or face further marginalization."[15] At the end of the day, these skeptics believe nothing has really changed, only that the marketing for capitalism has improved.

John Gray is not sure we have thought deeply enough about globalization.[16] He does not argue against globalization being a historical process under way for centuries. Yet he believes that there is another formulation of globalization that is an ideological construct, a political project seeking to create and sustain a global free market. Gray believes that this second meaning of globalization is deeply flawed and needs to be challenged. He is concerned that Globalization II may be a "false dawn."

Gray argues that capitalism is the last of the twentieth century's three utopian visions now that communism and fascism have been discredited. This vestige of the Enlightenment suffers from the same weaknesses as all utopian projects: the "power over" practices of empire and a Promethean attitude toward the environment. Furthermore, Gray argues that capitalism is as unstable today as it was going into World War I and the Great Disruption. Among what he calls the disordering effects of capitalism, Gray points to the fact that entire occupations are disappearing from the workplace, more and more of the workforce lacks economic security, the risks of unemployment and retirement are being transferred to individuals in the name of free market reform, and uneven access to work is leading to more crime and overcrowded prisons.[17] Intriguingly, his concerns were made well before the global financial crisis of 2008; the struggles of Greece, Italy, and Spain in the recovery; and the true depth of economic disruption and income inequality within nations now associated with globalization. We will have to wait and see.

Benjamin Barber introduces a more conflictual view of globalization in which culture matters more than economics or technology. He describes a

14. Hirst and Thompson, *Globalization in Question*, 1–18.
15. Waliggo, "Call for Prophetic Action," 254.
16. Gray, *False Dawn*. John Gray, formerly a supporter of neoliberal capitalism, became disillusioned in the face of its human cost. He is professor emeritus of European thought at the London School of Economics and Political Science.
17. Ibid., 71–74.

An African View

J. N. K. Mugambi, professor of philosophy and religious studies, University of Nairobi

Africans have continued to be treated like extensions of the history of other peoples. The time has come for them to be authors of their own history. The end of the cold war provides an opportunity for Africans to critically review the methodological presuppositions of the reigning ideology, which, in an endeavor to thwart any rivalry, presents "globalization" as a norm to which everyone everywhere should conform.

Mugambi, *Christian Theology and Social Reconstruction*, 7

world with two opposing forces: forces of integration pulling us to the center of a globalized world and forces of disintegration that are resisting globalization by retribalizing the world often through violence—"McWorld" versus "Jihad."[18] On the one hand, Barber sees a world with globalizing economies and technology and a thin global culture that feels mostly Western. On the other hand, he sees a fragmenting world in which each ethnic group (Kurds, Basques, Tuareg, Uighurs, and others) wants its own country and feels deeply alienated from the larger world—"people without countries, inhabiting nations not their own, seeking a small world within borders that will seal them off from modernity."[19] Barber does not make a prediction as to which view will win, but he is worried about the fact that neither option is necessarily democratic.[20] We will have to wait and see.

Like Barber, Samuel Huntington argues that culture, not economics, will have the final say in the twenty-first century and that this will lead to a "clash of civilizations." He observes that princes and kings fought each other up until the late eighteenth century. During Globalization I, nations fought each other. During the Great Disruption, two world wars were fought over competing economic globalisms and the globalism of nationalism. Now in Globalization II, Huntington argues that "the fundamental conflict in this new world will not be primarily ideological or primarily economic. The great divisions among

18. Barber, *Jihad vs. McWorld*, 219–35. Benjamin Barber is a senior research scholar at the Center on Philanthropy and Civil Society of The Graduate Center at the City University of New York.
19. Barber, "Jihad vs. McWorld."
20. Barber, *Jihad vs. McWorld*, 20.

humankind and the dominating source of conflict will be culture."[21] Globalization feeds this conflict between civilizations because it is experienced as a Western, and even Christian, imposition that is eroding the power of nations and cultures. Since Huntington's proposal, we have witnessed a breakdown in the Middle East between Sunni and Shia Islam and the emergence of the so-called Islamic State (ISIS) and its call for a return of a Muslim caliphate. We will have to wait and see.

A number of Christian theologians and ethicists fall loosely within this camp of those who are less than optimistic about globalization. They too are deeply suspicious of capitalism as an ideology and a practice and see capitalism and globalization as synonymous. Kathryn Tanner posits that the Christian story contains an alternative economic vision.[22] She argues that the biblical story presents "principles for the production and circulation of the good and what they are to mean for human life in God's service."[23] Drawing on the prehistory of capitalism in the West and practices in some of today's nonindustrialized societies, she presents the principles of a "theological economy" as an alternative to the present system. This "economy of grace" is presented as a noncompetitive alternative to capitalism.

Pamela Brubaker reduces globalization to neoliberal capitalism and narrows her assessment to an evaluative framework: "Who wins and who loses?"[24] However, this zero-sum understanding of economics overlooks the fact that the world's economic pie has increased fifty times in the last two hundred years with a greater percentage ending up in the Global South. Her proposal calls for a "people's globalization" that pushes up against political and economic power in favor of a "people-and-earth-centered globalization."[25]

Cynthia Moe-Lobeda argues that neoliberal capitalism has become so powerful that it has disabled our political system to such an extent that society's moral agency is crippled. She argues that moral agency is needed to provide a counterbalancing power that subverts, resists, and offers "socially just and ecologically sustainable alternatives" to the neoliberal expression of capitalism. She calls for an "active, embodied love [that calls people] to

21. Huntington, "Clash of Civilizations?" Samuel Huntington was emeritus university professor at Harvard University and director of its Center for International Affairs.

22. Tanner, *Economy of Grace*, xi, 29. Kathryn Tanner is professor of systematic theology at Yale Divinity School.

23. Ibid., xvi.

24. Brubaker, *Globalization at What Price?*, 37. Pamela Brubaker is professor of Christian ethics at California Lutheran University.

25. Ibid., 114, 38.

political participation on behalf of life and against what destroys it."[26] Her alternatives to capitalism suffer from the same weaknesses as those of Brubaker and Tanner.

While all three of these thinkers have weaknesses in their understanding of modern economics, something common to many theologians and Christian ethicists,[27] they correctly express a deep concern for the ethics of globalization, its tendency to be swayed and shaped by the powerful, and its seeming inability to deal with issues of justice, inclusion, and care for the environment. All three also affirm the importance of civil society and political participation as a means of ethically shaping globalization.[28]

Things Fall Apart

With apologies to Chinua Achebe, the phrase "things fall apart" applies to the most skeptical reactions to the trajectory of globalization. Not only will globalization fail to bring us to the promised land, but it can only prevail in limited ways or places as the world becomes more violent and turbulent. This may in turn cause globalization to fail.

Robert Kaplan surveys the world and concludes that "scarcity, crime, overpopulation, tribalism, and disease are rapidly destroying the social fabric of our planet."[29] He focuses on what I have described as the dark side of globalization. He concludes that poverty, weakened nation-states, scarcity, and conflict will join unhelpful demographics (too many youth in the Global South and too few working-age adults in the West) in overwhelming globalization, except in those places where people are rich enough to insulate and protect themselves—rich pockets in a Hobbesian world of hunger and violence.

In an updated assessment, Kaplan observes that the European Union—a child of twentieth-century globalization—is under siege.[30] Southern European countries feel marginalized and abused in the aftermath of global recession. In 2016, Britain decided that being in the European Union was no longer in its best interest. Nationalist parties in Europe are emerging in force in the

26. Moe-Lobeda, *Healing a Broken World*, 3–5. Cynthia Moe-Lobeda is professor of Christian ethics at Pacific Lutheran Theological Seminary.

27. Atherton, *Transfiguring Capitalism*, 5.

28. I will return to these shared concerns when I explore the theological limitations of globalization in chap. 12 and the proposals of Stackhouse and Groody for an ethical and spiritual architecture to shape globalization in chap. 13.

29. Kaplan, "Coming Anarchy." Robert Kaplan is a senior fellow at the Center for a New American Security and a visiting professor at the United States Naval Academy.

30. Kaplan, "Europe's New Medieval Map."

Muslim Perspectives on Globalization

A Suspicious Perspective

Ali Mohammadi and Muhammad Ahsan, Nottingham
Trent University

Contemporary globalization did not emerge as a "natural" development,
but rather as a created entity driven by major global players through [global]
agencies such as the IMF, World Bank, WTO, and the global media. The
obvious objective of all these organizations and their activities is to control
the entire world, particularly the Muslim world.

Mohammadi and Ahsan, *Globalisation or Recolonisation?*, 142

Globalization Is Dangerous but Inevitable

Abu Sadat Nurullah, instructor in sociology, University
of Alberta

Globalisation poses a challenge to Islamic culture and identity because
globalisation promotes the transmission of information through the media
and this has resulted in the dominance and hegemony of Western culture
over the rest of the world. This poses a challenge to Islamic ways of life, values, and principles. However, as globalisation is inevitable, Muslims should
take the benefits and opportunities provided by globalisation in spreading

face of over one million refugees from the Middle East and North Africa.
Putin's Russia has invaded parts of Ukraine and is threatening the Baltic
states. Things fall apart.

Stanley Hoffman also sees a bipolar world, but of a very different kind. He
suggests that September 11 and the emergence of global terrorism means we
are facing a "clash of globalizations," not "civilizations."[31] One part of the
world clearly rejects globalization. Many Muslims, both Sunnis and Shias,
see globalization as an unholy marriage of materialism, immoral values, and
Christianity. Almost everything associated with globalization—its economics,

31. Hoffmann, "Clash of Globalizations." Stanley Hoffmann was emeritus university professor at Harvard University and founded its Center for European Studies.

and demonstrating the unique traits of Islamic cultural identity around the world though various means.

Nurullah, "Globalisation as a Challenge to Islamic Cultural Identity," 45

Globalization Does Not Have the Final Word

Mohd Abbas, department of general studies, International Islamic University, Malaysia

History indicates that before the coming of modern globalization, the Muslims had their own version of globalization. During the Muslim era of globalization which coincides with the Golden Age of the Muslims, the West benefited immensely from the scholastic works produced by Muslim scientists and scholars. . . .

Muslims should have an open-mind to examine all that comes from the West and should pick and choose whatever is relevant to their needs and discard all that are dangerous and harmful to their existence as a community and nation. Certainly the Muslims cannot live in their own enclaves in total seclusion and isolation running away from globalization. They must view globalization as a challenge and look for solutions to overcome the problems that come along with globalization. The West on its part should cast away its past mentality of colonizing and intruding into the affairs of the East. It should not impose its hegemony on the East through colonization, neo-colonization or even through globalization.

Abbas, "Globalization and the Muslim World," 275, 295

politics, technology, and cultural values—is *haram*.[32] Islam stands over against globalization as a matter of faith and morality.

There is an interesting irony here. The technological side of globalization—the open access to information through the internet and social media—is *haram* for many Muslims, but is embraced by global terrorism and is empowering it. ISIS is "using marketing and digital communication tools not only for 'socializing terror' through public opinion . . . but also for making terror popular, desirable, and imitable."[33] Fueled by grievances from its colonial past

32. *Haram* is an Arabic term meaning "forbidden (by Allah)" according to the Qur'an and the Sunnah.
33. Lesaca, "On Social Media."

and Islam's internal divisions, a puritanical Islamic vision of globalization is emerging in the form of a caliphate without borders that uses the tools of globalization to recruit, raise money, and finance global operations.[34]

Recently, Michael Ignatieff added a second element to this theme of cultural and religious disintegration in terms of what he calls "the new world disorder."[35] There are two forces working against the triumph of globalization envisioned by the optimists. On the one hand, there is the violent reaction of ISIS and al-Qaeda, as Hoffman has described. On the other hand, there is an alternative form of capitalism—authoritarian capitalism—emerging in places like China and Russia. The irony is that globalization and its global market system allow these countries to enjoy the economic benefits of capitalism—thereby buying the peace of their citizens—while holding onto their totalitarian political systems. This also allows them to pursue less than peaceful foreign policies, as evidenced by the recent experiences of Georgia, Crimea, Ukraine, and the islands of the South China Sea. Together, these two counterforces to globalization result in "the tectonic plates of [today's] world order . . . being pushed apart by the volcanic upward pressure of violence and hatred."[36] Things fall apart.

What is the future of globalization? Will it move toward its promised land, remaining an ambiguous Western phenomenon, or will it fall apart (see fig. 8.1)? I have no idea, and neither should you. If one embraces the adaptive complex system view of globalization that I have proposed in this book, then one needs to accept two challenges. First, one should try to be less like a prophet and more like a learner. The world and all of us in it are going to have to learn our way into the future. Second, as Christians, we don't have to know what's going on in order to love our God and our neighbor. Even if the signs of the times are chaotic, inconsistent, and incoherent, we do know the final outcome of history, and we can be faithful to our mission to be witnesses to the saving power of Jesus Christ and the emerging justice and peace of God's kingdom.

The Last Two Hundred Years in a Nutshell

In the two hundred years of the Second Era of Globalization, the world's population increased sixfold, and yet, quite incredibly, the percentage of

---

34. Ignatieff, "New World Disorder." Michael Ignatieff previously taught at Harvard University, was leader of the Liberal Party of Canada, and is now rector and president of Central European University.
35. Ignatieff, "New World Disorder."
36. Ibid.

people living in chronic poverty was reduced from 95 to 22 percent. Economic thinking evolved from the original proposals of Adam Smith into the laissez-faire capitalism in Globalization I, the social welfare capitalism in the last half of the Great Disruption, and the neoliberal expression of capitalism of today's Globalization II. The economic center of the world moved from China and India to Great Britain in Globalization I, and then to the United States during the Great Disruption and for much of Globalization II. Now China is poised to become the world's largest economy once again. The economic actors have shifted from empires to nation-states and, now in Globalization II, away from nation-states toward transnational corporations, international networks, and individuals. The driving social imaginary moved from religion to science in Globalization I, to social welfare statism in the Great Disruption, and to free markets and individual identity in Globalization II. The population center of the Christian world moved from Europe to the United States and then to the developing world or Global South. A lot changed in the last two hundred years.

At the same time, as Branko Milanović reminds us, globalization had two faces in this two-hundred-year period. On the one hand, there was a lot of good news for the poor and for everyone else. The Western worldview changed in ways that opened the door to the sciences, technological innovation, and economic growth. Large numbers of human beings became more aware of their agency and creativity and became productive actors. On the other hand, the world experienced two world wars, a cold war, six genocides or intentional famines killing more than a million people each, and a global economic depression and a great recession. Up until the end of World War II, the spread of globalization coincided with the era of the empires in which the European nations, the United States, Russia, and Japan "played God" as they competed for new territories and as new technologies created economic and military advantage, while the Global South was deliberately denied the benefits of industrialization. This expression of globalization did not come to an end until after World War II.

For some, there is only good news resulting from globalization. For others, globalization has meant disastrous human cost. Both views are right, and both are incomplete. For Christians, this points to a critical underlying truth. Globalization is a human effort that, in its best expressions, can make the world better off materially, but it cannot eradicate the impact of human sin. What we have seen in this chapter is pretty much what one would expect from a world damaged by original sin and empowered by original good.

As We Move On

If you are still reading this book, I expect your head is tired and your brain is somewhat fried. We've looked at emergent social systems and at the confusion and ambiguity of the phenomena called globalization. It did not help when we had to accept the fact that that no one is in charge of globalization and no one—aside from God—knows where it is going. There are as many perspectives and analyses as there are scholars and critics. The impact of globalization is a rich and varied combination of good news, not so good news, and things that are still emerging for which the kind of news is not yet clear. I wish I could have reduced all this to a simple story with a clear direction, but this is simply not possible.

In the next two chapters I will switch my focus to globalization and the poor. While the good news in this chapter is that the poor have improved materially in the last two hundred years, there is still a lot to do. The number of our fellow human beings living in poverty, oppression, and exclusion represents a serious ongoing challenge. I will then outline what has been called a globalization of humanitarianism that developed in the aftermath of the Second World War. The ideas of poverty eradication and development have become global preoccupations.

Questions for Discussion

1. Which of the three views of globalization seems most on target for you? Why?
2. Which of the three views of globalization does your church or denomination find most appealing? Why?
3. On the basis of your preferred view of globalization and its future, what missional actions might you and your church take to engage globalization in a meaningful way?

Section 5

GLOBALIZATION AND THE POOR

9

Globalization's Response to Poverty

The previous two chapters outlined the good and not so good news that contemporary globalization has brought over the last two hundred years. It is a mixed picture, but at least in a material sense, the news for the poor has been one of steady improvement. Now I will examine the state of the world's poor today and describe how much work remains to be done. I will trace the origins of the idea of development or poverty eradication, which was birthed in the aftermath of World War II, and its evolution during Globalization II. This chapter will conclude with a quick summary of the institutions that are part of a global response to poverty.

The State of the Poor Today

There Is a Lot Left to Do

There are still too many people in God's world whose life is insecure and whose survival is a daily challenge. We know this is not what God intends for God's creation. Over 800 million people are still living on less than $1.25 a day, and over three billion on less than $3 a day, or just over $1,000 a year.[1] Compare this to the poverty line in the United States of $16 a day.[2]

1. World Bank, "Poverty: Overview."
2. This per person rate is based on the poverty line for a family of four. United States Department for Health and Human Services, "Poverty Guidelines."

Almost 2.5 billion people do not have adequate sanitation facilities, and almost 1 billion people resort to open defecation. Water scarcity affects more than 40 percent of the world's people. In 2012 almost 800 million adults were illiterate, as were just over 100 million young people. In spite of declining rates in child mortality, almost six million children died before reaching age five in 2015. In 2015, one in seven children under five were underweight, and growth was stunted in one in four children because of malnutrition.[3]

About 1.3 billion people live on ecologically fragile land. Nearly four billion people, the majority of whom live in developing countries, do not have access to the internet. As we noted in chapter 3, the dark side of globalization is harming the poor. Digital technology, a global financial system, and differing regulations and performance by border controls has enabled human trafficking and drug smuggling on an unprecedented scale. The poor are especially susceptible to being drawn into criminal behavior in order to stay alive.

Where Are the Poor?

Almost 80 percent of the world's chronically poor were living in South Asia and sub-Saharan Africa in 2012, while eight of the ten countries with the highest percentage of people living in chronic poverty were in sub-Saharan Africa.[4] Just under 150 million chronically poor were living in East Asia and the Pacific Islands. Fewer than 44 million of the world's extremely poor live in Latin America, the Caribbean, Eastern Europe, and Central Asia combined.[5] This geography of poverty reveals what has been called the "poverty paradox." Over half the people living on less than $1.25 a day live in middle-income countries with growing economies: India, Nigeria, China, and Indonesia.[6] Finally, it is important to remember that three-fourths of the world's poorest people live in rural areas. This is often overlooked in what seems like a rapidly urbanizing world with its slums and favelas.

Their Unhelpful Contexts

The contexts in which many of the world's poor live too often reinforce or even enable their poverty. Focusing assistance on the poor themselves without attending to their contexts is shortsighted. One needs to understand the

3. Statistics taken from UNDP, *Human Development Report 2015*, 4–5.
4. NationMaster, "Population below Poverty Line."
5. World Bank, "Poverty: Overview."
6. Summer, "Where Do the World's Poor Live?"

negative roles of conflict and violence, ineffective governance, criminal activity, and the threat of living outside the formal economy.

The World Bank has forecast that almost half the world's poor are expected to live in countries affected by fragility, conflict, and violence by 2030.[7] Violence and war create poverty by displacing people, destroying infrastructure, keeping children out of school, empowering criminals, and killing productive adults. While poverty rates are declining for much of the world, countries affected by violence are lagging behind. It is estimated that for every three years of continuing violence, poverty reduction lags by almost 3 percent.[8]

Quality of governance—the rule of law, good policing, and provision of public services—matters, too. A map of the index of state capability shows that low governance capability and chronic poverty go together.[9] Sixteen of the most fragile states are in sub-Saharan Africa, and conflict is a characteristic of the top ten.[10] The bottom ten countries on the Corruption Perception Index include six African nations, one country in Latin America, two in Asia, and Iraq in the Middle East.[11] A report on illegal financial flows shows that every dollar of foreign aid going into the developing world is dwarfed by the ten dollars of capital leaving the same countries illegally.[12] Poor governance hurts the poor.

Finally, there is a more nuanced and important perspective on the contexts in which the poor live. Economist Hernando de Soto focused his research on the poor living in the informal economy in Peru. The informal economy is an important context for poverty that we need to understand since it "comprises more than half of the global labour force and more than 90% of Micro and Small Enterprises (MSEs) worldwide."[13] This economy is a survival-of-the-fittest, Darwinian world in which the powerful exploit the weak without restraint. It has no rule of law, no legal protections, no social services, and little responsible policing. Extortion is the norm. In much of the Global South, the informal economy makes up as much as 40 percent of the national economy. This is the shady side of globalization.

De Soto made three important discoveries. First, in spite of the inhospitable conditions of the informal sector, de Soto's research discovered the vitality, creativity, and entrepreneurial nature of Peru's urban poor. The myth that the

7. World Bank, "Fragility, Conflict and Violence."

8. World Bank, *World Development Report 2011*, 4.

9. *Economist*, "World in 2011."

10. Fund for Peace, "Fragile States Index 2015." The Fragile States Index combines twelve social, economic, and political indicators.

11. Transparency International, "Corruption Perceptions Index 2015."

12. Baker and Joly, "Illicit Money," 62.

13. ILO, "Informal Economy."

The Poor as Entrepreneurs

Hernando de Soto, Peruvian economist

Men and women who through almost superhuman hard work and without the slightest help from the legal state [in fact, in the face of its declared hostility] have learned how to create more jobs and more wealth in the zones in which they have been able to function than the all-powerful state. They have often shown more daring, effort, imagination, and dedication to the country than their legal competitors.

De Soto, *Other Path*, xvii

poor are lazy and stupid was demolished. This discovery is important to the plans for poverty eradication that we will explore in the next chapter. Second, while the poor are risk-taking entrepreneurs, their future is limited. De Soto showed that the informal businesses of the poor cannot grow in the informal sector because of their vulnerability to theft, extortion, and any crisis.[14]

Finally, de Soto exposed the exclusionary nature of the formal economy in Peru (and in other Latin American countries). A mercantilist bargain was made by which the government is kept in power as long as the government protects the economic advantage of the rich families who control the major segments of the economy.[15] De Soto documented the raft of rules, fees, and procedures created by government regulation that make legal registration of a local market or vendor's license a time consuming and costly ordeal. These convoluted processes can involve fifty to a hundred steps, dozens of different government ministries and departments, and two to four years' worth of income in fees and bribes to accomplish.[16] The purpose of these regulations is to protect rich families from competition by deliberately creating barriers that prevent the poor and middle class from becoming part of the formal economy.

With this brief overview of the context in which today's poor live and the extent of the remaining challenges to eradicate poverty, it will be helpful if we have an understanding of the evolution of ideas and practices of development.

14. De Soto, *Other Path*, xix. Hernando de Soto is an economist and founded the Institute for Liberty and Democracy in Peru.
15. Ibid., 201.
16. Ibid., 131.

The Global Response to the Poor

Origins of the Idea of Development[17]

Development as an idea has its roots in the nineteenth-century globalization of compassion that I described in chapter 7. The resulting globalization of the question "Who is our neighbor?" created a new moral imaginary that understands the whole world as the domain for works of compassion. For the most part, this found expression in works of charity and social welfare in the nineteenth century as well as the human rights movement in the twentieth.

In the aftermath of the devastation of World War II, Europe had been rebuilt and was taking off economically. The post-war pressure to award independence to former colonies was undeniable and under way. At the same time, soldiers and war correspondents, who had been all over the world and had seen things previously unreported, were returning home with stories of far-off places and "exotic" non-Western cultures. The global technologies of radio and then television began to beam the words and images of very poor, distant places into the homes of people in the West, and the idea of loving our neighbor began to globalize.

A new idea with a global horizon began to emerge: if Europe and Japan could be rebuilt, then perhaps something could be done about poverty in the poorer parts of the world. This new idea was called "development" and was an extension of the West's understanding of compassion; one could work to end poverty, not just to care for the poor in the midst of their poverty. This led to a second insight: perhaps the economic and technological dimensions of globalization could be put at the service of the poor. Over time, the governments of the West began to believe that it is "the moral duty of Western industrialized countries to take active steps to help those who are more backward technically (and culturally) to advance along the road of progress."[18] This was one of the better instincts of globalization in spite of one shortcoming and one blind spot.

First, we need to remember that this commitment to development was also part of the Cold War strategy of the West during the last decades of the Great Disruption. Sometimes Cold War strategy called for guns and proxy wars; sometimes the strategy took the form of development aid. Helping poor nations in the Global South was a way of keeping them out of the Soviet orbit. The idea of development was not altogether altruistic.

17. Some of the material in this section is from chap. 2 of my *Walking with the Poor* (Maryknoll, NY: Orbis, 2011) and is used with permission.
18. Tyndale, *Visions of Development*, 156.

FIGURE 9.1 Modernization theory

Second, these Western "altruists" were unclear as to what they meant by the term "development." We need to remember that, while the West understood itself as "developed," it had a poor understanding about how this development had happened.[19] The story of the economic and technological transformation of Britain, Europe, and the United States that I told in chapters 5 and 6 was not available in the 1950s. Furthermore, the West was still shaken by the fact that the twentieth-century track record of globalization had included two world wars, a global economic depression, and the Holocaust. Nonetheless, the idea took shape that the "underdeveloped" world should "develop" by emulating the West.

In the 1960s, Walt Rostow wrote his "non-Communist manifesto" that outlined his proposal for the West's path of development in the form of five stages of economic growth.[20] It became the blueprint for the Western development efforts of the time. The goal of development was understood as modernization (Westernization), and the measure of development was the size of a nation's economy.

The basic assumption of what became known as modernization theory was that the traditional culture and values of poor societies needed to change and would change as they encountered a modernizing world of urbanization, public education, and integration into the Western economic system (see fig. 9.1). Traditional values, judged as not being conducive to economic growth, would fall away, and new "modern" values would take their place. Poor economies would begin to grow as a "modern" economy emerged—the globalization promise in the language of fifty years ago. There are still echoes of this theory today, as we shall see later in this chapter.

19. Historians today are still investigating the many causes of this radical change in human history.

20. Rostow, *Stages of Economic Growth*. W. W. Rostow was professor of economic history at the Massachusetts Institute of Technology and served in the Kennedy and Johnson administrations.

Evolution of the Development Theories

While modernization theory held sway for a while, it eventually lost its luster as the culturally and economically myopic creation that it was. Other theories of development emerged. Dependency theory, with its neo-Marxist and Latin American roots, argued that the West was the source of the underdevelopment of the South and that modernization theory and development aid were just fig leaves to cover up this unchanging neocolonial, capitalist reality. The goal of development for both theories was still economic growth, but the means of development was now a choice between socialist or capitalist economics.

In the 1980s, development practitioners, weary of arguments about global economic history and theories, began articulating an approach to what they called "people-centered development." This grounded-theory approach emerged from what they had been learning on the front lines working among the poor.[21] Small alternative theories, limited by time and place, began to emerge, and increasingly the idea of development as economics alone was called into question.

Two examples may be helpful. Robert Chambers argued for an understanding of poverty as entangling systems that called for a response focused on encouraging what he called "responsible well-being."[22] John Friedmann insisted that, while the kind of grassroots development programming that Chambers proposed was needed, it was not enough.[23] For Friedmann, the poverty of poor households was a result of not having enough social and political power to develop themselves and insist on the services they deserved from the state. What was needed was to organize the poor into associations and networks that would make them increasingly hard to ignore as important players in civil society; only then could the poor push back against the political and economic systems that limited their initiative. While issues of access, vulnerability, and social power became more central to the development conversation, the central measure remained the size of the national economy.

21. Grounded theory is a social sciences methodology that constructs theory from the analysis of data or experience. It is the opposite of the traditional model in which the researcher chooses an existing theoretical framework and then collects information only to show if the theory applies or not.

22. Chambers, "Responsible Well-Being"; Chambers, *Whose Reality Counts?* Robert Chambers is a research associate of the Institute of Development Studies at the University of Sussex with long field experience in rural India and Africa.

23. Friedmann, *Empowerment*. John Friedmann is professor emeritus in the School of Public Policy and Social Research at UCLA with extensive Latin American urban planning experience.

Development as Freedom—Amartya Sen

People themselves must have responsibility for the development and change of
the world in which they live.

—Amartya Sen[24]

In the 1990s, a welcome shift began to take place in the measures of development. A development economist from India, Amartya Sen, began working with
Mahbub ul Haq, a Pakistani economist in the United Nations Development
Program, to create a new index for assessing development with the declared
purpose of moving development economics from its focus on GDP alone to
a more people-centered approach. The resulting Human Development Index
(HDI) added life expectancy, as an indicator for health, and literacy, as an
indicator for knowledge and education, to GDP as a measure of standard
of living. Development was no longer focused on economic growth alone.

Sen also studied the relationship between famines and democracy and
demonstrated that there has never been a major famine in a functioning democracy.[25] This discovery led to his seminal book, *Development as Freedom*,
in which Sen announced his conclusion that poverty is better understood as
being the result of deprivation of human freedom. Things like low income,
lack of education, ill health, and lack of access to credit and social services
make people less free, as does lack of freedom in their political context.[26]
"What people can positively achieve is influenced by economic opportunities,
political liberties, social powers, and the enabling conditions of good health,
basic education, and the encouragement and cultivation of initiatives."[27]

For Sen, human well-being is best understood not by what people consume
(economics) but by what people *are* and *do*, such as being literate, healthy,
and economically active and participating in the decisions affecting their
community. Sen calls these kinds of things *functionings*.[28] Functionings are
the basic stuff of human life, such as having enough to eat, having adequate
housing, breathing clean air, and drinking clean water, as well as higher-value
ideals such as possessing self-respect and enhanced dignity, participating in
community life, and feeling safe. The human rights tradition insists that all
human beings have the right to function in this way. So does the biblical account. For the prophets, the test of the proper functioning of society and the

24. Sen, *Development as Freedom*, 283. Amartya Sen is professor of economics and philosophy at Harvard University and was awarded the Nobel Prize in development economics in 1998.
  25. Ibid., 16.
  26. Ibid., 4.
  27. Ibid., 5.
  28. Ibid., 75.

FIGURE 9.2 Development as freedom

governing of the powerful was the well-being of the widow, orphan, alien, and the poor (Ps. 72; Isa. 1:17, 23; 3:13–14). If the poorest can function, then the society, its economics and politics, is fulfilling its mission reasonably well. But surely there is more than just survival in God's intent for human beings.

Sen argues that we must go beyond just the idea of functionings—what people are and do—and extend our development concerns to include human *capabilities*, which he describes as what people are *able to do* or *choose to do*.[29] He argues that to experience human well-being we must have the freedom (capability) to choose what we wish (or are called) to become and have the means to get there. Human beings are intended to develop and thrive, not just survive. Sen is arguing that human well-being needs to be understood as people having the capability (freedom) to seek functionings in their world that they themselves deem valuable. Surely this is consistent with God's call for human beings to survive, be productive, and act as cocreators after God in creation.

For Sen, freedom is both the goal and the means to human development (see fig. 9.2).[30] The goal of development is to create the environment and conditions within which every person has the freedom to seek the better human future he or she desires. Freedom is the means of development in two ways. First, the poor themselves must be the actors if their capability is to be increased. Second, we must support the poor by removing impediments to their being actors and making choices, things that Sen calls "unfreedoms."[31]

With Sen's work, an ethical dimension became central to assessing development theory and practice for the first time. If people have more freedom to choose and act, they are experiencing positive change; if they are less free, the development policy or process is suspect. Increasing human liberty and

29. Ibid., 30, 87.
30. Ibid., 35.
31. Ibid., 17.

agency is now central to the development task, and economic growth is just one domain among others. This should remind us of Adam Smith's argument that natural liberty is the key to increasing the economy of a nation. Sen extends the idea of freedom to human agency as well. For this work, Sen was awarded the Nobel Prize in development economics.

Sen's view of the importance of human freedom and human agency echoes a Christian anthropology to a significant, but not complete, degree. Although Sen is not working from a Christian frame, the biblical idea of being made in the image of God lies at the heart of understanding the central importance God gives to human agency—the freedom and responsibility to act and create. Sen's view and the Christian view part ways with the further Christian understanding that the freedom God grants to human beings, including the freedom to tell God we don't believe in God, is not the unlimited freedom of the autonomous Western self. Rather, it is a freedom to give up some of our freedom because we can better love God and our neighbor when we do.

With the broad acceptance of Sen's approach in the 1990s, the size of a country's economy was correctly made a means, not an end. Economics had found its proper, more incidental, place in a new multidimensional understanding of poverty eradication that now includes ethical values and empowered human agency. The purpose of wealth is not to have wealth but to enable a person or household to pursue the kinds of capabilities they have reason to value.[32] No longer is Western modernization the development ideal. The understanding of well-being and how it is to be pursued are to come from the poor themselves.

In the last decade, the language of human well-being and increasing human and communal capabilities has become normative. The struggle now is to figure out what human well-being actually is and how one goes about increasing it. The development conversation may now be ready to join the other conversations on human flourishing, including religious conversations. More on this in the next chapter.

What Do the Poor Have to Say?

Well-being is a full stomach, time for prayer and a bamboo platform to sleep on.

—A poor woman in Bangladesh[33]

The post–World War II evolution and reframing of the idea of development took place primarily among academics from the North, who were eventually

32. Ibid., 14.
33. Narayan-Parker et al., *Crying Out for Change*, 264.

joined by academics and then practitioners from the South. It was not until the late 1990s that some began to wonder if listening to the poor articulate their own descriptions of poverty and human well-being might be a useful counterpoint. After a decade of hectoring by NGOs and development academics, the World Bank began to accept the idea that its staff of economists, funded by the world's wealthiest countries, might be a little too far removed from the real world of the poor. Working with the advice of Robert Chambers, a team of researchers was sent out to listen to over sixty thousand of the world's poorest people. In the early 2000s, the Voices of the Poor project published three books with their findings.[34]

In addition to listening to the poor speak about how poverty, oppression, and injustice negatively affected their lives, the researchers also asked questions about what the poor believed human well-being to be. As one might expect, more food, better health, and access to education quickly made the list. Human well-being without the basics of survival is impossible to imagine. More surprising was the finding that having enough materially for a good life does not mean asking for very much. The material desires of the poor were modest: "But at least for each child to have a bed, a pair of shoes, a canopy over their heads, two sheets—not to sleep like we do on the ground."[35]

But the conversation quickly moved beyond these more obvious material desires. Many of the expressions of well-being were relational: social well-being is central to human well-being for the poor.[36] The desires for being able to take care of one's family, experiencing harmony in the family and community, having friends, and helping others showed up regularly in the interviews. This is not a surprise to Christians, as the Bible makes it clear that we are relational beings, not autonomous economic decision makers or lone wolves.

Less expected by the researchers, many of the descriptions of what makes for well-being were psychological in nature.[37] These included a desire to feel better about oneself and a wish for a sense of dignity and respect, as well as having peace of mind, lack of anxiety, happiness, and satisfaction with life. Even more of a surprise to the Western researchers was the finding that "a spiritual life and religious observance are woven into other aspects of wellbeing."[38] Once again, this should not be a surprise to Christians, but it is news to secular folk. Maybe we do have something to offer our secular friends.

34. Narayan-Parker et al., *Can Anyone Hear Us?*; Narayan-Parker et al., *Crying Out for Change*; Narayan-Parker and Petesch, *From Many Lands*.

35. Narayan-Parker et al., *Crying Out for Change*, 25.

36. Ibid., 26.

37. Ibid., 26–27.

38. Ibid., 38.

The Global Institutions Responding to the Poor

In chapter 7 I described the emergence of a globalization of compassion in the nineteenth century, which resulted in a family of new institutions whose mission was charity, protection, and social welfare. The International Committee of the Red Cross, Caritas, Baptist World Aid, and the American Friends Service Committee were examples. For the most part, these agencies were in the relief and/or peacemaking business. Institutions with a focus on development would come later but belong in this same humanitarian tradition.

In the immediate aftermath of World War II, three new international institutions—the World Bank, the International Monetary Fund, and the General Agreement on Tariffs and Trade (called the Bretton Woods institutions)—were formed to reestablish the global market and trading system that was dismantled during the Great Disruption. As the commitment to help poor nations develop emerged in the 1950s and 1960s, the mandate of these three organizations began to shift toward creating the conditions that would encourage economic growth and thus contribute to poverty eradication.

Originally constituted to make reconstruction loans to post-war Europe, the World Bank shifted its focus to the developing world in the 1960s. Today it has two primary goals: to decrease the percentage of people living on less than $1.90 a day to no more than 3 percent within a generation and to promote shared prosperity by fostering the income growth of the bottom 40 percent in every country. The World Bank Group, a family of five financial institutions, works toward these goals by providing financial loans and grants as well as technical assistance to developing countries around the world. While the bank's official goal is to reduce global poverty, its articles of agreement require that its decisions be guided by promotion of foreign investment and international trade.[39] The underlying assumption is that economic globalization and poverty eradication are inseparably linked. Not everyone agrees with this, as one might expect.

Following the competitive currency devaluations that had contributed to the Great Depression of the 1930s and with the end of the Second World War, the International Monetary Fund (IMF) was created to reconstruct an international monetary system, the system of exchange rates and international payments that enables countries to trade with each other. Today the IMF's primary role is to ensure the stability of the international monetary

---

39. The World Bank Group "belongs" to its 188 member nations. It is governed by a board of governors, who are the ultimate policymakers at the World Bank. The five largest shareholders each appoint an executive director, and votes are proportional to the amount invested in the bank by each country. The United States, Japan, China, Germany, France, and the United Kingdom control almost half the votes.

system, which it does by fostering global monetary cooperation, facilitating international trade, promoting high employment and sustainable economic growth, and reducing poverty around the world.[40]

In the aftermath of the Thatcher-Reagan Revolution, the dominance of neoliberal economics resulted in the World Bank and the IMF insisting that the two institutions impose what came to be known as the Washington Consensus on emerging economies. During the 1990s, the resulting development mantra was simple: market-friendly reforms—globalization—will lead poor nations to economic growth. In the name of reducing poverty, countries seeking loans had to accept neoliberal economic conditions: open up their markets by removing tariffs, allow their exchange rates to be determined by the global market, open up for foreign investment, privatize state-run industries, and reduce public sector spending.

The Washington Consensus made some macroeconomic sense in the long term in that many of these economies did begin to grow. But in the short term and at the microeconomic level, where the poor live, the Washington Consensus was a disaster in the Global South.[41] Reforming labor markets meant decreasing minimum wages for people who were already poor. Reducing public expenditures led to reduced health services and fees for what used to be public services. Public schools were forced to charge school fees, something that Western nations do not do. The result was that tens of millions of poor children in the Global South were unable to go to school. Village health centers had neither health workers nor medicine. One development expert called the Washington Consensus the "globalization of vulnerability."[42] Bottom line, the Washington Consensus was not good news for the poor.

The General Agreement on Tariffs and Trade was the last of the three intergovernmental organizations established at Bretton Woods. Its mission was to create rules for liberalizing trade. Seeking global agreement on the rules of free trade proved to be a long and arduous process. Seven rounds of negotiations took place before the Uruguay Round (1986–1994) led to the establishment of the World Trade Organization (WTO) in 1995.

The primary function of the WTO is to create and monitor rules of international trade. Its overriding purpose is to help trade flow as freely as possible—so long as there are no undesirable side effects. The underlying assumption is that free and fair trade increases economic development and the

40. IMF is also made up of 188 member states, each of which appoints a governor to the board of governors. Voting power is proportional to who funds the IMF, with over 40 percent of the votes belonging to the United States, Germany, Japan, China, France, and the United Kingdom.

41. Rodrik, "Goodbye Washington Consensus."

42. Ramalingam, *Aid on the Edge of Chaos*, ix.

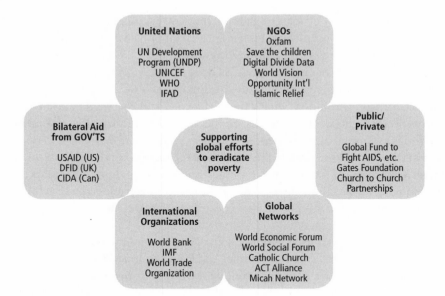

FIGURE 9.3 The globalization of poverty response

well-being of the poor. The WTO operates a system of trade rules and helps nations settle disputes without trade wars. Ruled by consensus, the WTO is a place where member governments try to sort out their trade problems through negotiations.

In addition to these three international organizations, the West's growing commitment to development aid eventually spawned a largely incoherent and unmanaged delivery system that emerged in bits and pieces—adaptive social systems again (see fig. 9.3). This inchoate system includes United Nations agencies, government agencies, INGOs, global networks, and public/private contributors.

The United Nations system has a number of organizations that are part of this development delivery system. The central focus lies within the United Nations Development Program (UNDP), which works to reduce poverty, inequalities, and exclusion by helping countries develop the policies, leadership skills, partnering abilities, institutional capabilities, and resilience needed to sustain development. Sister UN agencies focus on children (UNICEF), health (WHO), and agriculture (FAO and IFAD).

Bilateral aid between governments represents another set of major players. Many developed nations created their own development agencies to provide funding and technical assistance to this new task of development. The United States Agency for International Development (USAID) was created in 1961 and the British Ministry of Overseas Development (now Department for International Development) in 1964.

During this same period, a number of secular and Christian INGOs, originally founded to do humanitarian relief, began to add development activities to their ministry portfolios. These included Oxfam, CARE, Catholic Relief Services, Caritas, Church World Service, and World Vision International. More recently, Action Aid, Tearfund, and Islamic Relief, along with specialist INGOs such as Opportunity International (microfinance) and Lifewater International, joined the fray. All of these were a result of the processes of modern globalization.

The Catholic Church is perceived by some—including some Catholics—as being, among other things, an important global development agency,[43] making major contributions in the areas of education, health care, and economic development.[44] In addition, numerous Catholic INGOs focus on development work: England's Catholic Agency for Overseas Development (CAFOD), Ireland's Trocaire, and over 165 agencies that make up Caritas International.

More recently, a number of efforts were launched that do not fit neatly into a niche. The Global Fund to Fight AIDS, Tuberculosis and Malaria is proving very effective. The Bill and Melinda Gates Foundation brings the skills of the technology sector to technical areas of development, seeking to promote innovation. There are an increasing number of church-to-church development programs, something that would have been impossible before the advent of the communication dimension of Globalization II.

Finally, we need to take note of global networks that have turned their attention to development and poverty eradication. The World Economic Forum, a network of the rich and powerful, promotes poverty eradication efforts that align with its fervent belief in the good of economic (neoliberal) globalization. The World Social Forum is a network whose members take a diametrically opposite view, that neoliberal capitalism and globalization are harming the planet, increasing poverty and income inequality, and excluding those on the margin, especially indigenous peoples and migrants. Mainline Protestants and Roman Catholics are quite active in this network. The ACT Alliance is a coalition of 137 churches and faith-based organizations working together in over one hundred countries to promote development and inclusion of all. The Micah Network is an international network of mostly evangelical Christians and Christian agencies whose mission is to promote "integral mission," a view of the gospel that seamlessly integrates evangelism and social action.

43. Calderisi, *Earthly Mission*.
44. Gifford, *Christianity, Development and Modernity in Africa*, 85.

Summing Up

While there has been some good news for the poor in today's globalizing world, this chapter reminds us that there is still much work to be done. This chapter outlines the story of development thinking from its emergence in the aftermath of World War II. From development understood largely as infrastructure such as dams and roads, to a single-minded focus on economic growth, and finally to Amartya Sen's fresh and liberating insight about development of freedom, the idea of development and its practice evolved and reinvented itself, often in response to its failures. A conversation that was largely limited to Western politicians and technical specialists expanded with a major effort to listen to the poor themselves. To support, fund, and assess the resulting development efforts around the world, a fragmented family of global institutions has emerged who now span the globe with an annual budget in excess of $100 billion. In light of this story and the current structure in place to carry it out, we will now turn to contemporary thinking on development and poverty eradication.

Questions for Discussion

1. What is your reaction to Amartya Sen's proposal for "development as freedom"? What appeals to you? What does not?
2. Where might you expect to find churches and Christians working within the global network of poverty response (recall fig. 9.3)? Are there places where we might do more?

10

Contemporary Thinking on Development

Something significant changed in the practice of development in the first fifteen years of the twenty-first century. From within the development aid delivery system, a lot of research has been done into what works and what does not. While we are far from a state of comprehensive knowledge, this evidence-based research agenda is now driving development thinking and practice in a way that was not the case in the twentieth century. In addition to the research done by the major international organizations such as the World Bank and UNDP, an important new perspective has been added in the form of the Poverty Action Lab at MIT, which has introduced random trial experimentation to the research agenda.[1]

In this chapter on contemporary thinking on development, I will summarize the proposals of three major voices—Jeffrey Sachs, William Easterly, and Paul Collier. All three accept the idea of global markets and technology

---

A portion of this chapter is drawn from Bryant Myers, *Walking with the Poor* (Maryknoll, NY: Orbis, 2011), chapter 2, with permission from the publisher.

1. Founded by MIT professors Abhijit Banerjee, Esther Duflo, and Sendil Mullainathan, the Abdul Latif Jameel Poverty Action Lab (J-PAL) is a network of 131 affiliated professors from over forty universities. Its mission is to ensure that policy is informed by scientific evidence (see https://www.povertyactionlab.org/about-j-pal).

as givens. After introducing Lawrence Harrison and the contested issue of culture and poverty, I will introduce two important voices from the Global South—Hernando de Soto, who points to the importance of property rights in making capitalism work, and Muhammad Yunus, who proposed the idea of the right to credit. I will then introduce Abhijit Banerjee and Esther Duflo, who have alerted us to the importance of understanding why the poor make the choices they make, as well as to the idea of using rigorous testing to determine what works and what does not in development interventions. I will then briefly describe how the technological dimension of globalization is enabling and speeding up development among the poor. I will close the chapter by introducing an emerging conversation on faith and development and how Christians and secular development folk might find ways to enrich each other's work in development.

Global Proposals for Poverty Eradication

Delivering Development—Jeffrey Sachs

In *The End of Poverty*, Jeffrey Sachs argues that some nations—representing one-sixth of humanity—are locked in a poverty trap created by the interactions of disease, geographical isolation, and a limiting environment.[2] He argues that these countries cannot escape from this trap without outside help; they simply do not have the resources or the capability. All the other factors that exacerbate the impact of the poverty trap—demographics, governance, culture, innovation, finance, and geopolitics—can be managed over time, but only if the poverty trap is broken.[3] Thus, these countries will need significant external help—a big push.[4] Development programming should be designed using what Sachs calls "clinical economics." Sachs is testing his delivery approach in a number of Millennium Villages in different parts of the world—the jury is still out on their effectiveness.[5]

Sachs called for a "global compact to end poverty" that set a goal for rich countries to invest 0.7 percent of their GDP in the UN Millennium Develop-

2. Sachs, *End of Poverty*, 53. Jeffrey Sachs is the director of the Earth Institute and University Professor of sustainable development at Columbia University. Sachs was the UN special advisor on the MDGs from 2000 to 2006.

3. Ibid., 56.

4. Ibid., 19, 208.

5. The Millennium Villages Project is a demonstration project of Sachs and the Earth Institute at Columbia University in partnership with the UNDP. These demonstration projects are intended to validate (or not) that Sachs's integrated approach to rural development can be used to achieve the MDGs. See http://millenniumvillages.org.

ment Goals (MDGs).[6] This would have meant upwards of $175 billion annually for development assistance.[7] This aid would be coordinated through a revamped aid system that includes the World Bank, the IMF, UN agencies that support development, and government agencies for development.[8] Sachs's proposal rested on two underlying assumptions: poverty eradication is a moral responsibility of the developed world, and enough money and technology is the ultimate solution to poverty.

Discovering Development—William Easterly

In his book *The White Man's Burden*, Easterly points out that, during the sixty-odd years of development assistance that I summarized in the previous chapter, over $2.3 trillion has been spent on foreign aid.[9] While some progress has been made, it has been very uneven, and 800 million people are still living in chronic poverty. At the same time, the countries that have shown the most progress in economic growth—the Asian Tigers between 1960 and 1990 and China and India more recently—did not follow the development formulas of the West (the Washington Consensus), nor did they receive much foreign aid. Intrigued, Easterly decided to change the strategic question from Sachs's "How much foreign aid do we need to eradicate poverty?" to "What is the best use of foreign aid for development?"[10]

Easterly's perspective on the means of development is also markedly different from Sachs's. Easterly does not believe in the effectiveness of top-down, global planning for development. He sees this as a holdover from the colonial era reflecting the idea that "the West knows best." Contrasting what he calls Planners with Searchers, Easterly believes social problems are better solved as close to the action as possible by innovators who try and fail and try again—these are the Searchers. Planners, on the other hand, live in

6. The MDGs, adopted in 2000, were the world's first time-bound and quantified targets for addressing extreme poverty in its many dimensions—low incomes, hunger, disease, lack of adequate shelter, and exclusion—while promoting gender equality, education, and environmental sustainability. At the end of 2015, there was substantial progress. The goals for gender parity in primary school and access to clean water were met, and the goals for reducing extreme poverty and increasing primary school enrollment were narrowly missed. Child and maternal mortality were halved, missing their goal of two-thirds. UN, *Millennium Development Goals Report 2015*, 4–7.

7. Sachs, *End of Poverty*, 218.

8. Ibid., 255.

9. Easterly, *White Man's Burden*, 4. William Easterly is professor of economics at New York University, is codirector of its Development Research Institute, and was an economist for the World Bank from 1985 to 2001.

10. Ibid., 4, 11.

Washington, London, or Beijing and assume they know enough to be able to figure out global solutions and then determine what needs to be delivered to the poor. Searchers know they will never know enough and instead look for what is being demanded and try to meet that need.[11]

Easterly, a fan of Edmund Burke and the British Enlightenment, opts for a bottom-up, discover-what-works, learn-your-way-into-the-future approach to development that assumes that incremental discovery is a better fit in a complex, dynamical world about which you can never know enough. Thus, Easterly's solution to poverty calls for modest plans, local searching, and a lot of energy spent on evaluation.[12] Take small steps, do things in several ways, and see what actually happens. Feed those things that are working; starve those that are not. Complex adaptive social systems again.

The Bottom Billion Are Different—Paul Collier

Collier comes to the development conversation from a different angle altogether. In his book *The Bottom Billion*, he begins by asking which countries are languishing in terms of economic growth and then asks what is distinctive about them compared to countries that are growing economically.[13] He demonstrates that about one billion people live in fifty-eight countries that have suffered from negative economic growth since 1970, while all other nations are experiencing some form of economic growth (albeit at differing rates). Seventy percent of the bottom billion are in Africa, and the rest are spread around the world.[14] Examining the common issues these countries face, Collier identifies four poverty traps: chronic conflict, the negative impact of abundant natural resources (the resource curse), bad governance, and being landlocked with bad neighbors.[15] These four traps result in the likelihood that these countries will be left behind by the globalization that is lifting people out of poverty in places like Indonesia, India, and China. Furthermore, Collier notes that none of these traps will be overcome solely by a large input of foreign aid (Sachs) or by bottom-up problem solving by Searchers (Easterly).

Collier's diagnosis leads him to a family of proposed solutions. Landing between Sachs and Easterly, Collier believes foreign aid can help, but only

11. Ibid., 14–19.
12. Ibid., 53, 193, 375.
13. Collier, *Bottom Billion*. Paul Collier is professor of development economics at Oxford University.
14. Haiti, Bolivia, the Central Asian countries, Laos, Cambodia, Yemen, Burma, and North Korea. Ibid., 6–7.
15. Ibid., 5–6.

if it is used selectively.[16] Development aid injected into a conflict situation is clearly a formula for misuse or ineffectiveness. Aid that allows governments to continue misusing revenue from their natural resources also seems unwise. Collier argues that aid should be targeted at development programs that encourage the reduction of conflict and/or reward improved governance.

Two of Collier's proposals have to do with creating a global policy environment at the international level that encourages economic growth and good governance. Because many of the current trade policies of the developed world prevent Southern countries from gaining access to Northern markets, especially for agricultural products, Collier's first proposal calls for changing trade policies in the North to enable countries in the Global South to become connected to and benefit from international markets.[17] His second proposal calls for creating international laws and charters that encourage transparency and thus discourage corruption. He calls for international charters, or rules, for budget transparency, managing post-conflict situations, and international investment.[18]

Collier's final proposal is the most surprising. Where conflict is an endemic barrier to development, Collier wonders if military or police intervention may be a necessary development measure to create the security necessary to enable the other elements of his development proposal to be effective.[19] Needless to say, this unusual suggestion has not received much of a welcome. But it is unclear what else might help with the problem to which Collier has so aptly called our attention.

Collier is also worried that globalization might be arriving too late for the countries of the bottom billion.[20] He worries that the rapid economic growth and sheer population size of China and India might make it impossible for the smaller latecomers of the bottom billion to find a niche in the global economy even if they were freed from their various poverty traps. Fortunately, this does not appear to be the case. Since 2000 many countries in sub-Saharan Africa have seen sustained economic growth that is often among the highest in the world.[21] Furthermore, "low-cost, low-capital manufacturers, such as apparel producers, have already left China in droves, moving not just to Southeast Asia, but increasingly the Middle East and Africa."[22]

16. Ibid., 100.
17. Ibid., 157.
18. Ibid., 135.
19. Ibid., 124.
20. Ibid., 79.
21. AfDB Group, OECD Development Centre, and UNDP, *African Economic Outlook 2015*, 17.
22. Morris, "Will Tech Manufacturing Stay in China?"

Culture and Development—Lawrence Harrison

With the necessary and appropriate dismissal of the original version of modernization theory and its thesis that traditional cultures are poverty cultures while modern Western cultures are not, it became inappropriate to discuss culture and development for quite a long time. While the idea of connecting culture and development still makes some folks very nervous, it is an important question that needs attention.

In the mid-1980s, Lawrence Harrison reported a series of case studies from Latin America that, he argued, supported the proposition that culture was one obstacle to economic development in the region and therefore cultural values and practices needed to become part of the social analysis before development programs were designed. He also argued that these same cultural values have a profound influence for good and for ill on the effectiveness of social, and particularly economic, institutions.[23] This is significant since a strong case has been made for the importance of such institutions to economic growth in the West.[24]

Harrison's second conclusion provoked more controversy. He noted that economic development in the last fifty years has been geographically uneven and that culture provides a significant part of the explanation in two ways. First, he believes that "the society that is most successful at helping its people—all its people—realize their creative potential is the society that will progress the fastest."[25] Echoing Deirdre McCloskey, whom we met in chapter 5, this means that those cultural values that encourage people to be creative and productive; that reward merit, risk taking, and saving; and that encourage trust and transparency tend to support economic growth. Cultural values that limit any or all of these are simply less supportive of economic growth.

This renewed conversation on poverty and culture has several weaknesses. First, the idea that people live within a single cultural frame is just not true. We all live and move within a complex and fluid set of cultural and subcultural realities. Second, modern values are not exclusively located in outsiders, nor do traditional values find expression only among insiders. Thus, the conversation gets complicated and muddy in the real world.

While this new conversation on culture and development affirms that cultural change needs to come from within and not from without, the culture and development conversation naively ignores how little we really understand

23. Harrison, *Underdevelopment*, 3. Lawrence Harrison was a senior researcher and director of the Cultural Change Institute at the Fletcher School at Tufts University.
24. North and Thomas, *Rise of the Western World*.
25. Harrison, *Underdevelopment*, 2.

how cultures actually change. There is no agreement as to whether economic growth changes cultural values as Sachs suggests[26] or whether cultural values enable economic growth as David Landes claims.[27]

A related question on culture and development brings the issue of cultural values into the domain of the practitioner. "To what extent should changing cultural values be integrated into conceptualizing, strategizing, planning and programming of political and economic development?"[28] The desirability of making cultural change a goal of development is viewed with considerable suspicion by Sachs, de Soto, and Sen. Cultures do not appear to change at the pace of development programs and their very short lifetimes. In light of the history of Western colonialism and assumptions about the superiority of things Western, the step of trying to change culture seems a step too far for many.

Recent Insights

From macro-level theories and strategies for eradicating poverty, we now turn to a group of new discoveries that are influencing the practice of development. All of the following take it for granted that the economic and technological dimensions of globalization represent the best chance of helping poor nations, but, in contrast to the Washington Consensus, they focus on the microeconomic level—the place where the poor live and act. They address the question of how globalization can in fact connect with the lives of ordinary poor people.

The Mystery of Capital—Hernando de Soto

How does the Global South get connected to today's global markets? In the year 2000, Hernando de Soto began to explore what he called the "mystery of capital," wondering why capitalism works in the West and not so well elsewhere.[29] The first part of his discovery goes back to the story of Britain's nineteenth-century development and a change in how property was understood. Land or any physical asset became more than just something to be owned and exploited. The idea emerged that land could be an asset whose value could be leveraged. One can keep the land, take out a loan based on its value, and start a new business that endeavors to earn a profit—the creation of wealth. The idea of capital was born.

26. Sachs, *End of Poverty*, 317.
27. Landes, *Wealth and Poverty of Nations*, 516. David Landes is professor of economics and history at Harvard University.
28. Harrison and Huntington, *Culture Matters*, xxx.
29. De Soto, *Mystery of Capital*.

De Soto argues that capital is denied to many poor in the Global South today. Why? In order to turn an asset into a source of capital, one has to be able to prove that one owns the underlying asset. De Soto determined that a system of property rights in the West provides this kind of proof to a lender. De Soto argues that this is where the Global South is stuck. For the most part, a system of property rights and the legal means to enforce them are largely missing in many parts of the world where the poor live. The systems of communal ownership, government ownership, or conflicting or undocumented ownership in the Global South make for what de Soto calls "dead capital," since no one will loan money on something that one cannot prove one owns.[30] De Soto estimates that the world's poor are sitting on dead capital worth forty times more than all the foreign aid delivered since 1945.[31] The path to economic growth and connecting with the world's capital markets begins here.

The Power of Credit—Muhammad Yunus

Yunus is a Bangladeshi professor of economics and founder of the Grameen Bank. In the midst of a famine in the 1970s, Yunus met a poor woman who made bamboo stools on the street outside his university and wondered if his economics had anything to offer her in her poverty. To his surprise, he learned that the woman was not looking for a handout. She wanted to make things that people would buy but was limited by the high interest rates of money lenders and the fact that no bank would loan money to someone with no address and no assets.[32] Like de Soto, Yunus realized that without access to credit or simple savings programs, the poor could not earn a livelihood or build capital and were thus excluded from the benefits of globalization. This led him to two important proposals.

First, free from any experience in banking, Yunus had a liberating insight: the poor might be good credit risks under the right conditions, and the amount of credit the poor needed to become productive parts of the local economy was relatively small. The result is the well-known story of the Grameen Bank, which today has over nine million members—98 percent of whom are women—who borrow and save. The bank has made 8 million microenterprise loans with an 89 percent repayment rate.[33] The Grameen

30. Ibid., 6.
31. Ibid., 4.
32. Yunus with Jolis, *Banker to the Poor.*
33. Statistics taken from the Grameen Bank August 2016 report, which can be found at http://www.grameen.com/index.php?option=com_content&task=view&id=453&Itemid=422.

model launched a global movement of microfinance institutions, including the Christian NGO Opportunity International.

Yunus's second major innovation is what he calls a "social business," in contrast to nonprofit charities. Yunus argues that simply transferring money from the nonpoor to the poor through a nonprofit charitable arrangement has a serious weakness. The scale and sustainability of such an approach is limited by how much the nonpoor give and how long they give. Will there ever be enough charity to help two billion people living on less than two dollars a day? Yunus offered an alternative that he calls "social businesses." In comparison to a for-profit business, the mission of a social business is to create a social good in contrast to profit maximization. Investors recover their investments but do not receive dividends. In every other way, social businesses are run just like for-profit companies—they recover their full costs, including the cost of capital to grow, through affordable interest rates and/or two-tiered pricing (one subsidized price for the poor and another higher price for the middle class). Yunus calls these "non-loss, non-dividend companies" and offers them as the missing element of capitalism.[34] Today, a family of twenty-five Grameen companies provide services like microcredit, health and welfare, sales and distribution of handloom products, small-business loan guarantees, information technology training, and mobile phone service.[35]

Discovering What Works—Abhijit Banerjee and Esther Duflo

Minds on the margins are not marginal minds.

—Anil Gupta[36]

Sen and Sachs take a macro view of poverty, looking at global patterns and seeing poverty as a global problem. Easterly operates out of the same macro frame but prefers a local trial-and-error discovery process and promotes the importance of evaluation. Esther Duflo and Abhijit Banerjee have taken Easterly a step further.[37] Don't design and implement a single development solution and evaluate at the end of the project when adjustments are no longer possible, they argue. Instead, test a family of solutions within a single program, including a test of no solution at all. Begin monitoring results immediately

---

34. Yunus, *Creating a World without Poverty*, 21–29.
35. Ibid., 78–79.
36. Gupta, "Challenge of Scaling Indian Innovation."
37. Banerjee and Duflo, *Poor Economics*. Abhijit Banerjee is professor of economics at MIT. Esther Duflo is professor of poverty alleviation and development economics at MIT. They are codirectors of the Abdul Latif Jameel Poverty Action Lab at MIT.

to see what works, and then reallocate resources toward the successes and starve the ones that are not as effective.[38] Instead of trying to create a single approach for poverty eradication, Banerjee and Duflo opt for figuring out what works and does not work in a particular context—microsolutions. They watch what the poor actually do.

For example, it is known that sleeping under bed nets reduces malaria. Sachs says we should distribute free bed nets. Others disagree, saying that the poor need to pay something in order to value a bed net and thus use it properly. Still others say bed nets need to be produced and sold locally in order to create a sustainable supply. Rather than argue this out at an agency headquarters, Banerjee and Duflo would suggest focusing on a contiguous area in which all three approaches are tried in different groups of villages followed by monitoring the results to determine which option performs best.

Duflo and Banerjee offer a significant qualification to Hernando de Soto's conclusion that the poor are very entrepreneurial. While microfinance loans have a successful record, it has been a puzzle why successful microfinance experiences have not led to an increasing number of successful small businesses. Rather than debating this in the abstract, Duflo and Banerjee used random-control research and direct observation among poor people who were doing well with small loans. They reported two major findings. First, like de Soto, they found that the chronically poor in the informal economy exhibit constant risk taking and experimentation; they are entrepreneurial. But once their livelihoods become more secure, the poor report becoming more risk adverse. Putting your livelihood at risk by trying to leverage its success into a small business appears to be both too hard and too risky. Apparently, just as is the case in the West, not everyone is comfortable with an entrepreneur's life.

Let's look at one further example of what can be learned from asking the poor why they make the decisions they do. Banerjee and Duflo report that one of the reasons the poor make what appear to be bad decisions is that they do not know what they do not know. Lack of knowledge, in contrast to flawed decision making, is often what leads to such seemingly bad decisions.[39] Duflo and Banerjee discovered that decision making among poor people is often influenced more by their circumstances than by anything else. Counteracting the idea that the poor lack intellectual capabilities, they discovered that chronic poverty, insecurity, and scarcity narrow the horizons of the poor, so they sacrifice the future to the urgent present or allow the convenient to

38. This approach is explained in a TED video: Duflo, "Social Experiments to Fight Poverty."
39. Zwane, "Implications of Scarcity."

trump the less convenient.[40] Findings like these contribute to two new lines of inquiry, the "cognitive consequences of poverty"[41] and the psychological impact of chronic poverty on the poor.[42] These insights are reshaping how we think about helping the poor. We do not know as much as we think we know. Listening to the poor matters.

Information and Communications Technology for Development (ICT4D)[43]

Information is poor, scarce, maldistributed, inefficiently communicated and intensely valued [by the poor].

—Clifford Geertz[44]

The poor are often information poor, and they have few options for getting the information they need. A University of Ghana study found that almost one-third of the riders on a bus in the north of the country were going somewhere to get a piece of information. If they don't go and get it, they have few options. They can consult a shaman or hope someone will visit who has the information they need, or they can do without it. The barriers to getting information are largely technological. Telephone service is unreliable, as is electricity. Lack of access to affordable computer hardware and user-friendly software are often problems, as is the assumption that technology users are literate.

The good news is that the technological dimension of globalization is changing this very quickly. While technological innovation in the West took time to develop and become commonplace, today the challenge is how to integrate existing technology in a sensible way into poor countries. We've already noted the rapid spread of cell phones and smartphones. The Grameen Bank set up a telecommunications company and gave small loans so that one woman could earn income by being the "phone lady" in her village. Grameen Telecom is extending phone service in Bangladesh faster than the government is. M-Pesa, a money transfer system developed in Kenya, allows users with a mobile device to deposit, withdraw, and transfer money and to pay for goods and services (through Lipa na M-Pesa).[45] M-Pesa is used by over two-thirds of the mobile-phone owners in Kenya and half in Tanzania.

40. Banerjee and Duflo, *Poor Economics*, 205.
41. Shaw, Mullainathan, and Shafir, "Some Consequences."
42. Haushofer and Fehr, "On the Psychology of Poverty."
43. Often referred to as ICT4D.
44. Geertz, "Bazaar Economy," 28.
45. M is for mobile and *pesa* is Swahili for money.

It now operates in Afghanistan, South Africa, Senegal, Nigeria, Ghana, India, and Eastern Europe. Opportunity International uses similar tools to service their loan clients. Together these innovations are fundamentally transforming the landscape of financial services in Africa and possibly in the West as well.

The innovative application of new technology keeps growing. MFS Africa, a South African start-up, has developed a mobile phone payment platform that has been embraced by the continent's biggest telecommunications operators and their 500 million customers. This will allow quick and inexpensive movement of the hundreds of millions of dollars of remittances that flow globally from one country to another and from city to village.[46] In an effort to combat the costs of middle men and corruption, India deposits government pension and scholarship payments directly into the bank accounts of about 245,000 people in twenty of the nation's hundreds of districts.[47]

This innovation in information and communications technology assists in the area of public health as well. In Zambia, a rural doctor gets help from a doctor in Peru about a puzzling case of cholera through an email exchange mediated by a low-flying satellite. In Uganda, health huts in the remote countryside, with no landline and miles from a city, upload epidemiological data daily via satellite into a national health system. In African neo-Pentecostal churches, pastors download sermons from the United States and Britain. Churches are taking advantage of these changes to maintain easy and inexpensive communications with sister churches and partner churches in the Global South. Skype and the new money-transfer technologies make the mechanics of church-to-church partnerships much easier.

Faith and Development

Where Are the Christians?

You may be wondering why I have not shared a Christian proposal for poverty eradication. The answer is simple. There are no global proposals by Christians for ending poverty in the world. Before I explain why, let me contradict this claim to some degree.

While there are no global Christian poverty-reduction strategies per se, the gospel of Jesus Christ and God's kingdom does include the elimination of poverty, but as a consequence of something that God does, not by human endeavor or global strategies. When Christ comes and the kingdom of God is

46. Wexler, "Mobile-Payment Boom."
47. Harris, "Money for Poor."

on earth, "there will be no more death or mourning or crying or pain, for the old order of things has passed away" (Rev. 21:4). Furthermore, in this time between the ascension of Jesus and his coming again, our review of the history of globalization reveals that the church, through its theological anthropology and moral vision, has encouraged the emergence of changes that improved the living conditions of human beings. "The deeper historical evidence suggests that the classic Roman Catholic, Reformation, and, now, the newer Evangelical and Pentecostal traditions tend to generate an ethos that foments modernization, a fact that is arguably traceable to a basic attitude toward the duty to convert souls, societies, and gain stewardly dominion over the ecosphere in a fallen world."[48] The activity of God redeeming and restoring creation includes poverty eradication along with the other elements of the gospel.

Now back to the absence of Christian proposals for ending poverty per se. There are a variety of reasons for this. We begin with the fact that churches tend to focus their efforts on the neighbors they know. Their development work with the poor is micro and local.[49] This micro-level involvement does not lend itself to global proposals. Scanning the landscape for what churches are doing reveals a bits-and-pieces affair, highly decentralized, almost church by church, denomination by denomination, and tradition by tradition. There are an increasing number of church-to-church development efforts that are well intentioned and personally transformational. Sometimes these bring about good development, but they often lack the technical excellence of secular work.

We need not feel badly about this. Jesus said that the kingdom emerges from tiny seeds, from small things (Mark 4:28–32). Perhaps we should allow God to pursue God's strategy for eradicating poverty by saving and restoring the world while we pursue the more modest task of loving our local neighbors and those far-away neighbors whom we have come to know in a globalizing world. Perhaps we need to trust that God will make all our small things into a big thing, an emerging kingdom even.

A second reason for the lack of a Christian contribution to development theory and practice is that churches and Christians tend to delegate their development efforts to Christian development agencies, such as Tearfund, World Relief, Food for the Hungry, and World Vision International, or to Christian agencies with a focus on certain sectors, such as Opportunity International in microfinance and Lifewater International with its focus on water, sanitation, and hygiene. While these activists and agencies do sometimes write and even do research, they too limit their focus to the micro level of development

48. Stackhouse, *Globalization and Grace*, 243.
49. Fikkert and Mask, *From Dependence to Dignity*.

programming. Often their engagement with secular development theory and research is uneven. This is because they, like the churches, tend to remain within our Christian subculture, which is largely disconnected from secular thinking and experimentation. Too often Christian development folk only meet with other Christian development folk.

The final reason is also understandable. Most Christians in the academic world are either theologians who have little contact with a practical discipline like development studies, or they work in the social sciences of anthropology, sociology, or psychology. These social sciences have the most potential for helping the church function competently in the world (although churches do not always avail themselves of this knowledge). The net result is that very few Christians working within the development studies discipline feel free enough to bring their theology to the table.

The good news is that things have begun to change.

They Are Suspicious but Curious

The international development community, a generally secular and modern lot with suspicions about religion, has begun a slow process of engaging with those who are doing what has come to be called "faith-based development." The first opening occurred in 1980 when the journal of the Society of International Development devoted a special issue to the relationship between religion and development and then proposed a new research agenda on the topic.[50] Almost twenty years later, the archbishop of Canterbury and the president of the World Bank launched the World Faiths Development Dialogue. This led to a multiyear process of meetings and continuing exploration.[51] Subsequent research called attention to the fact that faith-based civil society organizations (we call them churches and agencies) were major, if not the largest, contributors to social welfare in much of the Global South.[52] In 2005 a five-year Religions and Development Research Programme[53] was launched by a consortium that included the Universities of Birmingham and Bath along with other British institutions and partners in the Global South. The program has already completed a series of interesting working papers on religion and development from the perspective of sociology, anthropology, and economics.[54]

50. Clarke, "Faith Matters."
51. Marshall and Van Saanen, *Development and Faith*.
52. Clarke, "Faith Matters," 37, 41.
53. Funded by the UK government's Department for International Development.
54. Its reports can be found at http://www.birmingham.ac.uk/schools/government-society /departments/international-development/rad/publications/index.aspx.

Most recently, a serious challenge has arisen from within the secular development studies community itself. Séverine Deneulin, a Catholic, and Masooda Bano, a Muslim, have called for a "rewriting of the secular script" of development.[55] They are encouraging the development community to go beyond the currently accepted instrumental view—that religion may somehow contribute to development—to a more organic view. Exploring Christian and Muslim understandings of human development, Deneulin and Bano demonstrate that working for development is intrinsic to religious experience and purpose. They drive home the point that, for the Christian and Muslim religious traditions, "there is no separation between religion and development. Development is what adherents of a religion do because of who they are and what they believe in."[56]

Deneulin and Bano point to significant "overlaps between the religious and secular traditions on development issues" in the areas of human dignity, social justice, poverty, relief, concern for the earth, equality, and freedom.[57] While there are also areas of significant and possibly irreconcilable differences, Deneulin and Bano wonder if a conversation between these two perspectives on faith and development might create value, and they propose using interfaith dialogue as a model for carrying out such a conversation.

In metaphorical terms, the secular development folk seem to be discovering the theological front yard of the religious traditions that are doing development. They have wandered in, intrigued by some of the plants and trees they find there. Rather than retreating behind the door of our house, fearful that these secular folk cannot understand the content, rationality, or revelation behind our development theology and practice, we need to go out and welcome them in. We need to recover our confidence as Christians, lost in the face of the overwhelming corrosive power of modernity, and believe once again that we have something to offer to the development conversations today.

We Are Also Suspicious and Need to Be More Curious

Christians are also suspicious. Our experiences with secular folk, especially of the academic variety, have not always been encouraging and have sometimes been dismissive and territorial. We did not volunteer to be relegated to the spiritual or religious realm, after all. But, in light of secular movement in our direction, we need to consider becoming more open and curious.

As pointed out in an earlier chapter, the deep irony in the history of the idea of development is that the secular world of development studies has,

55. Deneulin and Bano, *Religion in Development*.
56. Ibid., 4–5.
57. Ibid., 10–11.

for the most part, forgotten its origins. Humanitarianism and the idea of development emerged out of a largely Judeo-Christian view of God's world and how it works.[58] Sadly, many Christians have also forgotten this fact of history. Another fact deepens this irony: the same modernity that birthed the ideas allowing human beings to discover that they could change history, and that development and thus poverty eradication was possible, also reduced poverty to something entirely material, having to do mostly with lack of money and technology.

So while we may have shared origins at one time, we have drifted farther and farther apart for almost two centuries. We have significant points of disagreement, and for many it is unclear whether engaging one another is worthwhile. For example, secular understandings of the nature of human beings and their purpose in this world tend to be reductionist as the relational and transcendent dimensions of being human are usually overlooked or rejected. Then there is the question of who is poor. Are the poor only those suffering from material deficits? Is there a poverty related to having too much or being too powerful?[59]

The secular views of the causes of poverty do not seem sufficiently robust. They point to bad and unjust behaviors of individuals and social systems but have no compelling explanation as to the origins of this behavior—ignorance alone just doesn't seem adequate. Without an adequate explanation, solutions are hard. Education alone—modernity's proposed solution to most social problems—doesn't seem capable of improving the whole of the human condition.

Although the development proposals of Sen, Sachs, Easterly, Collier, de Soto, and Yunus have led us beyond economic growth alone, and beyond the historical tendency to have very low views of the poor and their potential, they share a common perspective: the modern worldview. They are all materialistic and technocratic, and reflect a firm belief in human reason, technology, and money as the key to solving the problem of poverty.

The secular and the religious points of view may be irreconcilable, and thus Christian and secular folk may have little to offer each other. But I wonder if these points of view might also be a reflection of modernity's commitment to the irrevocable divide between the spiritual world of religion and theology and the material, "real" world of poverty, economics, and politics. If the

58. Himmelfarb, "Idea of Compassion"; McCloskey, *Bourgeois Dignity*; Stackhouse, *Globalization and Grace*; Stark, *Victory of Reason*.

59. Former Archbishop Rowan Williams has said that, in pursuit of development, "we are not trying to solve someone else's problem but to liberate *ourselves* from a toxic and unjust situation in which we, the prosperous, are less than human." Williams, "New Perspectives" (emphasis original).

secular-religious divide is eroding, then perhaps a useful engagement might be possible. I am encouraged on this point by the curiosity and engagement of the development studies world with the matters of faith and religion that I just described.

Is There Value in Dialogue?

I believe that there is indeed value in dialogue, but I need to be clear about what I mean. The answer to this question is a bit different depending on whether we are talking about the micro level of designing and implementing development programs or the macro level of explanations of poverty and theories for seeking a better human future.

At the micro level of doing development among the poor, there are two compelling reasons to engage and to listen closely. First, we should take seriously the results of evidence-based evaluations and random control testing of development approaches. Secular development agencies learn more every year about what works and what does not work—at least at the material level—for the simple reason that they have more money and more academic resources with which to explore, examine, and evaluate development practice.[60] Best practice in water management, public health interventions, microfinance programming, and the like is best practice. There is no Christian best practice standing over against a secular best practice. To reject or be suspicious of such work on the grounds that it is secular assumes that God does not work or enable discoveries among any group other than Christians, a stance that is not biblical. God uses whom God will, and a passion for the poor and an instinct to innovate is innate in all human beings made in the image of God, not just Christians. We need to be willing to look for good news for the poor among any for whom development work is a passion or calling.

Second, there is a growing demand for interagency cooperation and co-ordination. Sooner or later, Christian development practitioners are likely to find themselves at the table with other development practitioners from secular and government agencies. We need to be able to understand each other and speak each other's language. A working understanding of contemporary secular development thinking and the research that lies behind it will make such conversations easier.

The primary challenge to learning from each other at the micro level is a cross-cultural problem. On the one hand, the development world of churches and Christian agencies is too often unaware of ideas, new techniques, and

60. The Poverty Action Lab at MIT should be watched regularly. They are the global leaders in random control assessments of poverty solutions throughout the world.

professional knowledge available from our secular friends. On the other hand, the world of secular development studies has little experience conversing with the world of faith and development. This belies a need for better cross-cultural engagement. Rowan Williams, the former archbishop of Canterbury, dryly observed that it would be helpful if we had better religious literacy among secular NGOs and activists and more humility and curiosity on the part of faith-based NGOs and their activists.[61]

A more nuanced challenge exists at the macro or conceptual level, the level of development theories. Embedded in theories and even some best practices are assumptions—about how the world works, who human beings are, and what a better human future might look like—on which we may not entirely agree. This makes engagement at the level of theory a two-edged sword for both perspectives, but especially for Christians. On the one hand, if we uncritically refuse engagement, we may stand in front of God someday and discover that we cut ourselves off from something good that God was doing in the world—something that God expected us to be part of. On the other hand, if we uncritically join in and emulate a secular proposal, we may find ourselves contributing to an agenda that is not what God desires for the world.

But if our philosophical and theological roots were once similar, then perhaps there is value in a more appreciative engagement with each other. This brings us back to the cross-cultural challenge. We Christians have been socialized to treat the secular world as wholly other and largely wrong; secular folk in governments and the academy have been similarly socialized, only the other way around—the two-tiered, material-spiritual worldview separates us once again. It will take deliberate effort to overcome this divide.

An Enriching Conversation

I think a useful conversation for both sides can take place if two things happen. First, each side must explore the other from an appreciative stance. This is what Rowan Williams was pleading for. What do we see that we can affirm? What ideas, assumptions, or values do we share? This is the conversation that Deneulin and Bano are attempting to start. Similarly, we need to get inside the proposals of Sachs, Easterly, Collier, and Sen, understand them on their own terms, and accept them as the best efforts of very smart and knowledgeable people. We gain nothing by simply dismissing them as secular ideas coming from secular folk and thus of no value to us.

61. Williams, "New Perspectives."

While I believe there is potential for useful conversation, this kind of dialogue is beyond my expertise and the scope of this book. But I do have a suggestion as to where to start. Focusing on our differing ideas of development, what each side understands development to be, and how it should be pursued might not be the best place to begin. It might be more fruitful to begin with a family of prior questions that would reveal our underlying assumptions about how the world works and why things are as they are. When I engage with secular proposals on development, I begin with a set of questions whose answers are very important to anyone who wants to engage deeply and seriously with what someone else is proposing. Sometimes the answers will be explicit, and sometimes they are undeclared or even unknown. The process of discovery with these questions is revealing and helpful for an appreciative engagement.

- What is a human being? What is the explicit or implicit anthropology?
- What are human beings for?
- Why is the human condition as it is? Why is the world as it is?
- What is the explicit or implied framework for understanding poverty?
- What is the understanding of the cause(s) of poverty?
- What does a better human future look like? Toward what end is development working?
- What process of change leads to this better future?
- What is the underlying perspective, faith commitment, or philosophical stance that drives the answers to the foregoing questions?

As a starting point for conversation, I offer an example adapted from Christian Smith and his important book *What Is a Person?* Smith argues that sociology would be helped if it unpacked its assumptions about the nature of the human person, the building block of the social systems that sociology studies. I wondered what Smith's exercise might look like in the context of development studies. So I created a simple outline of differing philosophical/theological perspectives, their view of the nature of human beings, and the resulting view of the better human future that development seeks (see table 10.1).

Obviously, one can hold several related perspectives; none of these is discreet. But laying perspectives out as table 10.1 does seems helpful in two ways. First, where you end up is often determined by where you start. This is nothing new, but it is a reminder that perspective matters and needs to be declared. All faith commitments—that is what a perspective is, after all—need to be labeled as such and should remain open to dialogue. One may claim

Perspective Is . . .	Human Beings Are . . .	Better Future Is . . .
Darwinian	Self-conscious animals	Procreate and die
Economic	Rational, value-maximizing individuals	Increase wealth
Marketplace	Acquisitive hedonists	Accumulate stuff
Postmodern romantic	Carnally desiring sensualists	Increase gratification
Sociological	Artifacts of structure and socialization	Change social structure
Buddhist	Illusions of individuality	Ignore poverty, release self
Christian	Made in the image of a God who loves	Love God and neighbor

Adapted from Smith, *What Is a Person?*, 7. Christian Smith is professor of sociology and director of the Center for the Study of Religion and Society and the Center for Social Research at the University of Notre Dame.

TABLE 10.1 One's Point of View Matters

to be a Darwinian on the basis of proven science, but the assumption that this is all there is to the human story is a faith claim. Second, declaring one's assumptions as to the identity of human beings—who they are and why they are here—may lead to interesting discussions about oversimplification or reductionism. The same outcome may well result from a comparison of views on the better human future.

One final reminder. None of these views is wholly wrong; each has some truth to it. This is where the conversation can begin. What is meant and not meant? In what ways might some of these views enrich others? How might some of these views assist others? The goal is to deepen our respective understandings of what development is or ought to be.

We are facing a new opportunity. The so-called secular development conversation is rediscovering religion and its importance to any idea of human well-being and social change. This product of postmodernity may mean that Christians and their religious perspective on development are positioned to make a fresh contribution to the development discourse, provided that we are willing to take our development practice and thinking into the larger development community.

The goal is to note differences but not to dwell on these alone. Naming and unpacking our differing assumptions and frameworks is likely to assist all perspectives. If the secular development studies world is in fact on the edges of our theological garden looking for things that might be helpful to the poor, perhaps we ought to begin a conversation with them. Might this be an invitation to an open-minded, nonjudgmental Christian witness?

We Christians need to be willing to come out of our self-imposed exile, stop being apologetic about being Christians, and begin to contribute the material that our faith tradition has to offer—it is considerable.

Summing Up

As we look back on this account of the history and current thinking about development from a global perspective, we find a mixture of good news and not so good news, of contradictions and opportunities. The good news is that the percentage of people living on less than two dollars a day has dropped from over 95 percent in 1820 to about 13 percent in 2012. In the twenty-four years between 1981 and 2005, the number of people in the world living in absolute poverty dropped from just under two billion to 900 million, with the largest declines in China, India, and more recently Brazil and Indonesia.[62] The not so good news is that almost 900 million people in fifty countries are deeply mired in poverty in very unhelpful contexts, in which it is unclear how development as we now understand it can take place.[63]

Furthermore, the good news is that global development assistance is at its highest level in history. The not so good news is that we are unclear on how best to use this foreign aid to facilitate effective and sustainable development.[64] The good news is that we know a great deal more about economic policies, participatory methods, good governance, and useful cultural values that enable development. The not so good news is that the development goal is "in the service of expanding the human ability to produce and have more—more stuff, more freedom, more years, more control."[65] The good news is that the number of nonpoor in the world is the highest in history. The not so good news is that they are struggling with obesity, consumerism, and a deteriorating natural environment.

Finally, the good news is that the evangelical church is caring more for the poor than at any time since Victorian England. The not so good news is that we are largely unaware of what has been learned about being effective in the long term.

Questions for Discussion

1. Which secular proposal for eradicating poverty seems to you to be most likely to succeed? Why?
2. What kind of better human future should Christian development work move toward?
3. What should you look for when choosing a Christian relief and development agency to support?

62. World Bank, "Poverty: Overview."
63. Collier, *Bottom Billion*, 5–7.
64. Easterly, *White Man's Burden*, 4, 11.
65. Hoksbergen, Curry, and Kuperus, "International Development," 30.

GLOBALIZATION AND THE CHURCH

11

Globalization and World Christianity

I now turn to the impact of globalization on world Christianity and the impact of world Christianity on globalization. I've already pointed out that the spread of Christianity is part of the First Era of Globalization. I also called our attention to the fact that Christianity is a globalism—a religious or ideological value system that makes a set of assertions about the way the world works and, most importantly, how it ought to be ordered.

The central concern of this book is how the Christian church and Christians will respond to globalization. I have described three basic options that churches and Christians might pursue. One option is to ignore globalization, putting our heads down and focusing only on local and spiritual things. A second option is to resist globalization as something that needs to be reversed or replaced. A final option is to engage globalization and celebrate the good it has done and work to overcome its weaknesses and failures. This chapter is intended to help set the stage for making this choice.

I begin with two preliminaries that form the foundations for how I will outline the story of the church and globalization. First, I will summarize how I understand the mission of the church, and second, I will return to complex adaptive social systems as they shed light on the history of world Christianity. Then I will briefly outline the history of how a small group of former Jews in Jerusalem were part of a movement that has taken root all over the world in the last two thousand years. With this story in place, I will make some observations about the way the global Christian church has changed dramatically

187

in the last one hundred years. The chapter will conclude with a description of the four broad mission frontiers that the church faces today.

Two Preliminaries

The Mission of the Church

The mission of the church in the world is not complicated. Matthew reports that Jesus instructed us to make disciples of all peoples (nations), baptizing them in the name of the Triune God and teaching them to obey everything Jesus commanded (Matt. 28:19–20). We are to be Christ's witnesses to governors, kings, gentiles (Matt. 10:18), and to the ends of the earth (Acts 1:18). Witness, make disciples, teach them to obey God's commands. Let's look at each of these in turn.

The word *gospel* means "message" or "good news," and news is not news unless it is announced. Proclamation of the good news of Jesus Christ and the coming of God's kingdom is required. But being a witness is not a question of clever or heartfelt words; we are not in the business of selling the gospel.[1] At the end of the day, we can only witness to what God has done in our lives and to what God is doing in history.[2] Whether or not people respond is the work of the Holy Spirit alone. Our responsibility is simply to share our story and God's story with an invitation to all to join God's story.

Evangelism should not be thought of as being different from or unrelated to discipleship. The command to make disciples suggests that the measure of mission is not how many people decide to become Christians but the degree to which those who do respond are being formed into living witnesses to Christ and God's kingdom. The central measure of the faithfulness of our mission should be "What kind of disciples we are making?" Our effectiveness in forming disciples who consume, vote, and volunteer in ways that reflect the actions of Christ during his ministry and the values of God's kingdom is a critical test of the church's engagement with globalization, as we shall see in the next two chapters.

What commands did Christ give us that we are to teach to others? We were commanded to love the Lord our God with all our heart and with all our soul and with all our strength and with all our mind, and to love our neighbor as we love ourselves (Matt. 22:37–40; Mark 12:30–31; Luke 10:27). Among the many commands in the Bible, named and implied, these two, we are told, are

1. Tennent, *Theology*, 18.
2. Newbigin, *Gospel in a Pluralist Society*, 129.

the central two—so central, in fact, that "all the Law and the Prophets hang on these two commandments" (Matt. 22:40).

Our mission to love God and to love our neighbor as ourselves is both a moral and a relational responsibility. As followers of a moral and relational three-in-one God, we are to speak to the moral and relational behavior of economics, politics, technology, and any other facet of globalization. Whatever the political theory, economic system, or cultural values, the church has a responsibility to contribute to an ethics that values human freedom, agency, and creativity and that acknowledges the transcendent and relational nature of human beings. The church and all religions must demand that no economic or political system can be judged to be moral if it tolerates anyone living a life that is not fully human.

This is the mission of the church in a nutshell—witness to the Jesus who preached good news to the poor, healed the sick, cast out the demons, and promised salvation to all who believe, and to the news that God's kingdom has been inaugurated on earth and that it will be the only kingdom on earth at the end of time. Invite people to a relationship with God and each other, and then disciple them around the central commandments of loving God and loving our neighbors. How this is expressed varies by context and one's gifts.

Making Sense of Our Christian History

In my introduction of complex adaptive social systems in chapter 2, I presented Niall Ferguson's suggestion that new structures in history emerge unbidden and unexpectedly. No one saw them coming, save God. We recognize them and give them a name only as we look back to make sense of what proved to be a transformative change. I suggested that this understanding of history unfolding unexpectedly might be useful as we look at the history of the Christian church.

Lesslie Newbigin has helpfully pointed out that in the early chapters of the book of Acts, evangelism was the "second act." First God acted, and then ordinary people asked questions about the miracles they had seen. Only then did the disciples explain what had happened by pointing to God and to the gospel (Acts 2:12; 3:11; 7:1).[3] Peter did not decide it was time for him to become an evangelist, nor did the church decide it was time to launch its first evangelism campaign or begin training missionaries. God acted without warning, and the disciples tried to keep up.

3. Ibid., 133.

The church then spread from Jerusalem in equally unanticipated ways. Fleeing persecution, Philip ended up in Samaria proclaiming the Messiah, and then God led him to the desert road where he ran into an Ethiopian eunuch and the gospel found its way to Africa (Acts 8:4, 26). Also fleeing persecution, other believers found themselves sharing the gospel in Phoenicia, Cyprus, and Antioch, much to the surprise and puzzlement of the church in Jerusalem (Acts 11:19–22). Paul was minding his own business as a Jew when the Spirit of Jesus changed his life and directed him toward his new mission to the gentiles. Believers then continued to witness and followers of Jesus appeared all over the world. The only one who understood what was going on was God. Eventually, Luke gathered up the stories, made sense of the church's early history of mission, and wrote the book of Acts. But, in the moment, the actions of mission were unrelated and seemingly incoherent. This sounds a lot like an emerging new structure in history.

Using this emergent framework for understanding the history of world Christianity has other benefits. First, we get away from the "great man" account of Christian history that reduces the Christian story to our favorite few heroes while ignoring the multitudes, whose names we often do not know, who acted faithfully as witnesses to Christ and God's kingdom over the last two thousand years. More importantly, this is an antidote to modernity's lie that human beings can somehow save themselves, that social change is simply a matter of clever human beings creating strategies and programs that lead to "progress." Second, the good news is that the success of what God is doing in history does not rest on our shoulders. God initiates and we participate, often without knowing exactly what it is we are contributing to. We are not expected to "be successful" or "change the world." This is the work of the Holy Spirit. We are expected simply to be faithful to the command to be witnesses and to love God and to love our neighbors as ourselves.

The last two hundred years of globalization represent as significant a historical transition as did the rise and fall of the Roman Empire, the radical economic and social transformation of Britain, or any other historical watershed. The impact of globalization on the Christian church is as significant as it has been on the rest of the world. God knows where globalization is going, and we do not. Thus, how the church should respond to this emerging future is by definition unclear and must be discovered. Because we are still in the midst of this transformational change called globalization, the theologies and mission strategies of earlier eras are unlikely to be as useful as they once were. We will need to be open to the leading of the Spirit and be willing to think new thoughts and pray new prayers. We will have to work hard to deeply understand what is happening and what it means; serious social and cultural analysis will need to be done.[4] But the one constant is our mission to be witnesses and to love God and our neighbor. These are things we can do without regard to how much or little we understand about what God is doing in the world.

Christianity: An Enduring Globalism

In chapter 3 on understanding globalization, I noted that there are ideologies, cultures, and religions that, when believed by sufficiently large numbers of people and institutions, can influence social change. I used the word *globalisms* to describe these ideological or religious understandings about the way the world works and how it ought to be ordered.[5] I noted two things. First, the dominant globalism of today is the belief in the efficacy of the neoliberal expression of capitalism and the validity of secular humanism. Second, Christianity, alongside the other world religions, is among the world's most enduring globalisms.

Remember that by definition a globalism makes a universal truth claim, and in the biblical narrative God's global claim is clear: the Bible announces that God is the world's creator, sustainer, ruler, lover, savior, and judge.[6] Abraham was told that he would be a blessing to all nations (Gen. 18:18). The Psalms tell us that the nations and their kings will bow down to God (Pss. 22:27; 72:11). The gospel is to be preached to the whole world (Matt. 24:14), and we are to be witnesses to the ends of the earth (Acts 1:8). We are to make disciples of all peoples (Matt. 28:19). At the end of time, all nations will come and worship before God (Rev. 15:4), and the nations of the world will walk by the light of the glory of God and the Lamb (Rev. 21:24). Consider what these claims might feel like to a non-believer, an atheist, a Muslim, or an adherent to any other faith.

Since this claim is God's and not ours, we must assume a stance of humility. When we go to the ends of the earth or to the end of the block as witnesses, we are not witnessing to our spirituality, theology, technology, economics, politics, or culture. We are simply witnessing to the good news that Christ and God's kingdom saved us and offers to save others. Sadly, this is unlikely to be the way we are perceived. The scope of God's claim is all-encompassing, and so Christians need to understand that we represent, however humbly, a compelling globalism that has been gaining adherents for over two thousand years. We need to be prepared to accept resistance and possibly the enmity of those who put their faith in a competing globalism.

4. All of these challenges are the focus of the last two chapters of this book.
5. Steger, *Globalization*; LCWE, "Globalization and the Gospel."
6. Bauckham, "Bible and Globalization," 27.

God Makes a Global Claim

Justo L. González, emeritus professor, Candler School
of Theology at Emory University

Radical monotheism requires a global perspective. The Judeo-Christian
doctrine of creation means that nothing exists beyond the scope and reach
of the one God. A radically monotheistic religion must be global precisely
because it admits of no other gods. . . . Christianity [is] a truly global religion,
expressing at once both the unity of the world in which it was formed and
the diversity within that world.

Thus emerged a religion with a truly global vocation.

González, foreword to *Globalization and Grace*, xxv–xxvi

We need to remind ourselves that Christianity is an atypical globalism in
that it always localizes. Through translation of the Bible and local theologiz-
ing, this globalism makes its home fully everywhere and anywhere, in every
language and in every cultural setting. The consequence is that, while Christianity makes a global claim, does mission everywhere, and unites all Christians, it does not create cultural homogeneity as does economic globalization
and do other globalisms such as Islam.

Finally, one additional element of Christianity as a globalism is relevant to
the next several chapters. The God who created, sustains, saves, and brings
human history to its fulfillment is a moral God, the God of the Ten Commandments and the two Great Commandments. The kingdom of God provides an
ethical framework to guide us and the kingdoms of this world toward what God
knows is the best human future. The church has no choice but to announce
this news and to speak about God's kingdom. Leaving the public square or
the institutions of society to the other globalisms is not a Christian option.

The Globalization of World Christianity

The Historical Trajectory

As soon as the church was told to go as witnesses to the ends of the earth
and make disciples of all peoples, the church became part of the process
of globalization as well as one of its outcomes. I have already outlined the

movement of Christianity from Jerusalem as a process of migration driven by the Holy Spirit, who goes where the Spirit wills. This continues today. From a Jewish center in Jerusalem, the church made its home among the gentiles as it spread west to North Africa, north to West Asia, Greece, and Rome, and east to Syria.

The unpredictable wanderings of the church and its gospel have continued for two thousand years (see fig. 11.1). From a marginal religion worthy of little more than persecution, the church, then mostly Greek speaking, suddenly found itself adopted by the most powerful empire of its time in the fourth century. Yet the early church in Europe almost faded away until the Celtic mission movement rekindled the faith on the continent. Between the ninth and fourteenth centuries, the Syrian (Nestorian) mission movement carried the gospel from the Mediterranean to India and China. The church then divided between Rome and Constantinople, and Europe became Christianized and carried out the crusades in the Middle Ages.

The Catholic mission era began with the age of discovery in the sixteenth century, and the gospel was preached, often coercively, in Latin America and Asia. In the nineteenth century, the era of Protestant missions emerged, often in partnership with the empires of Europe, and the gospel went to Africa and Asia.[7]

In a surprising turn at the beginning of the twentieth century, the Holy Spirit launched a Pentecostal renewal movement in different parts of the world all at the same time. The resulting Pentecostal mission movement launched a new wave of mission from churches in the Global South to the east and west in Africa and Latin America as well as taking the gospel back to their former colonizers in the North. By the end of the twentieth century, mission was from anywhere to everywhere.[8]

The Nature of Christian Mission

Two distinguishing features of the globalization of Christianity are important to note. First, the Christian church has always grown serially, taking root for a time in a particular place and then moving on.[9] The lands of the early church in the Middle East and North Africa are now primarily Muslim areas. By the year 1000, the church's center of gravity had moved to Europe,

---

7. The foregoing was developed from Neill, *History of Christian Missions*; Lapple, *Catholic Church*.

8. Walls, "Christian Mission," 202. Andrew Walls is former director of the Centre for the Study of Christianity and is professor of the history of mission at Liverpool Hope University.

9. Walls, *Missionary Movement in Christian History*, 22–25.

FIGURE 11.1 Globalization of Christianity

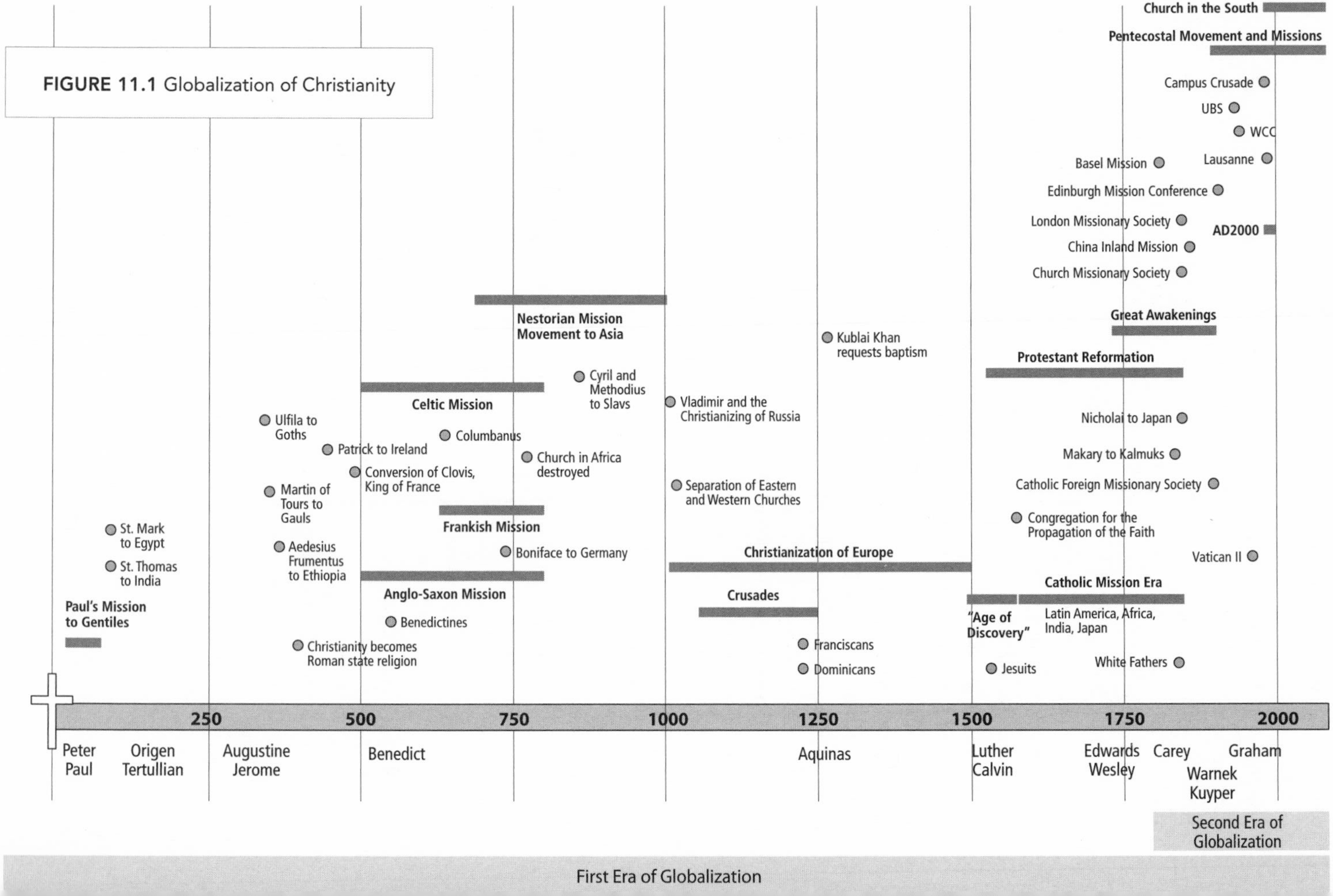

Adapted from Myers, Exploring World Mission, 18

and theology and mission practice were becoming largely European. By the mid-twentieth century, the church was withering in Europe while, to the surprise of proponents of secularization theory, Christianity was expanding rapidly in the Global South. These shifts were not really understood until well after they happened—emergent history again. The good news is that the church has undergone a series of reimaginings and adaptations in response to a changing world. This history of adaptation holds out the promise that the church will be led by the Spirit to new understandings in theological and missiological thinking and practice that will enable it to constructively engage the contemporary processes of globalization.

Second, in contrast to the teaching of other world religions, the Christian gospel has been able to translate itself across cultural and geographic boundaries without diluting the universality of its message. Andrew Walls points to the creative tension between the "pilgrim principle" and the "indigenizing principle" of the gospel. The former is the universal claim of the gospel that transcends the particulars of cultures and place, thus uniting us to an "adoptive past"—to the saints who went before us.[10] The latter is the remarkable fact that the gospel fully makes its home everywhere and anywhere, in every language and cultural setting. There has never been a permanent cultural center of Christianity, although this has not always been understood.

As the church changed over time, so did the way it thought about and practiced mission.[11] For the early church, the goal of mission was making disciples. It was a time of apostles and martyrs. The church was an eschatological community. As the church became gentile and Hellenistic, the goal of mission was a Christian life. It was a time of itinerant evangelists and healers, and the church was understood as a worshiping community. With the emergence of Christendom and the European medieval church, the goal of mission was to expand Christendom by compelling people to come in (cf. Luke 14:23). The gospel message was carried by a strange mixture of monks and conquistadors. The church had become an institution of power. With the Reformation, the gospel became the power to save all those who believe, and the goal of mission became personal renewal. The Protestant church was to be a reforming community. In the modern mission era (the Second Era of Globalization), the goal of mission was to save souls and improve quality of life in the here and now. It was a time of volunteer missionaries and an emerging south-to-south mission movement.[12] The church was understood as a civilizing community.

10. Ibid., 7–9.
11. The following is summarized from Bosch, *Transforming Mission*.
12. Hanciles, *Beyond Christendom*, 218.

And now today, as the third millennium is developing, it is not clear where the church in mission is going. It is increasingly a church of the Global South. For some, mission is simply seeking justice; for others, it is only evangelism; for others still, evangelism and casting out demons are at the heart of mission. Encouragingly, a growing number of people understand Christian mission as being about discipling the nations for spiritual and social transformation—a gospel of life, deed, word, and sign. Your author counts himself among this latter group. The important lesson from all this is that Christianity is a remarkably flexible globalism, ever adapting under the leadership of the Holy Spirit.

God Did Not Die

The story of the expansion of Christianity in the last one hundred years needs to be understood against secularization theory, which posited that as globalization and its markets, technology, and science grew ever more pervasive, religion would fade away as no longer necessary. Modernity was seen as a one-way street, and religion has been caught going in the wrong direction. After all, science is how we know things, liberalism has provided secular ethics to politics, pluralism has displaced religion's truth claims, and individualism and personal networks have undermined community.[13]

The facts argue otherwise. Over the last century, the number of Christians and Muslims has grown significantly and now accounts for over 55 percent of the world's population (see fig. 11.2). People who claim a religion of some kind account for almost 90 percent of the people on earth. Even traditional religions have not significantly faltered in the face of modernity and globalization. The only solace to secularization theorists was the emergence of almost 800 million "non-religionists" during the twentieth century, although the number appears to be leveling off over the last twenty years.[14]

While this is good news, the kinds of religion that not only did not go away but appear to be flourishing in the midst of contemporary globalization are sobering. Olivier Roy has noted that the major religious growth in the twentieth century has been in Pentecostalism, Muslim Salafism, fundamentalist Jewish movements, and a reformulated Buddhism and Hinduism, both of which have become quite militant. These movements tend to be morally and socially conservative, and Roy wonders if they may be the religious form (a globalism) best suited to react against globalization in this century.[15] Earlier

13. Summarized from Sacks, *Persistence of Faith*, 2.
14. Figures taken or calculated from Johnson et al., "Christianity 2016."
15. Roy, *Holy Ignorance*. Olivier Roy has written on secularization and Islam and is chair of Mediterranean studies at the European University Institute in Florence, Italy.

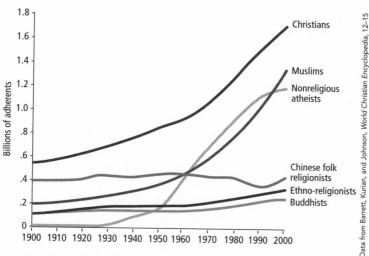

FIGURE 11.2 Who believes what?

in the book I listed fundamentalisms as one of the major fragmenting forces reacting to the integrating forces of globalization.

The Changing Shape of the Christian Church

What Changed?

It is no longer news that the Christian church has radically changed its shape over the last one hundred years. In 1900 there were around 600 million Christians in a world of 1.6 billion people. Over 70 percent of them lived in Europe (including Russia) and North America. Today this picture has turned upside down. Over 60 percent of all Christians live in Africa, Asia, and Latin America, while less than one-third live in greater Europe and North America.[16] This shift becomes even more pronounced when we take into account that these studies count self-identifying Christians as opposed to active Christians; the Western count is significantly overstated.

The bottom line is startling: Christianity is now a non-Western religion. Only the United States and Germany are in the top ten countries with the largest number of Christians. Brazil, Mexico, Russia, the Philippines, Nigeria, China, the Democratic Republic of Congo, and Ethiopia fill out the rest of the table.[17]

16. Johnson et al., "Christianity 2016," 5.
17. Pew Research Center, *Global Christianity*, 11.

In Today's World . . .

Though Christianity began in the Middle East, the region today has the lowest concentration and lowest number of Christians of any of the world's regions.

Indonesia, a majority Muslim country, has more Christians than the twenty countries in the Middle East and North Africa combined.

Nigeria has twice as many Protestant Christians as Germany, the birthplace of the Reformation.

Only two of the ten countries with the largest Protestant populations are in Europe.

More Catholics live in Brazil than in Italy, France, and Spain combined.

China is estimated to have more Christians than any European nation except Russia.

Pew Research Center, *Global Christianity*, 11

The cutting edge of global Christianity has changed just as dramatically. In 1900, almost all Christians were Roman Catholic or Protestant, the two primary streams of European Christianity for centuries. Today the fastest growing regions in the Christian world are Africa and Asia, while the fastest growing movements within global Christianity are the Pentecostals/charismatics and evangelicals.[18] While Roman Catholicism and traditional Protestant Christianity have not gone away, they are not as dynamic as they once were, with the exception of the charismatic renewal movements that have partially transformed each from within. This brings us to the unexpected new work of the Holy Spirit in the twentieth century.

After the shift of the center of gravity of the church from the West to the Global South, the second most significant and dramatic shift in the Christian world in the twentieth century was the emergence of the Pentecostal/charismatic movement. Within the first decade of the century, mass experiences with the Holy Spirit launched the Welsh Revival (1904), the Mukti Revival in north India (1905), the Azusa Street Revival (1906), one in Chile (1902), a revival in Calcutta (1907), and revivals in different parts of West Africa in the last part of the decade. In 1900 there were less than one million Pentecostals/charismatics in the world. Today there are over 650 million on all continents, close to 30 percent of all Christians and twice the number of evangelicals.[19]

18. Johnson et al., "Christianity 2016," 26.
19. Ibid.

This polycentric movement emerged unexpectedly; it was not the product of the traditional "from here to there" mission.[20] Pentecostalism globalized in less than a decade and yet was not a product of globalization by mission or migration.

Globalization and Pentecostalism have crossed paths in the last thirty-five years. Neo-Pentecostalism emerged in the 1980s about the same time as Globalization II reached full swing. Accounting for almost one-third of the Pentecostal/charismatic movement today,[21] neo-Pentecostalism is a self-generating phenomenon that emerged at the grass roots in the Global South. It is deeply contextual and is generally nondenominational or postdenominational.[22] This new expression of Pentecostalism is distinguished by a combination of Pentecostal worship, aggressive evangelism, and grassroots efforts in education, health services, and other social ministries.

Of considerable interest to secular social scientists, researchers of neo-Pentecostalism have been struck by its appropriation of several of the technological and economic dimensions of globalization. Evangelism campaigns employ the latest technologies, including social media. Movies, music, films, and television series are part of the church-based mission strategies in Nigeria and Ghana.[23] The conservative moral code that neo-Pentecostal churches require of believers and its training in life skills appear to some as a way of reorienting Pentecostals for a successful integration into the global market system.

We must be cautious, however, that we do not overdraw the connection between globalization originating in the West and neo-Pentecostalism. This assessment may be overly influenced by the "eye of the beholder" in two ways. Samuel Zalanga has argued the Pentecostal movement is a new kind of modernity "without the modern science and rationality that characterized the Western enlightenment in the West."[24] In addition, Ogbu Kalu wryly observes, "The ordinary Pentecostal in Africa is less concerned with modernity and globalization and more focused on a renewed relationship with God, intimacy with the transcendental, empowerment by the Holy Spirit and protection in the blood of Jesus as the person struggles to eke out a viable life in a hostile environment."[25]

20. Kalu, *African Pentecostalism*, 20.
21. Street, *Moved by the Spirit*.
22. Kalu, *African Pentecostalism*, 17; Miller and Yamamori, *Global Pentecostalism*.
23. Kalu, *African Pentecostalism*, 109; Freeman, *Pentecostalism and Development*; Gifford, *Ghana's New Christianity*.
24. Zalanga, "Religion," 43–62.
25. Kalu, *African Pentecostalism*, 191.

Neo-Pentecostalism has also been good news for the poor.[26] The social ministries of these churches have substantial reach. Mercy ministries provide food, clothing, and shelter. Emergency services respond to floods, famines, and earthquakes. Educational services include day care, schools, and tuition assistance. Counseling services provide help with addiction, divorce, and oppression. Economic development assistance includes microloans, supporting business start-ups, job training, and affordable housing.[27] Most important, however, is the change in how people understand who they are and what they can do, the same change that was critical to the economic transformation of Britain. In the case of Africa, this change is originating within the Pentecostal worship experiences. Drawing on ethnographies from three African neo-Pentecostal churches, researchers found that new Pentecostal Christians "begin to see themselves as part of God's people, a 'somebody' rather than a 'nobody,' a victor, not a victim. Most important of all, they begin to move beyond a passive fatalism and come to realize that they have agency in their lives."[28] Increased human agency again.

In summary, the last century has seen the Christian church experience a number of major missiological shifts. In the Global North, almost one million people opted for atheism or no religion at all and the church in Europe underwent a stunning decline.[29] At the same time, the numerical center of Christianity moved to the Global South, and Pentecostalism emerged unexpectedly, now accounting for almost a quarter of all Christians.[30] It was quite a century of change.

What Do These Changes Mean?

The implications of the center of gravity of the church moving to the Global South are considerable. We need to understand that the great majority of our Southern brothers and sisters are poor and persecuted. These majority-world Christians are generally more theologically and morally conservative than Western Christians, with the possible exception of American conservative evangelicals. They are much more comfortable with the supernatural and have a worldview closer to that of the Bible.[31] This often creates confusion in conversations with Christians from the West.

26. Myers, "Progressive Pentecostalism."
27. Miller and Yamamori, *Global Pentecostalism*, 42.
28. Freeman, *Pentecostalism and Development*, 13.
29. Barrett, Kurian, and Johnson, *World Christian Encyclopedia*, 4.
30. Pew Research Center, *Global Christianity*, 17.
31. Jenkins, *Next Christendom*, 216. Philip Jenkins is the distinguished professor of history and codirector of the program in Historical Studies of Religion at Baylor University.

The Implications of Change

Andrew Walls, former director of Centre for the Study
of Christianity, University of Edinburgh

In the multicentric Christian church, there can be no automatic assumption
of Western leadership; indeed, if suffering and endurance are the badges of
authenticity, we can expect the most powerful Christian leadership to come
from elsewhere.

The same may be true for the intellectual and theological leadership;
multi-centric mission has the potential to revitalize theological activity and
revolutionize theological education.

Theology springs out of mission; its true origins are not in the study or
the library, but from the need to make Christian decisions—decisions about
what to do and what to think.

Walls, "Christian Mission," 203

As the center of gravity of the church was moving to the Global South, the
historic movement of people from the West to the rest of the world changed
direction. Africa, Latin America, and Asia became net exporters of people to
the West in the form of migrant workers, asylum seekers, and, increasingly,
economic migrants.[32] Just under half of these migrants are our Christian
brothers and sisters, and many understand themselves to be missionaries to
a West that is losing its Christian way. Over a quarter of these migrants are
Muslim, which creates painful adjustment problems that resist easy solutions.

This new situation also has consequences for how we think about mission.
The most obvious is that mission is no longer a Western monopoly or privilege. Nor can non-Western churches be thought of as extensions of Western
missionary efforts; they are self-acting agents of mission and increasingly are
the major contributor to global missions.[33] Again, mission from everywhere
to everyone.[34]

This demographic shift raises several important theological issues as well.
First, there is the question of whose theology will guide our lives and mission efforts. Until recently, Europe did theology and the rest of the world did

32. Hanciles, *Beyond Christendom*, 177.
33. Ibid., 296.
34. Escobar, *New Global Mission*.

Self-Theologizing

Justo L. González, emeritus professor, Candler School
of Theology at Emory University

When mission theoreticians in past decades spoke of the "three selfs" as a goal
for younger churches, they included self-support, self-government, and self-
propagation. They did not envision self-interpretation or self-theologizing. . . .
The surprise of our generation has been that the younger churches have
provided insights into the meaning of the gospel and the mission of the
church that the older churches sorely needed.

González, *Mañana*, 49

contextual theology. This is no longer accepted. All theologies are by definition
contextual. But there is more to it than that. While more and more folks in
the West acknowledge the globalization of the church and give witness to
the shift from the West to the Global South, too many "remain theologically
provincial."[35]

Second, the theological questions are not the same. In the modern and
largely secular West, the critical theological issues focus on gender and sexuality, the dangers of consumption and materialism, and the challenges of
multiculturalism and pluralism. In the Global South, the pressing theological
questions are different: morality and holiness, poverty and justice, political
violence, the rule of law, corruption, and coexistence with primal or traditional
religion. To make this more complex, the two parts of the Christian world
tend to read their Bibles differently. In a heated discussion at a global meeting of Anglicans from around the world on the topic of sexuality, an African
bishop asked his Episcopalian colleague in exasperation: "If you don't believe
the Scriptures, why did you bring them to us in the first place?"[36]

Finally, this shift in the center of theological thinking may hold out hope
to the Western church and its captivity to the two-tiered, material-spiritual
worldview that I have referred to repeatedly in this book. The churches and
theologians of the Global South are not as deeply captive to this worldview,
even though exposed to it through their experiences with Western education. I
suspect that this is one of the reasons that the Pentecostal movement has taken

35. Tennent, *Theology*, 16.
36. Jenkins, *New Faces of Christianity*, 1.

root so quickly and pervasively. Even most Protestant and Catholic churches in Africa are sympathetic to a seamlessly integrated material and spiritual world. Perhaps it will be our brothers and sisters in the Global South who will help us in the West recover the biblical vision of such a world.

This raises important questions for pastors, students, and academics. Whose material are you reading? What voices are you listening to? Are Kwame Bediako, Ogbo Kalu, Lamin Sanneh, Mercy Oduyoye, Emmanuel Katongole, Nimi Wariboko, René Padilla, Samuel Escobar, Roberto Goizueta, Justo González, Ruth Padilla DeBorst, Hwa Yung, Vinoth Ramachandra, Melba Maggay, Andrew Sung Park, Martin Luther King Jr., and Howard Thurman on your reading list? Are you keeping an eye on the theology and missiology journals in Africa and Asia (and Latin America, if you can read Spanish), or *Pneuma* and the *Journal of Pentecostal Theology*? You are what you read, after all.

The Frontiers of Mission Today

The traditional mission frontier is still in play. We are still to go to the ends of the earth as witnesses to Christ and God's kingdom. The gospel needs to be taken to those places where people have never heard the name of Jesus, whether that is over there or nearby. Most of those who have not heard the good news are poor; they need to hear and see a gospel of word and deed. Yet while the good news is getting an eager response in the Global South, it is fading away among the rich and secure, especially in Europe and more recently in the United States.[37] These places are clearly mission frontiers, as Lesslie Newbigin alerted us and as the Gospel and Our Culture Network continues to remind us.[38] It is an open question as to whether churches in the West have mission strategies and ministries adequate to reach the rich and secure. This concern is highly relevant to the missiological challenges of globalization addressed in chapter 14.

A second frontier is the Muslim world and its 1.7 billion believers. We are mostly aware of their presence in the Middle East and North Africa, but the five countries with the most Muslims are not Arab: Indonesia, India, Pakistan, Bangladesh, and Nigeria.[39] Christianity and Islam have a history of one rising while the other falls. The most recent shift took place as the modern mission movement accompanied Europe's colonial expansion, which redrew the map of the Muslim Middle East when the Ottoman Empire collapsed. This

---

37. Jenkins, *Next Christendom*, 220.
38. Newbigin, *Gospel in a Pluralist Society*. Gospel and Our Culture Network: www.gocn.org.
39. Pew Research Center, "Global Religious Landscape."

historic enmity is the central problem for a mission strategy for witnessing in the Muslim world.

But there is a deeper challenge. Forecasts suggest that Christianity and Islam will make up two-thirds of the world's population by 2100.[40] A survey of global mission leaders reported that evangelizing Muslims was their second-highest priority. The disquieting news was that two-thirds viewed Muslims unfavorably, believing that Islam is more prone to violence than any other religion and that Muslims are unfriendly to evangelical Christians.[41] How are we to love our Muslim neighbors if we are afraid of them? What is the responsibility of our churches to help parishioners better understand Islam and engage Muslims positively? A major step in this direction has been taken by Evelyne Reisacher and her important contribution in the form of what she calls "joyful witness in the Muslim world."[42] A missiology of joy seems a new, more winsome message.

For the sake of peace, it is crucial for both Christians and Muslims to find a way to live in this world together. Jonathan Sacks calls for a "theology of the other" in which the ancient texts of both peoples are examined in a search to understand how to see God's face in strangers.[43] Amos Yong explores the possible contributions of the Christian understanding of hospitality and the Other.[44] Christian-Muslim relations must be at the top of missiological priorities in coming years.[45]

The third major mission frontier has to do with those who are harmed or ignored, intentionally or otherwise, by the processes or outcomes of globalization. Those who lose jobs and a sense of contributing as a result of the "creative destruction" of markets need to be recognized, retrained, and assisted in making the transition. Those who remain poor and on the margins need to be known by name and helped with strategies of personal development while they are cared for in the transition; social safety nets must not be an option. The victims of empowered criminality—the trafficked, exploited, and abused—need to be sought out, healed, and restored to society. The migrants who are simply seeking a safer and better life need to be welcomed and enabled to find a new home in a new land. Choices by corporations that heedlessly harm the weak and vulnerable need to be made public, resisted, and corrected. Policies of governments that fail to support and care for the

---

40. Johnson, Barrett, and Crossing, "Christianity 2012," 28.
41. Pew Research Center, "Global Survey."
42. Reisacher, *Joyful Witness*.
43. Sacks, *Not in God's Name*.
44. Yong, *Hospitality and the Other*.
45. Johnson, Barrett, and Crossing, "Christianity 2012."

poor and middle class need to be called into account in the public square or punished at the ballot box. All of this assumes a moral ecology that refuses to tolerate anyone living a less than fully human life.

The fourth mission frontier has to do with the missing dimension of globalization. The secular humanist underpinnings of globalization are unable to create a compelling and widely agreed upon moral frame that can shape the processes and outcomes of globalization toward ends that are good for human beings, societies, and the planet. Globalization tends to accept a kind of moral or ethical neutrality by relegating moral decisions to autonomous individual choice or simple pragmatics. This flaw in globalization has been identified as a missing moral ecology (Jonathan Sacks), global ethic (Hak Joon Lee and Hans Küng), or moral architecture (Max Stackhouse).[46] These critics all agree that the creation of such a moral ecology or spiritual architecture is the domain of religion. To make our contribution to this mission frontier, we will have to leave our safe Christian subculture and constructively reengage in the public square. The church is part of civil society, after all. This urgent need to participate in creating a compelling moral ecology, and the role of the faith communities in doing so, is the focus of the next two chapters of this book.

Questions for Discussion

1. In a modern West that is wealthy and less religious, what is your mission strategy for the rich and secure?

2. In a world where Christians fear and misunderstand Muslims, what is your strategy for helping folks in the pew better understand Islam and their Muslim neighbors?

---

46. Sacks, *Persistence of Faith*; Lee, *Great World House*; Küng, *Global Ethic*; Stackhouse with Paris, *Religion and the Powers of the Common Life*.

12

The Theological Limitations of Globalization

Globalization, *a priori*, is neither good nor bad. It will be what people make of it. No system is an end in itself, and it is necessary to insist that globalization, like any other system, must be at the service of the human person; it must serve solidarity and the common good.

Pope John Paul II[1]

In the final three chapters of this book, I shift my perspective. Heretofore, we have focused primarily on the processes and outcomes of the various dimensions of globalization. Now we examine globalization from a new angle—the globalisms of modernity and the neoliberal expression of capitalism that have been animating the Second Era of Globalization. This requires a theological examination of these globalisms to expose their limitations. These limitations reveal where the gospel of Jesus Christ and God's kingdom have good news to offer.

A word of warning: thus far, I have presented the processes and outcomes of globalization as a mixture of good news and not so good news, of original good and original sin. However, when it comes to the globalisms undergirding globalization today, the tone of the discussion now becomes more critical.

1. John Paul II, "Globalization."

207

The differences between the globalisms of modernity and neoliberalism and the globalism of the Christian faith are profound.

I have already made the point that globalization is a phenomenon that emerged unbidden from within the modern Western project of the Enlightenment, and thus most of the discussions and descriptions of globalization rest on a faith commitment to secular humanism. This means that globalization is by definition materialistic and that the transcendent has been ruled out. The temptation is to limit our theological engagement to simply announcing this fact and then walk away thinking our theological work is done. But if the church and Christians wish to shape or influence globalization, we need to examine globalization in more depth. We need to begin by naming and assessing its implicit theological assumptions. It may seem unusual to use the word *theological* when talking about an expression of secular humanism, but, again, we need to remember that these assumptions of globalization are in fact faith commitments, even if not religiously derived.

Globalization contains three significant theological limitations: a thin anthropology, a flawed understanding of power, and an inability to satisfy the human hunger for meaning and morality. Each of these needs to be examined from a Christian perspective. In this chapter I will examine globalization's flawed anthropology as well as its assumptions about the purpose of power. I will also suggest a diagnosis for why and how globalization is unable to offer a moral or ethical framework. I will close by making the case that such a spiritual and moral architecture is necessary if the good within globalization is to be sustained and the failings of globalization are to be corrected. Then, in the next chapter, I will examine a range of Christian responses.

Before going on, a word of caution concerning the meaning of the phrase "theological engagement" is needed. Thinking Christianly or theologically is a good thing; truth matters and the Bible is true. But there are a number of good reasons to wonder if *acting theologically* might be more important than just *thinking theologically*. First, we were sent on a mission to make disciples, to be witnesses to the ends of the earth, to act in the world. While better actions can result from better thinking, this is not always the case. Second, we often learn more from reflecting on our actions than we do by refining concepts or seeking better theories. This is especially true when our actions take place in a complex adaptive social system—the world of over seven billion individuals in two hundred nations speaking over six thousand languages. Learning our way into the future—acting and reflecting—may better fit our globalizing context than attempting to think or plan our way there. So our theological engagement with globalization ultimately needs to lead us to actions and practices.

Theology and Globalization

Daniel G. Groody, Holy Cross religious, professor of theology, University of Notre Dame

For the theologian, globalization offers a new hope for human solidarity and connectedness, which coexist against the reemergence of age-old human constants like greed, selfishness, and sinfulness. Theology can also be understood as an intellectual discipline that offers to the human community a navigation system for the human heart that helps us find the way to life-giving relationships that are foundational to building a peaceful world. . . . Like sonar, theology offers us insight to the world beneath the ocean surface by probing the deeper terrain of human nature in all its capacities for virtue and sin. . . . Like a global positioning system, it offers us insight into the transcendent realities by helping interpret the signals from above that can help us find our way from within our own social locations.

Groody, *Globalization, Spirituality, and Justice*, 21

A Flawed Anthropology

The thin and ultimately unsatisfactory anthropology undergirding globalization's economics and politics has been a consistent theme in this book. Human beings are more than rational, value-maximizing, economic beings. Were this not true, then we must hope that the "total good" is the same as the "common good."[2] In a sinful world with significant inequalities of wealth and power, this seems unlikely. Alternatively, a human being cannot be reduced to a social role among all other societal roles where one's contribution is defined for one and choice is not an option or even desirable.[3] Were this true, then we must assume that powerful states and corporations always act with the well-being of everyone in mind. Again, this does not seem to square with what we read in our newspapers or see in the news. These two reductionist anthropologies are unsupportable.

The greater failure of the secular materialist underpinning of globalization is that it ignores the relational nature of human beings. Yet, as noted earlier, Margaret Archer argues that it is only in our relational nature that

2. Archer, "*Caritas in Veritate*."
3. Archer's *homo economicus* versus *homo sociologicus* in ibid.

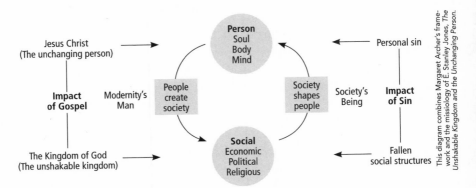

FIGURE 12.1 The impact of sin and the gospel, and the inseparability of individuals and society

our deepest human needs can be met. Caring for one another or being cared for, loving our neighbor and ourselves, all have their roots in our relational nature.[4] All of these qualities are valuable in their own right and cannot be bought with money or power or created with technology. Embracing the relational nature of human beings creates space for the unarguable importance of transcendence, human dignity, solidarity, human liberty, and the common good necessary to be fully human. These are all key elements of the best human future. Globalization by itself does not and cannot offer any of these.

To be fair, globalization gets its anthropology right in one sense. The values and assumptions undergirding globalization do affirm what we understand as the original good in human beings. Human beings are seen as creative problem solvers who can figure things out, make choices, and act on instincts for the common good. This understanding contributes to the good news in globalization. However, the implied anthropology of globalization fails to offer a believable explanation for the human condition as it is. Without a theology of sin, globalization has no explanation for greed, the hunger for power, hedonism, or selfish human choices. This is the point at which Christians have something to offer.

The biblical account has an explanation for the failings of human beings and their social systems as well as an antidote for both. Rejecting the either-or choice between the radical individualism of modernity's man and the social construction of human beings by a society bent on creating some ideal vision of a better future, the creation narrative understands people and society as

4. Ibid., 289.

being in an interactive relationship with one another (see fig. 12.1). People shape their society, and societies shape their members.

The impact of sin affects both individuals and society's structures; both are fallen and hence fail to live up to their potential for the ethical behavior and the justice that God intended. The problem of individual sin and the lack of justice are now explained. It is this two-level impact of sin that requires that we witness to both Jesus Christ (to save individuals) and the emerging kingdom of God (to redeem and restore our social world and God's creation). Christ and his disciples consistently linked the two (Luke 8:1; Acts 8:12; 28:23, 31; 2 Tim. 4:1; Rev. 12:10). There cannot be one without the other. Globalization's explanation and answer for this human problem are thin to nonexistent.

The Problem of Power

Power and use of power are central issues when it comes to acting theologically in response to globalization in all of its facets. Most of the concerns about transnational corporations, free markets, and powerful nations have their roots in asymmetries of power and a pretty consistent record of misusing power. Addressing and coping with the asymmetries and abuse demands a moral ecology to frame and shape globalization.

I need to return to my short presentation on power and inequality in chapter 2. A world with complete equality of power, wealth, or anything else is simply not possible, even in the kingdom of God. God did not create the world or human beings this way. I pointed to James Davison Hunter's affirmation that differences in giftedness, intelligence, or physical skill are not a mistake God made, but rather that human relations are inherently power relationships and that this is a good thing as it forces us toward interdependence; it is a driver for relationality and solidarity.[5] This conclusion aligns nicely with Paul's metaphor of the body and gifts in Romans 12, which suggests that the purpose of gifts and differences in power is to enable relational well-being, an interdependence that unites the various gifts of individuals for the well-being of the whole body. Setting equality aside, what then might a theology of power for a sinful world look like?

Let's begin with the source of power. Our power to name, organize, and create comes from God; it is not something we created for ourselves (Gen. 2). Our gifts, skills, and power are not ours, other than as a gift. This has implications. First, these powers are given to us by a God who loves us. Our

5. Hunter, *To Change the World*, 178. James Davison Hunter is professor of religion, culture, and social theory at the University of Virginia.

power as human agents is the product of an act of generosity on God's part.[6] Second, this power is given in the context of a moral order created by a moral God; any power we have or exercise has limits and constraints. Finally, since we are commanded to love God and love our neighbors as ourselves, we must understand that power is meant to be a means to an end, not an end in itself.

The biblical text supports these claims. Psalm 72 calls for a king endowed with justice who defends the afflicted, saves the children of the needy, and crushes the oppressor—power at the service of the least of these. Psalm 82 tells us that God judges the "gods" (those in power over nations and peoples) on a simple set of criteria: Did you defend the weak, uphold the cause of the poor and oppressed, and rescue the weak and needy? This is power *in service of*, not power *over*.

The prophets repeatedly judged the nation of Israel and its political and religious leaders on the basis of the faithfulness of their worship *and* the well-being of the widow, orphan, and the alien.[7] Power in service of the least of these. The greatness of a nation is not a function of economic growth, military power, or international influence.

How power is used matters in our globalizing world. When the powerful and the principalities and powers fail to care for the poor while defending the unjust, God announces that they "know nothing, they understand nothing. / They walk around in darkness; / all the foundations of the earth are shaken" (Ps. 82:5). Using power as an end, rather than a means, undermines the functioning of the world's economic, political, and social systems, it seems.

Richard Bauckham suggests that the Bible has twin narratives of power when it comes to globalization.[8] Abraham was to be a blessing to all nations—a globalization of blessing and salvation. But the stories of the abuse of power by Nebuchadnezzar in Daniel and the unrighteousness of the economic dominance of Tyre in Ezekiel, and the combination of both in the empire of Rome described in Revelation, reveal an alternative narrative of globalization by domination and exploitation. The problem, of course, is sin. Power used as a means of loving God and our neighbor becomes instead power as an end—the temptation to play God in the lives of others.

Jesus offers a different model for the use of power. His power came from his intimacy with and submission to God the Father. Jesus rejected the status, reputation, and privilege that accompany power. He used his considerable power

---

6. Middleton, *Liberating Image*, 278.
7. Myers, "Isaiah, Which Is It?," 23.
8. Bauckham, "Bible and Globalization," 27–43. Richard Bauckham is professor of New Testament studies at St. Mary's College, University of St. Andrews.

in service of compassion and inclusion—relational well-being again. Finally, Jesus's use of power was always noncoercive, respecting human liberty—even the liberty of those who chose not to believe him and even those who killed him.[9] Yet all the power in creation belongs to the slain Lamb, and only God's kingdom is left standing at the end of time. God's "weak" globalization of blessing and salvation is the only survivor at the end of the day. Sadly, we live between the times and so must engage a globalization in which both frameworks of power are at play.

The first part of the challenge is to discern what kind of power is in play—power *over* others or power *in service of* others—and the best human future. What form of power is being expressed or sought in the economic behaviors of globalization? In our behaviors? In our use of globalization's technology? In the politics of globalization? In our prayers for cultural change? The second part of the challenge is to discover how the fallen principalities and powers can be named and made visible, thus unmasking their ultimate powerlessness in the face of the gospel of Christ and God's kingdom.[10]

The Relegation of Morality and Ethics

> The moral fiber seems to go out of a society or a civilization if it is not sustained by a compelling vision of transcendence to continually fund its spiritual capital.
>
> —Max Stackhouse[11]

A process has been under way for quite a long time that has made universal moral frameworks harder and harder to come by. The spiritual and material worlds were last considered to be interpenetrating in medieval times. The power relationships of the day were simple: the religious and political realms were joined. Power belonged to the church and to the king, and both had power over everyone else. While this arrangement did not enable economic growth and was rather hard on common folks, it did allow the church, when it was at its best, to provide a common moral framework—however flawed—for the king and the king's subjects.

In the aftermath of the Protestant Reformation, Europe experienced almost 120 years of religious wars. As the Enlightenment emerged in the eighteenth century, the desire to avoid religious wars was joined by a growing confidence in

9. Foregoing summarized from Hunter, *To Change the World*, 187.
10. See Wink, *Unmasking the Powers*.
11. Stackhouse, *Globalization and Grace*, 78.

The Missing Piece

Jonathan Sacks, former Chief Rabbi of the United Hebrew Congregations of the British Commonwealth

Science, technology, the free markets and the liberal democratic state have enabled us to reach unprecedented achievements in knowledge, freedom, life expectancy and affluence. They are among the greatest achievements of human civilization and are to be defended and cherished.

But they do not answer the questions that every reflective individual will ask at some time in his or her life. Who am I? Why am I here? How then shall I live? The result is that the 21st century has left us with a maximum of choice and a minimum of meaning. . . .

The world's greatest faiths offer meaning, direction, a code of conduct and a set of rules for the moral and spiritual life in ways that the free-market, liberal democratic West does not.

Sacks, "Swords into Plowshares," C1

human reason and observation, which led to new technologies and increasing wealth and health. Slowly, a new idea became normative. Perhaps it would be better if politics, science, and reason exercised authority in the material (real) world, while religion and the church (or churches) exercised their authority in the religious realm, limiting themselves to matters of the soul.

This seemingly helpful shift created a significant unintended consequence. Separating the spiritual world from the material world also separates religion, God, values, ethics, and spirituality from the physical world of politics, science, technology, the market, and civil society (see fig. 12.2). Revelation—the source of our theology and the grounds for our belief about who human beings are and why they are here—holds sway only in the spiritual or religious realm, while observation, reason, and individual choice become the only way we can know these things in the material world. Values are treated as private, personal decisions; they lose any universal claim. This loss of a shared moral vision creates a real dilemma when societies try to make ethical judgments about the activities in the political, economic, and civil society realms. It also makes it hard to balance the power of the state, the economy, and civil society because, at the end of the day, what is needed to do so is a shared ethical or moral vision.

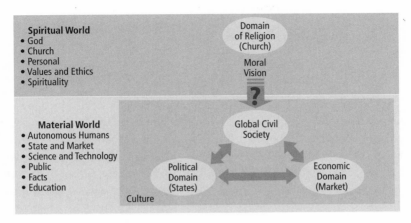

FIGURE 12.2 Where does a moral vision come from?

The Missing Moral Ecology of Globalization

As well as a physical ecology, we also inhabit a moral ecology, that network of beliefs, relationships and virtues within which we think, act and discover meaning.

—Jonathan Sacks[12]

The consequences of globalization's flawed anthropology, its misunderstanding of the purpose of power, and its having lost sight of the source of shared ethics and meaning proved to be a pivotal failing. Without a true and shared view of these important things, we struggle to answer the three most critical questions for which human beings need answers. Who are we? Why are we here? How then shall we act? A more detailed set of questions follows. How do we establish the worth of individuals beyond how much money they have; come to an understanding of society as a covenant, not a contract; or appreciate morality and ethics as a critically important communal endeavor that makes life worth living?[13]

Using a ship as a metaphor for globalization, Daniel Groody expands on the ethical poverty of globalization by asking three big questions: Who is the captain? Where are we going? What maps are we using?[14] As we've just seen,

12. Sacks, *Persistence of Faith*, 26. Jonathan Sacks is former Chief Rabbi of the United Hebrew Congregations of the Commonwealth and the author of many books.
13. Ibid., 10.
14. Groody, *Globalization, Spirituality, and Justice*, 18–19. Daniel Groody is a Catholic priest, a Holy Cross religious, and associate professor of theology and director of the Center for Latino Spirituality and Culture at the Institute for Latino Studies at the University of Notre Dame.

Assessing Globalization

Brian Griffiths, Lord Griffiths of Fforestfach

The cornerstone of Christian social teaching is the intrinsic dignity of every human being. It is this that forms the basis for human rights, democratic government and market economics. For Christians, the ultimate test of globalization is not economic growth, new technology, capital flows or increased trade, but how it affects the life and choices open to individuals. Closely linked to this is the idea of justice. For the Christian, justice is more than making sure the rules of the game are fair. It is also about results. It is about what happens to those who are not qualified to play the game. It is also about those who play but get injured. Justice is about the common good of all, not just the rewards of the successful. If globalization is to be just it is not enough that the poor be heard; the poor need to be empowered.

Griffiths, *Globalization*, 25

with faith and religion relegated to the private spiritual realm, the only places to turn for ethical guidance are the domains of economics, technology, and politics, and, as we have seen, they struggle for adequate answers. Economic decisions are made on the basis of what enhances economic growth or benefits an individual. Technology is governed solely by the effectiveness and efficiency of technique.[15] Politics is preoccupied with accumulating and exercising power. None of these has the capacity to create an ethical framework beyond simple pragmatics: if something works, it's ethical. Surely this is not enough.

Recalling my explanation of complex adaptive social systems, Groody's first two questions are ultimately unanswerable. In chapter 4, I made the case that no group of human beings, or family of institutions, is in charge of globalization—there is no captain on the globalization ship. As to globalization's destination, we have seen that it is not possible to know the end of an emergent phenomenon except in retrospect. Globalization is going where it is going and, aside from God, no one knows where it is taking us. So no one is in charge, and we are heading toward an unknown destination. But Groody's question about what nautical maps we are using can be and needs to be answered. (I will develop Groody's proposal in the next chapter.)

15. Ellul, *Technological Society*.

Even if we cannot plan our way to a stated end in an emergent system, and even if we cannot control the system, it does not follow that human beings are without power of choice and influence. After all, complex adaptive social systems are made up of large numbers of human beings, and if large enough numbers of people begin to change what they think and how they act, emergent systems adjust and create new structures in response. The campaigns to abolish the slave trade and secure the right of women to vote are cases in point.

While we are unable to plan and direct our way into the future, we can learn our way into a better future. How might this be done? The same way each of us has lived out our lives. When we talk of a better future for ourselves and our families, we have an idea of what this future might be like and how to get there. With a general destination on the horizon, we take modest steps that we think make sense. Some steps work and many do not; much is uncertain and many things change. So we monitor our progress as we take each step. Does my undergraduate degree support my sense of vocational call or not? Does my first job reinforce my life's directions, or is a new direction needed? If I get married, how does that change things? Do our choices about how to raise our child seem to be working? In all of these situations, if things seem to be working, we take another step. If not, we change course and try something new. We discover our way into a better future. And so it must be for globalization.

This brings us back to Groody's map question. What kind of ethical framework should we use to navigate the globalization ship? What kind of moral framework provides a shared understanding of what a desirable present and future might be for all human beings? We need a way to assess the processes and impact of globalization in terms of whether they give life or diminish it, promote the common good or undermine it, protect the environment or harm it, promote justice or spread injustice, and protect the poor or exploit them. This in turn brings us back to globalization's failure to provide such a framework.

Jonathan Sacks, in his important book *The Persistence of Faith: Religion, Morality and Society in a Secular Age*, argues that the failure of the secularization thesis—that religion will fade away in the face of the modern world and the benefits of its science, technology, and economics—is the reason that globalization and secular humanism are unable to answer these questions about meaning and morality. Human beings are relational beings embedded in societies. Just and peaceful relationships matter; meaning and purpose matter. Enacting and sustaining a moral order is "one of the central, fundamental motivations for human action."[16]

16. C. Smith, *Moral, Believing Animals*, 11.

We need what Sacks calls a moral ecology, a moral environment that answers the question "How then shall I and we live?" He goes on to argue that a society's moral ecology is made up of "institutions, modes of behavior and 'habits of the heart' that are essential to the health of the *polis*, but that cannot be created by political [or economic] means."[17] The institutions to which he refers are the world's great religions, which are "concerned with ends, not means, moral imperatives rather than economic interests and duties rather than rights."[18] How else, Sacks wonders, do we go beyond our individual selves and form "communities of character"?[19]

A moral ecology establishes the environment within which the political and economic systems must work, not the other way around. Politics, technology, and economics are not autonomous and must not be allowed to act as if they were. Economics, technology, and politics need to serve the well-being of human beings, not the other way around. Alone, they cannot establish virtuous ends. So what then do we do?

In the next chapter I will examine a constellation of answers to this critical modern question. I will begin with a Protestant proposal made by Max Stackhouse as a result of his eight-year research project on globalization with contributors from around the world and from a number of faith traditions. I will then introduce a Roman Catholic contribution made by Daniel Groody, a scholar at the University of Notre Dame working within the tradition of Catholic social teaching. Finally, I will connect Stackhouse and Groody to an important contribution on how cultures change by James Davison Hunter, a prominent figure in the sociology of religion and the sociology of culture, with much of his work dedicated to the study of evangelicalism and cultural change.

Questions for Discussion

1. In what ways have you experienced not being treated as a relational human being by the political or economic systems of this world?
2. In what ways have you felt that someone or some organization was exercising *power over* instead of *power in service of* some part of your life?
3. To what degree do you feel that the institutions of economics and politics function within a shared ethical system?

17. Sacks, *Persistence of Faith*, 12.
18. Ibid., 20.
19. Ibid., 14.

13

The Christian Engagement with Globalization

Love in truth—*caritas in veritate*—is a great challenge for the church in a world that is becoming progressively and pervasively globalized. The risk of our time is that the *de facto* interdependence of people and nations is not matched by ethical interaction of consciences and minds that would give rise to truly human development.

Pope Benedict XVI[1]

It seems fitting that a book on globalization, the poor, and Christian mission focus its last two chapters on the missional call to the church and the Christians within it. After all, it is an article of faith that God—Father, Son, and Holy Spirit—is at work in today's globalizing world on God's project of redemption and restoration that ends with the coming of the kingdom of God on earth. We know better than to place our faith in ideology, technology, economics, politics, or culture; these are all as flawed as we are.

We left the previous chapter with some insights into how the implicit theology and values of the twin globalisms of globalization fail to address the deepest questions of human meaning. We noted a failure in anthropology (who we are, why we are here, how we should live, and what is our best

1. Benedict XVI, *Caritas in Veritate*, §9.

The Church and Reconstruction

Social Analysis without Theology
Max Stackhouse, professor emeritus of reformed theology
and public life, Princeton Theological Seminary

Insofar as most social analyses of that emerging global [civil society] are no
longer attentive to any theological perspective, the principalities, thrones,
authorities, and dominions behind and residually in them tempt scholars to
cynical analysis, and the multitude follows their arrogance, idolatry and injustice. They have no fundamental basis for a reconstructive vision [of society].

Stackhouse, *Globalization and Grace*, 18

From Liberation to Reconstruction
J. N. K. Mugambi, professor of philosophy and religious
studies, University of Nairobi

In Africa, the theme of [liberation in] Exodus made much sense as long as
people viewed their oppression in terms of external pharaohs enslaving their
subjects. . . . The civil strife in Africa after 1990 can be viewed as the first phase
of a process of social reconstruction on the continent. The role of religion
in this process of reconstruction was publicly acknowledged throughout the
continent. Christianity, Islam and African Traditional Religions were all recognized as social forces that could be mobilized for reconstruction.

Mugambi, *Christian Theology and Social Reconstruction*, 29–30

human future), in understanding the use of power, and in providing a spiritual
and moral vision by which we can navigate our way toward the future. How
then can Christians and others of faith contribute to overcoming these failings? How might the church and Christians help the world move beyond the
narrow pursuit of money, power, and technology, beyond just seeking longer
lives to seeking lives worth living? Where might the path toward this project
of social reconstruction begin?

I do not plan to offer a single proposal for the simple reason that globalization is too complicated and multilayered for any single approach. Instead I
will explore three broad proposals for responses that churches and Christians

might employ in this age of accelerating globalization. We should not be surprised that God has prepared God's people to make a multifaceted and multilayered family of responses. It is not an accident or an oversight on God's part that today's polycentric church is made up of many traditions working from a variety of Christian theologies, carrying out many variations of Christ's mission in a myriad of cultures and lived experiences. God was not surprised by globalization, and we need to believe that God's church has been prepared to respond in many ways to its complexity.

As a foundational principle for this discussion of the church's response to globalization, I begin with a reminder from the story of the transformations in nineteenth-century Britain at the beginning of the Second Era of Globalization. The church, while its theology played a liberating role in economics, politics, and social change, played an even more critical role by remembering its central mission: "The great saints of the church have revolutionized society because they have given the world a new metaphysical vision, a world and life view anchored in the transcendent. They have provided not simply programs of social change, but a sense of meaning and purpose to existence."[2] More economic justice, fairer and more representative politics, and a restored natural environment are all important, but, at the end of the day, a transcendent vision of whom and whose we are, why we are here, and how we are to act is the church's most important contribution.

A Protestant Contribution—Max Stackhouse

In the first decade of the twenty-first century, Max Stackhouse led an eight-year study on globalization at Princeton's Center of Theological Inquiry.[3] Rejecting the idea that globalization is a kind of second fall that needs to be resisted and overcome,[4] Stackhouse argues that the biblical narrative suggests that globalization should be understood as a historical process reflecting both God's grace and our disobedience, original good and original sin, things that are for life and things that degrade or demean life. Stackhouse reminds us that God's ultimate response to our great disobedience was grace, not judgment,

2. Bloesch, *Faith and Its Counterfeits*, 52.
3. This study led to the multivolume *God and Globalization*: Stackhouse with Paris, *Religion and the Powers of the Common Life*; Stackhouse with Browning, *Spirit and the Modern Authorities*; Stackhouse with Obenchain, *Christ and the Dominions of Civilization*; Stackhouse, *Globalization and Grace*. Max Stackhouse was emeritus professor of reformed theology and public life at Princeton Theological Seminary.
4. Advocates of liberation theology tend to fall in this category, as do some mainline Protestant theologians and social ethicists. I briefly described a few in the latter part of chap. 8.

demonstrated by a covenant God made with human beings that is still in play today. Further, God's ultimate act of grace—the death, resurrection, and coming again of Jesus and God's kingdom on earth—is the final word in human history. Stackhouse concludes that "the vision of that end is the New Jerusalem, a cosmopolitan and complex urban civilization into which all the peoples of the earth can bring their gifts. This is the key to a theology of history and thus to the dynamics of globalization."[5] At the end of history, God's love overcomes; God completes God's project of redemption and restoration.

Stackhouse begins his definition of globalization in much the same way as I have here: a global set of political, economic, technological, cultural, and social dynamics. But then he adds something new. He argues that globalization is also "influenced and legitimated by certain theological, ethical and ideological motifs,"[6] and thus an ethical and spiritual dynamic needs to be part of its definition. The distinction between globalization and globalisms that I made earlier in this book may be useful for analytical purposes, but in reality the two are inseparable. The processes and outcomes of globalization reflect the morality and meaning of its twin globalisms: modernity and neoliberal capitalism. They are not ethically neutral nor free of assumptions, in spite of what many secularists believe. The thin and inadequate ethical and spiritual dimensions of globalization that I described in chapter 12 need to be addressed and corrected.

Global Public Theology

As with Jonathan Sacks, the failure of the secularization thesis is where Stackhouse begins his argument in favor of what he calls the need for a "global public theology." He suggests that the cause of the resurgence of religion today is a "widespread search for a guiding and ethical worldview" that can provide a "comprehensive vision of morals and meaning for souls and civilizations."[7] More importantly, Stackhouse argues that many in today's world "fail to grasp the way in which religion shapes the public ethos of civilizations." He reminds us that "Christian faith, and Protestantism particularly, until quite recently, generated those forces that are driving globalization in its several social, political, cultural and professional dimensions."[8] Accepting the complexity and pluralism in today's world, Stackhouse calls for an ethical frame "that is simultaneously complex enough to take account of the incredible

5. Stackhouse, *Globalization and Grace*, 32.
6. Ibid., 8.
7. Ibid., 21.
8. Ibid., 6.

myriad of cultures and beliefs while being simple enough to shape the loyalties of peoples."[9]

For Stackhouse, creating this shared ethical vision must rest on a deep and sustained theological engagement that examines and challenges the inadequacy of the underlying assumptions and values of globalization that were named in the previous chapter. A global public theology begins with a spiritual vision that addresses globalization's reductionist anthropology, misunderstanding of the purpose of power, and lack of a robust and broadly accepted ethical framework. The heart of Stackhouse's proposal is that the task of religion and theology is "to provide a reasonable proposal with regard to the moral and spiritual architecture and the inner guidance systems of civilizations."[10]

How does such a global public theology come into being in today's world? Stackhouse calls for the development of a shared spiritual-ethical architecture in a world of many religions. This poses a distinct challenge today as we have a global economy and global technology but no global religion. Different religions and thus differing bases for morality and meaning are a fact of life that cannot be ignored. Nonetheless, Stackhouse argues that this is work that can only be done jointly by the world's great religions. While understandings of the nature of God and eschatological ends will forever separate the world's great faiths, Stackhouse argues that "at the level of deontology,[11] most of the world's religions, in fact, share a great deal about what is right and what is wrong."[12] Furthermore, all of them would disagree with modernity's material and secular framework. Therefore, together they must "identify the genuinely universalistic dimensions of divine reality and of human existence."[13] On the basis of these common theological affirmations, a global public theology must then "ethically guide, repair, or resist those developments [of globalization] that have proven to be deceptive, unjust or misdirected."[14] This is where a global public theology enables and supports active efforts at the redirection and transformation of globalization (see fig. 13.1).

This brings us to the question of how such a global public theology might break out of its captivity in the spiritual realm and have a chance to reconstruct the material (real) world. How might a spiritual and moral architecture

9. Ibid., 21.
10. Ibid., 84.
11. Deontology refers to the normative ethical position that determines the morality of an action on the basis of its adherence to a rule or rules.
12. Stackhouse, *Globalization and Grace*, 232.
13. Ibid., 84.
14. Ibid., 85.

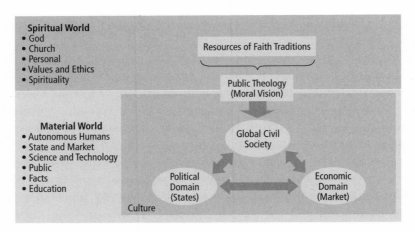

FIGURE 13.1 Global civil society as a missional agent

become the framework of guidance and limitations within which economics, politics, and technology function, as opposed to today's secular option of granting them autonomy?

Global Civil Society

While the domains of economics, technology, and crime are truly global, I pointed out that the political domain is not. Stackhouse sees this lack of a globalized political domain as an opportunity. "A worldwide set of . . . ethical dynamics, influenced and legitimated by certain theological, ethical and ideological motifs . . . are creating a worldwide civil society that stands beyond the capacity of any nation-state to control." This global civil society is potentially a moral force (see fig. 13.1).

Stackhouse believes that global civil society is the social location with the best chance for a global public theology to emerge, but it will be a challenge. A truly global public theology must be tested as to whether it has a broad public claim or is just a parochial word of wisdom from within one religious community. Stackhouse argues that if it is to exercise persuasive power outside the church or religious community, a proposal for a common public theology must "meet the test of public reception—according to what manifests the truth, justice, and mercy of God and what the public can internalize from it and weave into the fabric of the common life to enhance their moral, spiritual, and material existence."[15]

15. Ibid., 84.

This is not a call for majority-rules morality. It is a way of describing how such a genuinely public theology needs to be framed and presented in a way that people from differing religious or value perspectives can nonetheless agree that murdering, stealing, extracting wealth from the weak, and tolerating some people living in subhuman conditions is wrong. Global civil society holds the promise of being a place where this kind of work can be done and ultimately can become part of the economic and political processes of this world. Stackhouse points to the global human rights movement, the environmental movement, and the indigenous peoples movements as illustrating the potential for moral guidance to come from global civil society.

Stackhouse calls this a new form of missions, one that invites the peoples of the world to become participants in a global civil society that promotes a true view of human beings and their purpose and a resulting ethics of justice, inclusion, and empowerment. He argues that we need to more deliberately prepare the people in our pews to engage our globalizing world by becoming "partners in the moral guidance" of the processes and outcomes of globalization.[16] Stackhouse reminds us that the church and Christians did this before in medieval Europe, in the aftermath of the Reformation, and in Victorian England, when Christians campaigned against slavery and other ethical failures of the British Empire.

But can this happen in today's world? When churches, Christian agencies, and individual Christians unite into networks, coalitions, and even larger associations, their social influence correspondingly increases. And when focused on an issue that is attractive within the larger civil society, this social influence can nudge the world toward a new direction or stance.

Jubilee 2000 and its campaign for debt relief for poor nations in the Global South is a case in point. Shortly after Pope John Paul II mentioned the idea of a Levitical Jubilee in his apostolic letter "As the Third Millennium Draws Near" in 1994, two British Christians, Martin Dent, a great-great-great-grandson of a British abolitionist, and Bill Peters, a retired British ambassador, took the same Old Testament idea as the name of a campaign for debt relief, hoping that Jubilee 2000 might become the twenty-first-century equivalent to the abolition movement. Several Christian aid agencies in Britain, including Tearfund, provided crucial early support. Quickly, the Anglican and Catholic churches joined in, as did secular groups like Oxfam, a group of rock stars, and eventually the British government's Department for International Development.[17]

16. The foregoing is a summary from ibid., 246.
17. Summarized from Hoover, "What Would Moses Do?"

Ultimately, Jubilee 2000 was embraced by aid organizations in the Global South, human rights groups, labor unions, and religious groups. What began as a Christian movement allowed itself to become an inclusive movement where anyone was welcome if they believed in the justice of debt relief in the negative aftermath of the Washington Consensus. Jubilee 2000 "owes its success and inspiration to the Bible. . . . At the end of an increasingly secular century, it has been the biblical proof and moral imagination of religion that have torched the principles of the hitherto unassailable citadels of international finance."[18] Ten years later, Jubilee 2000 was assessed as "one of the most successful international, non-governmental movements in history."[19]

Hak Joon Lee provides an important qualification to Stackhouse's proposal for a global ethical vision mediated through global civil society. Lee reminds us that we live in a sinful world in which decisions about what is normative and right are intimately connected to the issue of power, including the power to influence the choice of norms as well as the power to choose to ignore them.[20] There is a danger that global public theology and civil society may focus on getting the norms right and neglect the need to work for the actual transformation of the power structures in this world. Lee reminds us that Martin Luther King Jr. "engaged both in ethical deliberation [persuasive public theology] and political practice [non-violent actions with large numbers of people]."[21] I am not sure that Stackhouse would disagree, as he described King as a "worldwide symbol of public theology in activist mode,"[22] but political activism in Stackhouse is more implied than declared. Nevertheless, Lee's concern also points us to another important limitation.

It is possible to imagine the emergence of a global ethical vision that stands over against globalization's ethics of pragmatism. As we have seen, religions have shaped the ethical behavior of societies before. But it is much harder to imagine correcting the misuse and abuse of power that is a result of personal and social sin. We have been able to address specific problems like slavery, apartheid, and debt relief for a time, but the underlying causes—fallen human beings and their fallen social structures—remain, and therefore these problems tend to recur. The ultimate and complete solution to power and sin awaits the return of our Lord. Only when the weak power of the slain Lamb ushers in God's kingdom in its fullness at the end of time will we see universal justice

18. Hutton, "Jubilee Line That Works," 30.
19. Roodman, "Arc of the Jubilee."
20. Lee, *Great World House*, 11. Hak Joon Lee is professor of Christian ethics at Fuller Theological Seminary.
21. Ibid., 16.
22. Stackhouse, *Globalization and Grace*, 92.

and peace. It is important for us to accept that there will always be limits to our efforts at social change. We can create signs of the coming kingdom here and there, but at the end of the day, fallen human beings cannot save themselves.

A Roman Catholic Contribution—Daniel Groody

For Roman Catholics, there is already a kind of public theology in the form of a one-hundred-year tradition of moral theology addressing social issues arising within the Second Era of Globalization. This section will begin with a summary of this tradition and will then introduce a proposal by Daniel Groody that echoes much of what we have just seen from Max Stackhouse and then extends it.

Catholic Social Teaching

In the aftermath of the economic, political, and social changes in nineteenth-century Europe, the Roman Catholic Church found itself facing a very different kind of world as the century closed. The role of the Catholic Church—and indeed any church or Christian theology—was viewed with increasing skepticism. Rapid changes in industrialization and urbanization created disruption and suffering in the lives of ordinary people, which led to a growing suspicion of capitalism, in spite of economic growth. Modernity placed its faith in the supremacy of human reason, and the resulting critical philosophies

The Moral Perspective

Pope John Paul II

The Church's social doctrine is not a "third way" between liberal capitalism and Marxist collectivism, nor even a possible alternative to other solutions less radically opposed to one another: rather, it constitutes a category of its own. . . . Its main aim is to interpret these realities, determining their conformity with or divergence from the lines of the Gospel teaching on [human beings] and [their] vocation, a vocation which is at once earthly and transcendent; its aim is thus to guide Christian behavior. It therefore belongs to the field, not of ideology, but of theology and particularly of moral theology.

John Paul II, *Sollicitudo Rei Socialis*, §41

were pushing religion off the public stage. The effectiveness of science and technology was having the same effect. The materialistic and critical voices of Marx, Darwin, and Freud made religion seem less and less important. As I described earlier, religion was relegated to the spiritual realm and was expected to eventually go away altogether.

Into this context of a diminishing role for the church and religion in society, Pope Leo XIII wrote *Rerum Novarum* (New Things) in 1881. His encyclical addressed the new ideas about the role of reason, labor, capital, private ownership, and the new modern state. It reaffirmed the importance of the family, the relationship between employee and employer, and the roles of both the church and the state when it comes to the poor. *Rerum Novarum* criticized both socialism, dismissing it on the grounds that it "subordinated individual liberty to social well-being without respect for human rights or religious welfare," and capitalism, which had "released the individual from social and moral constraints."[23] The moral vision problem again.

Avoiding the modern temptation to dismiss the old in our enthusiasm for new thinking and discoveries, Catholic social teaching unfolded as an ongoing conversation of reaffirmations and reinterpretations of earlier encyclicals within the social-teaching tradition.[24] Pius XI (1931), Paul VI (1971), and John Paul II (1991) each built on foregoing theological affirmations that were unchanging, while responding with fresh theological insight to the "new things" that had emerged within the processes and outcomes of globalization and the development of nations in the hundred-year period following *Rerum Novarum*.[25]

Overall, some seventeen to twenty documents make up this living tradition of Catholic social thought. Taken together they provide a consistent yet adaptive Christian moral perspective on globalization, economics, and public policy as well as the well-being of all, with particular attention to the poor.[26] The importance of sharing the good news of Christ and God's kingdom was never far from sight. "Without the perspective of eternal life, human progress in this world is denied breathing space. Enclosed in history, it runs the risk of

23. O'Brien and Shannon, *Catholic Social Thought*, 13.

24. If you are not familiar with Catholic social teaching, the following will help you get a toe in the water: the introduction and chaps. 1–3 of Vatican II's *Gaudium et Spes*; parts 4–5 on authentic human development in John Paul II, *Sollicitudo Rei Socialis*; and §§25–29 on economics, businesses, and the market in *Centesimus Annus*. See also Coleman and Ryan, *Globalization*, 18–19.

25. Pius XI, *Quadragesimo Anno*; Paul VI, *Octogesima Adveniens*; and John Paul II, *Centesimus Annus*.

26. Paul VI, *Populorum Progressio*; John Paul II, *Sollicitudo Rei Socialis*; Benedict XVI, *Caritas in Veritate*.

being reduced to mere accumulation of wealth."[27] This tradition maintains a consistent commitment to a whole gospel.

Catholic social teaching also provides some nuance when thinking about the role of the church in the world when it comes to issues of social concern. Paul VI accepted the idea that the church and the state (and presumably he would agree to include the market) are different powers, and thus each is supreme in its own sphere of competency.[28] Benedict XVI stated that "the Church does not have technical solutions to offer and does not claim 'to interfere' in any way with the politics of States. She does, however, have a mission of truth to accomplish . . . for a society that is attuned to man, to his dignity, to his vocation."[29] So while the state and the market have their own responsibilities and the church will not offer a Christian economic or political system, the church does have a moral obligation to speak to the world about the truth about God and about humankind. Thus, the church has a critical role in the public square.

Key Themes of Catholic Social Teaching

The following introduces six themes relevant to globalization that emerge consistently in Catholic social teaching:

1. Truth about God and human beings
2. Human dignity
3. Common good
4. Subsidiarity (liberty)
5. Solidarity
6. Option for the poor

The *truth about God and human beings* forms the basis of a Christian anthropology. The truth about God is that God is the creator, sustainer, redeemer, and restorer of creation and that God chose to make humankind in God's image. God is the God of history, and God's kingdom will be history's end. The truth about us is that we are relational and moral beings who are thus responsible for God's world and for the well-being of each other. We are to create and act in ways that make the world conducive to human well-being. As I observed in the last chapter, this is the point at which contemporary

27. Benedict XVI, *Caritas in Veritate*, §11.
28. Paul VI, *Populorum Progressio*, §13.
29. Benedict XVI, *Caritas in Veritate*, §9.

globalization and its underlying commitment to secular humanism fails most completely.

The idea of *human dignity* rests on the fact that God made every human being in God's image and that God's Son died for the redemption of every human being. Every human being has inherent worth, value, and a singular identity in God's sight. The chief concern of Catholic social teaching is to speak on behalf of those for whom this is not the case: "Catholic social teaching pays particular attention to those in society whose dignity is diminished, denied or damaged or those who, when they are no longer deemed useful, are rejected and discarded or those who are dehumanized in their jobs."[30] This affirmation of human worth and dignity also means that globalization and its many social institutions must be assessed in terms of their contribution to enhancing (or diminishing) the dignity of all human beings.

Common good rests on two related biblical ideas. First, our loving God intends a livelihood that is life-giving and good without regard to our productive value or any other secondary identifier. Second, because we are relational human beings, it follows that our relationships must work for the well-being of all; this is the meaning of justice, as we will see in a minute.[31] No autonomous modern self here. This in turn implies a moral test of all social institutions— the state, the market, the church, and civil society. Are they creating a set of social conditions within which everyone and every group can flourish? The common good is "built around the vision of a peaceful society. . . . Peace is a fruit of justice and integrally related to the development and empowerment of poor people and poor countries."[32]

Subsidiarity is an awkward word but an important idea. The focus is on the importance of human liberty to God: "It is a fundamental principle of social philosophy, fixed and unchangeable, that one should not withdraw from individuals and commit to the community what they can accomplish by their own enterprise and/or industry."[33] The idea of subsidiarity, combined with that of human dignity, establishes human agency and human freedom as twin principles that should not be encroached upon or eroded by higher social institutions—not the state, the market, or any part of civil society, including the church. Subsidiarity validates and undergirds the idea of voluntary civil society in which people freely associate with and work for policies, ideas, and

30. Groody, *Globalization, Spirituality, and Justice*, 109.

31. Groody speaks of internal and external justice. Internal justice is being rightly related "with God through the saving work of Jesus Christ." External justice is about being "restored to right relationships with God, themselves, others, and the environment." Ibid., 26–27.

32. Ibid., 108.

33. Pius XI, *Quadragesimo Anno*, §79.

programs that they deem important. The history of Britain's emergence in the nineteenth century is an example of the principle of subsidiarity being discovered and released.

Solidarity as a principle of Catholic social teaching is a more recent theme, generally associated with John Paul II. It reflects the simple biblical idea that we are all part of the human family and that, as relational beings, we are all responsible for the well-being of all (1 Cor. 12:25–26).[34] The incarnation was God's coming close to those whom God loved and who could not help themselves. Jesus's call to love our neighbors as ourselves defines the meaning of solidarity, especially when there is no limit as to whom our neighbors might be (Luke 10:25–37). This is not a call for a warm and fuzzy sense of concern but a command to stop, cross over to the other side of the road, and change the circumstances of someone who is suffering or has been wronged.

Solidarity is deeply connected with the idea of the *option for the poor*, a term that arose with Vatican II and particularly in liberation theology. The idea draws on the central ethical focus that Jesus declared in the Beatitudes. It reflects the fact that Jesus chose to carry out the great majority of his ministry in Galilee, a marginal part of Israel inhabited by the marginalized of Jewish society. This shift in social location creates a different view of the poor and an undeniable call to act on their behalf: "Love for others, and in the first place love for the poor, in whom the Church sees Christ himself, is made concrete in the promotion of justice. Justice will never be fully attained unless people see in the poor person, who is asking for help in order to survive, not an annoyance or a burden, but an opportunity for showing kindness and a chance for greater enrichment."[35]

One final observation before moving on to Groody's theological examination of globalization. It is important to note that Catholic social teaching is not monolithic. It was written to provide some middle ethical axioms[36] that the church and people of goodwill might use to think and act theologically about social change in a pluralistic context. The evidence of the space created by this middle-axiom approach is that two quite different readings of Catholic social teaching have emerged, each varying its points of emphasis on the six themes just summarized.

34. John Paul II, *Sollicitudo Rei Socialis*, §38.
35. John Paul II, *Centesimus Annus*, §55.
36. The idea of middle axioms was proposed by J. H. Oldham (Oldham and Visser 't Hooft, *Church and Its Function in Society*). Standing between our theological and faith commitments, which we are loath to change or adapt, middle axioms are intermediate theological statements intended to help us navigate what Oldham called "creatively practicing the politics of the kingdom in an increasingly secular world." While Stackhouse does not use the term, it is consistent with what he called a "public theology."

The most well-known perspective is that of liberation theology and its deep suspicion of capitalism, which creates a preference for a strong state, if not a socialist one, committed to comprehensive policies of social welfare for the poor. This perspective places its emphasis on the truth about God and humankind and on human dignity while placing heavy emphasis on the common good, solidarity, and the preferential option for the poor.

The second perspective, sometimes called "theoconservatism," also places its emphasis on the truth about God and humankind and on human dignity, but then focuses largely on subsidiarity and the importance of human liberty.[37] Drawing on Catholic social teaching's criticism of socialism, supporters of this view are deeply suspicious of government efforts to improve the human condition and prefer economic development for the poor to be carried out by the private sector in contrast to either government or multilateral aid. Nonetheless, this group is also sharply critical of any attempt to absolutize free markets on the grounds that the "liberal market philosophy is an inadequate basis for globalization because it fails to provide a moral and cultural foundation that respects fully the dignity of the human person."[38]

Globalization, Justice, and Spirituality

Working within the Catholic social teaching tradition, Daniel Groody has contributed a proposal for the theological and ethical engagement of the values, processes, and outcomes of globalization. He writes, "[Catholic social teaching] offers an invaluable set of ethical coordinates that can help steer the ship of globalization in the right direction [toward justice]."[39] Groody's proposal has some common ground with that of Stackhouse. Both assume the possibility and usefulness of a global public theology, both believe that all religions need to contribute to this moral theology, and both understand the importance of civil society.

Catholic social teaching began as a self-consciously Catholic theological tradition, but it did not remain that way. With *Gaudium et Spes* (Joy and Hope),[40] encyclicals began to be addressed to the church and to "all people of goodwill."

37. This largely North American project has its roots in Michael Novak's *Spirit of Democratic Capitalism* and includes George Weigel, Robert P. George, Richard John Neuhaus, and Anglican Lord Brian Griffiths. This perspective is actively promoted today by the Acton Institute in the United States.

38. Griffiths, *Globalization*, 18.

39. Groody, *Globalization, Spirituality, and Justice*, 118.

40. One of the four Apostolic Constitutions resulting from the Second Vatican Council in 1965.

Catholic social teaching began to aspire to become a public theology, in the sense that Stackhouse defines it, in a world of religious pluralism. In some places this aspiration is actually becoming the case. Catholic social teaching is commonly used among many faith-based NGOs, including Protestants and those of other faiths. The International Forum on Globalization, representing a wide spectrum of NGOs, adopted core principles that "echo [Catholic social teaching] without using religious language"[41] in its report titled *Alternatives to Economic Globalization: A Better World Is Possible.*[42]

Groody's proposal goes a step beyond Stackhouse and global civil society as the means of shaping or influencing globalization. Groody is aware of the fact that, while Catholic social teaching is becoming increasingly well known outside the church, "most Catholics, especially the laity, remain largely untouched by it, both in their faith and their daily work lives."[43] As a consequence, Groody enlarges his focus for social action to include the people in the pew, the laity, as he calls our attention to the importance of worship and spiritual formation.

Groody names three theological issues as being critically relevant to engaging globalization. The first is what he calls the central theological question: In which God do I believe and put my faith? The marketplace gods of capitalism, socialism, or consumerism? The political gods of democracy, communism, or any single issue that is my sole passion? The gods of identity—my nation, my ethnicity, my religion, my gender? The gods of me—my well-being, my self-esteem, my autonomous happiness-seeking self? Groody argues that the central failing of globalization is not atheism but idolatry. "One of the primary tasks of Christian theology is to distinguish the God in whose image and likeness we are made from the god of our own making."[44]

The answer to "Which God?" leads Groody to his central theological affirmation. What is the "super-story" that shapes all our human stories? Some say the super-story of our times is globalization.[45] For others it is the implied super-story of "modern media, the visual imagination it engenders and the underlying values in this imagination."[46] But for Christians, the super-story is far bigger than just more stuff and more fun. The human super-story is the biblical story about God and our being in relationship with God and each other, the story that "took a decisive and definitive turn

41. Coleman and Ryan, *Globalization*, 265.
42. Cavanagh, *Alternatives to Economic Globalization.*
43. Coleman and Ryan, *Globalization*, 262.
44. Groody, *Globalization, Spirituality, and Justice*, 23.
45. T. Friedman, *Longitudes and Attitudes*, 3.
46. Groody, *Globalization, Spirituality, and Justice*, 25.

in the life of Jesus of Nazareth, whose life, death, and resurrection are *the* super-story and the defining revelation of who God is and what it means to be human."[47]

Once we are clear on whose we are and who we are, we face what Groody calls the theological imperative—justice. Groody defines justice relationally; we are to be rightly related to God (inner justice or loving God) and to each other and God's creation (external justice or loving our neighbor).[48] Thus, injustice is the result of our relationships not working for our well-being or that of others.[49] Free human beings who seek justice will live in a way that creates or enhances life rather than destroys or diminishes life.[50] "God's justice is not principally about vengeance or retribution, but about restoring people to right relationships with God, themselves, others and their environment."[51] These three theological imperatives are critical to developing what John Paul II called the "globalization of solidarity."[52]

At this point, we might expect a proposal in terms of what the church, the laity, and "people of goodwill" might do, but Groody surprises us. Instead of further developing a response to globalization, he turns to worship, the Eucharist, and spiritual formation. For Groody, there is no dichotomy between liturgy and working for justice, no two-tiered worldview with worship addressing spiritual things and justice working in the "real" world. We need to understand that "liturgy and justice are both the celebration of right relationships."[53] He reminds us that it is in the Eucharist, the communion supper, that we celebrate and remember the work of God in us (internal justice) and God's mission for us in the world (external justice). The sacraments are the way we encounter God and the values of God's kingdom. The liturgy and the Eucharist prepare us for our mission: "The eucharist [is] a graced event that celebrates God's transformative activity in the world and the Christian calling to participate in [God's] transformation."[54]

For Groody, worship and liturgy are about creating right practices, not just right thinking. "Ritual is (should be) a structured, purposeful, interpersonal activity directed toward the internalization of certain values and beliefs. . . . The purpose of Christian liturgy is to enter more deeply into the meaning

---

47. Ibid. (emphasis original).
48. This framework also dissolves the material-spiritual duality of the modern worldview. Our relationships are material and spiritual, horizontal and vertical.
49. Myers, *Walking with the Poor*, 143–44.
50. Groody, *Globalization, Spirituality, and Justice*, 24.
51. Ibid., 27.
52. John Paul II, *Ecclesia in America*, §55.
53. Groody, *Globalization, Spirituality, and Justice*, 213.
54. Ibid.

of who we are, to whom we belong, and where we are going."[55] As we have seen in the last chapter and with Stackhouse, the economic and technological dimensions of globalization have given us more and more control over our external world yet offer little to the inner world of human beings—who we are, why we are here, and how we are to live. "There are enduring human questions that globalization has largely ignored and left unexplored. These questions deal with loneliness and belonging, good and evil, peace and division, healing and suffering, meaning and meaninglessness, hope and despair, love and apathy, justice and injustice, freedom and slavery, and ultimately life and death. . . . These values are the concern of spirituality."[56]

Groody describes spiritual disciplines as the most important avenue we have as Christians to "make the invisible heart of God visible in the world."[57] The heart, he argues, is the place where we encounter God, and this encounter compels us to follow Jesus by "making the mind and heart of Christ one's own."[58] He envisions a process of spiritual formation using the disciplines that shape us on the inside in a way that drives us into the world to love God and our neighbors. The key to renewing our relationship with God and ultimately with our neighbor are the spiritual disciplines: fasting, prayer, community, solidarity, and simplicity.[59]

The foregoing summarizes Groody's proposal for how the church and Christians can engage the assumptions and values of the globalisms undergirding contemporary globalization (see fig. 13.2). Like Stackhouse, Groody says that, in addition to Catholic social teaching, we need to draw on the resources of other faith traditions for a common moral vision.[60] Both Groody and Stackhouse point to *Toward a Global Ethic: An Initial Declaration*, an outcome of the Council for a Parliament of the World's Religions, as an example of the possibility of creating a common ethical vision.

This brings us to Groody's proposal for how such a common moral vision can be lived out in a transformative way in globalization's world of economics, politics, and civil society. Groody takes a different first step than does Stackhouse. He begins with the formation of the laity in the pews and the parish. Worship and spirituality, when truly transformational, should change the way parishes and ordinary people in the pews spend their money, volunteer their time, and act as citizens in the political arena. We are all actors in

55. Ibid., 215.
56. Ibid., 240.
57. Ibid., 241.
58. Ibid., 243.
59. Ibid., 247.
60. Ibid., 124.

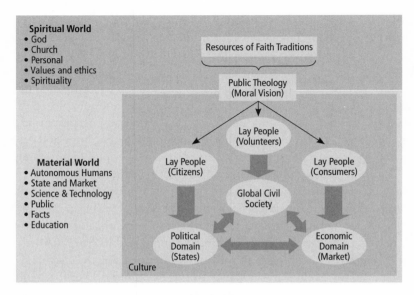

FIGURE 13.2 Releasing the laity as faithful witnesses within

the domains of globalization—in the market, politics, and civil society. All Christians can witness to Christ and God's kingdom and can love God and our neighbor in all three domains.

This is not to say that Groody would disagree with Stackhouse about global civil society. The church as an institution can organize or join networks, coalitions, and associations of Christians and others of goodwill as a way of creating social power. This is how large numbers of Christians and others of goodwill can be active in civil society where the focus is on how to better love our neighbors. But individual Christians have their own individual areas of influence that go well beyond civil society—areas where they can be witnesses to the gospel.

Changing Culture—James Davison Hunter

The proposals of Stackhouse and Groody assume that the culture of globalization can be changed by undertaking two broad initiatives. First, create a common global spiritual and moral architecture that speaks to the missing values and unacceptably thin anthropology of globalization. Second, spread this new moral vision both through actions in civil society—the social domain of the church—and through the actions of individual Christians whose

---

The Power to Change

James Davison Hunter, professor of religion, culture, and social theory, University of Virginia

As to our spheres of influence, a theology of faithful witness obligates us to do what we are able, under the sovereignty of God, to shape the patterns of life and work and relationship—that is the institutions of which our lives are constituted—toward a shalom that seeks the welfare not only of the household of God, but of all. That power will be wielded is inevitable. But the *means of influence* and the *ends of influence* must conform to the exercise of power modeled by Christ.

Hunter, *To Change the World*, 254 (emphasis original)

---

discipleship and spiritual formation has prepared them to act Christianly in the way they vote, consume, and volunteer their time and money. This is well and good, but there may be more that we could be doing.

James Davison Hunter, in his important book *To Change the World*, calls Christians and churches to be a "faithful witness within," a call and practice for all Christians, not just clergy or activists. This sounds very much like what Groody has proposed, but Hunter enlarges the mission field beyond just the way we vote, consume, and volunteer. Hunter encourages all Christians to become a faithful witness within whatever places they may be able to influence—their families, neighborhoods, professional organizations, cultural institutions, workplaces, or any other social gathering place where God has placed them. By "faithful witnesses within," Hunter is also calling Christians to go beyond just announcing that Christ is Lord. Christians must also witness to the (emerging) kingdom of God by working for the implementation of kingdom values—fairness, justice, flourishing, inclusion, truth, transparency, and the biblical use of power. We are to work for kingdom-like social change in whatever social situations or institutions God has placed us. To further develop this idea of a faithful witness within, Hunter uses a biblical metaphor and then calls our attention to the importance of the culture-forming power of certain kinds of institutions as well as aesthetics.

Hunter provides a biblical metaphor for a "faithful witness within" in the form of God's call to Israel when Israel was in exile in Babylon: "Seek the peace and prosperity of the [pagan] city to which I have carried you into exile. Pray to the LORD for it [the pagan city], because if it prospers, you too will prosper" (Jer. 29:7). Reflecting on Hunter, I see two contributions to a Christian response to globalization and its globalisms. First, we are to be faithful witnesses within the cultural context of globalization, not try to escape it or resist it or allow ourselves to become culturally captive to it. We are to seek the well-being of globalization and those that worship at its shrines. This echoes Stackhouse's view that globalization is a providential grace in a fallen world and that the "church particularly is called to preach, teach and cultivate this grace."[61]

Second, the Babylon metaphor suggests that wherever we are in our globalized world, God is at work and so we too must be working as faithful witnesses within whatever context God has placed us; this is our individual mission field. Being a faithful witness within does not mean passive conformity but rather "a constructive resistance that seeks new patterns of social organizations that challenge, undermine, and otherwise diminish oppression, injustice, enmity, and corruption and, in turn, encourage harmony, fruitfulness and abundance, wholeness, beauty, joy, security, and well-being"[62]—God's shalom and the values of the kingdom of God.

Hunter is rather put off by what he sees as the tendency of too many American churches and Christians to simply assume that the way to be faithful witnesses is to try to influence or shape the political realm.[63] His view of history suggests that trying to influence the political realm has two weaknesses: Christians and their mission can become co-opted or simply played, and the evidence that cultures change this way is thin. Hunter argues for an alternative understanding of culture change that recognizes that the institutions of society have far more potential to influence culture than do individuals alone. He believes that Christians are ignoring this opportunity.[64]

Hunter posits that the "key actor in history is not the individual genius but rather the networks [of large numbers of individuals] and the institutions that are created by such networks."[65] Thus, for Hunter, cultural change is created by a practice of faithful witness that "generates relationships and institutions that are fundamentally covenantal in character, the ends of which are the fostering of meaning, purpose, truth, beauty, belonging, and fairness— not just for Christians but for everyone."[66] This begins with the gifts that

61. Stackhouse, *Globalization and Grace*, 241.
62. Hunter, *To Change the World*, 247–48.
63. Ibid., 3–33.
64. Ibid., 32.
65. Ibid., 38.
66. Ibid., 263.

The Arts Are Needed Too

James K. A. Smith, professor of philosophy, Calvin College

We don't just need teachers and preachers and scholars and "doctors" of the church to *tell* us what to do; if the gospel is going to capture imaginations and sanctify perception, we need painters and novelists and dancers and songwriters and sculptors and poets and designers whose creative work *shows* the world otherwise.

J. Smith, *Imagining the Kingdom*, 163 (emphasis original)

God has given people—arts, music, drama, social media, math, persuasion, conceptualization, mobilization, quiet service. Being faithful witnesses within means using these gifts within the institutions of education, of business and commerce, of guilds and professional associations, and of art and architecture, literature and music, movies and media.

The Decisive Importance of Prayer[67]

History belongs to the intercessors, who believe the future into being.

—Walter Wink, *Engaging the Powers*, 304

With no intention of distracting from my summary of proposals for Christian engagement with globalization, I need to make two critical qualifications. The first is obvious but needs to be named. Our human efforts are limited; we cannot save ourselves or God's creation. We have an essential role to play, but at the end of the day God must do what God has set out to do: redeem and restore God's world. Second, the "prince of this world" (John 12:31), while defeated by Christ on the cross, still holds sway until the end of history and Christ's return. There is a powerful liar who is working against every effort to save or transform, any attempt to create a normative ethical framework or spiritual architecture, or any attempt to add the transcendent reality of God to the globalisms animating globalization. Only God can (and has) dealt with

67. I am indebted to my wife, Lisa Myers, for reminding me (once again) of the importance of prayer in the work of changing the world and for her insights from a lifelong profession as a spiritual director and student of spirituality.

this adversary. These two facts bring us to the decisive importance of prayer as our first priority and highest calling as God's partners in God's mission of restoration and redemption.

Let's unpack this a little. First, Paul encourages us to pray continually (1 Thess. 5:17). This seems an impossible command for an individual, but fortunately Paul was addressing all "brothers and sisters." From its beginning, the church as a whole has been praying the prayer that Christ taught us. Today, across the world and at all times of the day, some of the over two billion Christians are praying for the world and the coming of God's kingdom in its fullness. Furthermore, praying continually is also a way of living more and more deeply into an awareness of God's presence in and through us on behalf of the world.

Second, Christ gave us something quite specific for which to pray: "Your kingdom come, your will be done, on earth as it is in heaven" (Matt. 6:10). Our common prayer for the completion of God's project of redemption and restoration is more than an act of petition. It is an act of subversion.[68] Intercession, as Walter Wink reminds us, "is spiritual defiance of what is, in the name of what God has promised. Intercession visualizes an alternative future."[69] Thus, praying that God's kingdom come is not just "an ineffectual longing for the gulf to be bridged"[70] between the world of today and the kingdom of tomorrow; it is an act of mission by which we re-vision ourselves and our world.

Third, we are to pray against the principalities and powers who make globalization seem so seductive and attempt to validate globalization's claim of being "good news" while deceptively hiding globalization's invitations to accumulation, domination, and exploitation.[71] We are to pray for the unmasking of the faith claims of modernity and neoliberal capitalism—that human beings are alone in the world and must save themselves and that God and the transcendent are holdovers from a more primitive time and are neither real nor efficacious. We need to pray for the Holy Spirit to enable people to come to know who they truly are and what they are here for—that they have an inspiring vocation and that there are rules to live by that make justice and peace possible. We need to pray for the emergence of a global public theology whereby the religions of this world provide the moral and spiritual architecture that allows us to replace the thin gruel of ethical pragmatism provided by economics, politics, and culture alone.

Fourth, and possibly the most important, prayer is an invitation, not just an obligation. It is in prayer that we can discover that God is already praying within

68. Leech, *True Prayer*, 82.
69. Wink, *Engaging the Powers*, 298–99.
70. Elliott, *Praying the Kingdom*, 22.
71. Wink, *Engaging the Powers*, 311.

us.[72] When we pray, especially when we are attentive to God in silence, we find ourselves entering into the very life and heart of God. This is the only place where we encounter the deep grace of Father, Son, and Holy Spirit, the only place where we can see the world and ourselves as God sees us now and where we can see what God intends for us at the end of time. Finally, it is by being attentive to God in prayer that we discover that loving God and loving our neighbor, while conceptually different, are in fact two dimensions of the same thing.[73]

> The purpose of prayer is not to uncover divine solutions to the social and economic problems . . . of the world. Prayer does not displace the task of creative, intelligent, and compassionate . . . civic collaboration or political action. . . . Prayer [is] a profound expression of who we are as men and women; it is a sign of our having been made for one another, and it reveals the mystery within humanity which all of us share.[74]

Fifth and finally, prayer transforms us. Remember, we are as flawed as the world is. Sin is ubiquitous. So our mission in the world must begin by looking for the plank in our own eyes (Luke 6:42). This too is the work of prayer.

> Prayer is . . . a spiritual grace that facilitates human transformation. . . . The desire to change the world begins with a commitment to change ourselves. . . . As it grounds and connects us to God, prayer informs, reforms, and transforms us and all other relationships, allowing God to guide, shape and influence our decisions, and accomplish in us some of the highest work of the human heart.[75]

The choice we face is not between passive prayer and missional action. Rather, the choice is about how we will live into our prayers and pray ourselves into action. Our first duty is to open ourselves to God's heart, to pray for the coming of God's kingdom, and then to make whatever small contribution God enables us to make.

Summing Up

There is no single strategy or approach for a Christian engagement with globalization. Globalization is too complex, and the church is, too. The bottom line is that we are to seek the welfare of the society and culture in which

72. Ibid., 304.
73. Reiser, *To Hear God's Word, Listen to the World*, 50.
74. Ibid., 51.
75. Groody, *Globalization, Spirituality, and Justice*, 250–51.

God has placed us in this globalizing world. I hope the case built here will help everyone who claims Christ as Lord and looks forward to the eventual coming of the kingdom of God realize that they have a place and a missional calling somewhere in the midst of our globalizing world. We need to be faithful witnesses within our congregation, parish, or neighborhood; we need to pay attention to how we spend our money, vote, and volunteer; and we need to recognize our presence in the social institutions where society is creating the bits and pieces of itself and work there to shape the goals and practices of those social institutions toward more kingdom-like ends. Everyone has a gift to contribute that enables them to fulfill God's command to love God and neighbor. For some, the gift is prayer and fasting; for others it is activism and organizing networks; for others it is their art or music or poetry or film making. Working together or working quietly alone, each of us can witness to Christ and to God's kingdom.

The final chapter will examine the implications of becoming and being faithful witnesses in our globalizing world. We need to reexamine our understanding of mission in light of what we have seen thus far in this book.

Questions for Discussion

1. Make a list of the institutions—political, business related, educational, charitable, artistic, and so on—within which you are active.

2. What might a faithful presence within those institutions look like? How might you work to influence them toward ends that foster "meaning, purpose, truth, beauty, belonging and fairness—not just for Christians but for everyone"?

3. How might your church prepare and equip you for this kind of faithful witness within?

14

The Missiological Challenge of Globalization

I began this book by suggesting that the church and Christians today need to make a choice between three basic stances toward globalization: resisting globalization, ignoring globalization (with the exception of appropriating its technology for traditional mission), or engaging globalization. By now you know that I favor the third option. The church and Christians need to embrace the fact that globalization is the central missiological challenge of our time, and we are called to respond.

As I hope I have made clear, globalization is a complex and messy mixture of original good and original sin. We need the faith to believe that the values, processes, and dynamics of globalization are the objects of God's love as well as of God's project of redemption and restoration. Our mission is to become faithful witnesses to Jesus Christ and God's kingdom from within the institutions, structures, and domains of this globalizing world.

In the previous two chapters, I outlined the thinking of Jonathan Sacks, Max Stackhouse, Daniel Groody, and James Davison Hunter and their shared conclusion that the central failure of globalization is its inability to provide satisfactory answers to the questions of meaning: Who are we? Why are we here? How then should we live? The values and underlying assumptions of globalization offer little to ease the hunger in human hearts for a spiritual and moral vision. I then outlined proposals by Stackhouse, Groody, and Hunter that call for the church and Christians to be faithful witnesses to the good news of Christ's gospel and the emerging kingdom of God in our globalizing world.

This final chapter addresses the question of what the pervasive and growing reach of globalization and its ambiguities and complexities might mean to missiological thinking and practice. While the mission of the church has not changed, the values, processes, and outcomes of globalization in the twenty-first century have changed the context of mission. Globalization is expanding, stretching, intensifying, and accelerating our social relations, and these changes are changing us and the way we view the world. In a very real sense, the globalisms that are animating globalization—modernity and neoliberal capitalism—are offering a competing and seductive "good news." Christians now live in an era of "contested" mission, and too many seem unaware of this fact. This new mission context suggests that we need to reexamine our thinking about and practice of mission.

In what follows, I will propose three ways our thinking and practices need to change. First, our understanding of the mission field needs to be reimagined. The mission field is no longer just "over there" but is also inside the church and just outside its doors. All Christians everywhere are embedded in today's contested mission field. Second, we need to rethink our understanding of missionaries and their formation. I will argue, along with Groody and Hunter, that all Christians need to be formed and equipped to be faithful witnesses to Christ and to God's kingdom within whatever institutions—family, community, non-profit, business, artistic, or professional—God has placed them. Third, this in turn calls for a reexamination and reimagining of our processes of discipleship and spiritual formation.

Finally, in regard to being faithful witnesses within, I will call attention to two limitations that I believe need to be overcome. First, to carry out this reimagined form of mission requires that we recover the good news in the gospel in order to get a hearing in a suspicious world. Second, the church and Christians need to recover their confidence in the relevance of the church and its gospel to all areas of life without succumbing to the temptation of trying to recover its Constantinian past.

I will close the chapter and this book with a brief set of reflections that I hope will encourage and release all of us to make these changes and become the witnesses that God insists that we be.

The Mission Field Has Changed

For over five hundred years, the work of Catholic and Protestant mission consisted of taking Christ's gospel to people somewhere else in the world who had not heard it. Even as the church's geographic center of gravity moved to the Global South, the mission frame remained essentially the same. While mission was no longer from the West to the rest, but from anyone to anywhere, the task was still to take the gospel to those who had not yet heard it or had forgotten it. To carry out this mission, we steeped ourselves in the meaning and the person of the message, studied communication theory, developed our cross-cultural skills, and learned the importance of contextualization—all part of the standard missiological curriculum of the last fifty years.

As Christians kept their eyes narrowly focused on going to the ends of the earth with their message, they lost sight of the fact that the world was getting smaller and more tightly connected; the ends of the earth were coming to us. This change means that the missiological challenge of globalization is more complex than just finding new ways to use the techniques of globalization to carry out traditional mission. We must not overlook or ignore the fact that globalization is really something quite new in God's world.

Today there is a competing global offer of "good news." Globalization and its values have also gone to the ends of the earth. Globalization's message, media, and promises are attractive, accessible, and seductive. In a sense, the promises and seductions of the globalisms of modernity and neoliberal capitalism are evangelizing us. James K. A. Smith makes this point when he argues that "our imaginations are contested ground, pulled and wooed and shaped by competing stories about 'the good life,' tempted and attracted by affective pictures of what counts as 'flourishing.'"[1] All people, including Christians, are the targets of this new and tempting "good news."

To complicate this new reality, we need to acknowledge that, at least in a material sense, much of globalization's good news really is good news—less poverty, better health, better education, better access to more information, better connections to more people, and more choices. Furthermore, this competing good news is tangible news—it can be seen, touched, and taken to the bank. Today's mission field is a genuinely contested space. The implications are significant.

The presence of a competing offer of good news means that today's mission field begins inside the church itself, not outside its doors. This mission field lies in the hearts and minds of the people in the pews who are being shaped and formed all day, every day by the promises and seductions of globalization's twin globalisms. Christian mission needs to be reimagined to include helping the people in the pews develop the eyes to see and ears to hear that will allow them to separate what is true from what is not in the face of the fire hose of information, claims, and seductions they hear, see, and experience every day

---

1. J. Smith, *Imagining the Kingdom*, 162.

Discernment and the Holy Spirit

Kirsteen Kim, professor of theology and world Christianity,
Leeds Trinity University, UK

In a society taken up with desire for experiences of all kinds, pneumatology has great potential relevance. It also has the capability to broaden the contemporary penchant for experience beyond desire for individual fulfillment and temporal satisfaction. However, if it is to relate to contemporary society, pneumatology must recognize the Spirit's work beyond the boundaries of the church or the Christian heart. Furthermore, a theology of the Spirit for today must take into account the other spirits encountered in an increasingly pluralist world. It must raise awareness of, and help us respond to, the many worldviews and belief systems that we encounter today. Finally, it must offer guidance for Christians on which modern-day powers to support and which to resist, and how to do so ethically and effectively.

Kim, *Holy Spirit in the World*, 3

in a globalized world. They need a functional discernment that helps them separate false prophets from true ones, false idols from the one true God.

The second part of today's mission field begins not only over there, but just outside the door of the church in the lives, jobs, and recreation of ordinary Christian men and women who are working, shopping, volunteering, and creating in the world of contemporary globalization. Especially in the West, the church and its members are living in the heart of globalization's Babylon. We are strangers in an increasingly strange land that is not our own. Yet Hunter suggests that globalization is the "city" whose welfare we are to seek, whose flourishing will lead to ours, because, in the end, God is faithful. Our mission is to resist Babylon's temptations and yet be faithful witnesses in the midst of the values, processes, and institutions of globalization where we live. Chapter 13 outlined the many and diverse ways that we might be able to do this in our world as individuals and as groups.

This in turn suggests that mission in the midst of globalization must go beyond traditional mission theology and practices. I have already pointed to globalization's failings in terms of meaning and morality. Our good news must now reflect the gospel's better news in these critical areas of human life. Being able to expose the weaknesses of globalization's underlying ideas, assumptions, and rationales, of its failures of fairness and inclusion, of its inadequate way of knowing and making sense of things, must become part of mission practice. We must recall our Victorian forebears and once again engage the world of ideas. "Because [past] missionary discourse . . . has been dominated by so many geographic, territorially driven paradigms, our ability to recognize many of the most challenging new frontiers that face Christians in the twenty-first century has been hampered. Many of the most important frontiers are intellectual, social and epistemological."[2]

Today's mission field is made more complex by the claim of Sacks, Stackhouse, and Groody that creating a spiritual and ethical vision to guide the ship of globalization will require the ethical resources of all major faith traditions. Interfaith dialogue has always been a challenge for evangelicals, and this will be no exception. But we cannot avoid the challenge. Globalization is a global problem offering its own "faithless" good news, and no single religious tradition can gain a broad and compelling enough voice to counteract it on its own. Today's leaders and laity will need training and equipping to be able to work in such a pluralistic mission environment.

A Different Kind of Missionary

Since the mission field is no longer just "over there," and since the missional challenge in the world of globalization is about ideas and values, about meaning and morality, about relationships that work for or against well-being, it seems that we can no longer delegate missions to pastors and missionaries, to activists and Christian NGOs. The lay faithful need to discover that God is expecting all believers to be witnesses to Christ and God's kingdom every day and in every social location where they work, play, create, and seek well-being. Mission in today's world of globalization requires passionate and discerning disciples of Christ who think Christianly about what they consume, how they vote, how they volunteer, and what values they defend and promote in their workplaces and in their art, architecture, film, and music.

Preparing the laity for this kind of mission will require new understandings and skills. The first step in preparation may be the hardest. Too many Christians and churches are simply not engaged with globalization and thus are unaware or uncritical of its seductive good news. We need to find ways to get the issue of globalization—its globalisms, its meanings, and implications—on their mission radar. To do this, there may be value in exploring variations of

2. Tennent, *Invitation to World Missions*, 495. Timothy Tennent is professor of world Christianity and president of Asbury Theological Seminary.

Paulo Freire's approach of raising what he calls "critical consciousness."[3] We need to create new eyes to see and new ears to hear.

We then need to help people understand the challenge presented by globalization. We need discipleship formation that helps ordinary Christians understand the complex nature of globalization and how it works in the world and in our lives. All of us—leaders and laity—need to be willing to do the hard work necessary to understand the values of its twin globalisms and their assumptions about who we are, about social change, and about power and wealth.

Disciples who are faithful witnesses also need the theological and critical tools that enable them to recognize the implicit promises of globalization's modernity and neoliberal capitalism. What better human future do they promise? Today's disciples need to have a deep understanding of why the "good news" of globalization is not as good as it sounds. Once you have enough, you need something more. People need to know who they are, why they are here, and how they should live. We are meaning-making,[4] moral, believing[5] creatures, after all. God made us this way. These fundamental human needs cannot be satisfied by more wealth or power or by better technology. But thinking critically and conceptually is not enough. Today's disciples need more.

Disciples need to be able to recognize and name globalization's liturgies of formation, whether they are experienced in the form of malls, music, film, or social media.[6] This is the front line of mission where globalization is evangelizing us. "For [most] people in advanced capitalist countries, . . . their stories, narratives, images, and sound come from centralized, for-profit corporations—the so-called global culture industries. . . . [These] commercial 'orchestrators of attention' . . . are winning a contest that church leaders scarcely recognize as underway."[7] Disciples need a spirituality that empowers them to protect themselves. The antidotes to the promises of the twin globalisms must come from worship and liturgies that have been carefully crafted by those deeply aware of the nature of today's contested field of mission.[8]

Disciples must be empowered to discern and unmask the seductive power and promises of globalization. Disciples need to be able to understand whom it is that makes these temptations so powerful and seductive. There is a liar in

---

3. Freire, *Education for Critical Consciousness*; Evans, Evans, and Kennedy, *Pedagogies for the Non-Poor*.

4. Crouch, *Culture Making*, 24–25.

5. C. Smith, *Moral, Believing Animals*, 45.

6. J. Smith, *Desiring the Kingdom*, 23–25.

7. Budde, "Collecting Praise," 125–26. Michael Budde is professor of Catholic studies and political science at DePaul University.

8. J. Smith, *Imagining the Kingdom*, 25.

Worship and Desire

James K. A. Smith, professor of philosophy, Calvin College

[We need] to recognize the charged, *religious* nature of cultural institutions that we all tend to inhabit as if they were neutral sites. . . . [We need to] appreciate that the [shopping] mall is a religious institution because it is a *liturgical* institution, and that it is a pedagogical institution because it is a *formative* institution. . . .

Because our hearts are oriented primarily by desire, by what we love, and because those desires are shaped and molded by the habit-forming practices in which we participate, it is the rituals and practices of the mall—the liturgies of the mall and market—that shape our imaginations and how we orient ourselves to the world. . . .

[My core claim] is that liturgies—whether "sacred" or "secular"—shape and constitute our identities by forming our most fundamental desires and our most basic attunement to the world. In short, liturgies make us certain kinds of people, and what defines us is what we *love.* . . .

Being a disciple of Jesus Christ is not primarily a matter of getting the right ideas and doctrines and beliefs into your head in order to guarantee proper behavior; rather, it's a matter of being the kind of person who *loves* rightly—who loves God and neighbor and is oriented to the world by the primacy of that love. We are made such people by our immersion in the material practices of Christian worship—through affective impact, over time, of sights and smell in water and wine.

J. Smith, *Desiring the Kingdom*, 23–25, 32–33 (emphasis original)

this world; the deceptions of globalization's twin globalisms are not accidental. Disciples need to be made aware of the seductive nature of the principalities and powers and have the discernment and the spirituality to stand against the seduction of idolatry and false promises.[9]

Finally, if we take seriously Hunter's proposal about being faithful witnesses within all the cultural and social institutions within which God has placed

9. I do not have time or space to describe how Max Stackhouse uses Walter Wink's theological description of the principalities and powers as the organizing framework for his work on globalization. See Stackhouse with Paris, *Religion and the Powers of the Common Life*; Wink, *Engaging the Powers*.

us, we are facing a very different kind of cross-cultural mission. Within the institutional life of globalization, the folks with whom we work, play, and volunteer may not speak our theological language or share our Christian ethical values. We are going to have to learn to be comfortable working missionally in pluralistic or secular environments. Thus to be faithful witnesses within working for the emergence of kingdom values—justice, peace, righteousness, and inclusion—will require us to be bilingual in a sense, learning to speak our message in secular language, using secular ideas and arguments. Our goal is to uncover common ethical values, without our becoming less Christian as we do it. The net result is that all Christians will need the same kind of training that we used to reserve for missionaries. Everyone will need to be able to work cross-culturally, even within their own culture.

Discipleship Formation and the Spiritual Disciplines

As I discussed in some detail in chapter 13, Daniel Groody closes his proposal for engaging globalization with a focus on the importance of worship and spiritual formation in shaping disciples who love God and their neighbor in how they consume, vote, and volunteer. James Davison Hunter pleads for the formation of disciples who can act as "faithful witness within," working for adoption of the kingdom values of justice, peace, mercy, and inclusion in whatever spheres of influence God has placed them. The critical concern is whether or not our discipleship or formational approaches are up to the missiological challenge of globalization.

We have already noted the limited influence of Catholic social teaching in the parishes and among the laity in the Catholic Church.[10] This may have been what prompted Groody to end his proposal with its emphasis on liturgy and spiritual formation. There is a lot in Groody's material about worship and spiritual formation from which Protestants might benefit.

But discipleship that fails to transform and prepare Christians for faithful witness is not just a Catholic problem. I've already expressed concern for the paucity of sermon series or Bible or book studies focused on globalization within the Protestant community. It does not appear that our preaching and teaching or worship and sacraments are resulting in large numbers of people who wish to be God's transforming presence in a globalizing world. Further, there seems to be a lack of confidence in the quality of our discipleship itself: "Only 1 percent [of pastors] say 'today's churches are doing very well

10. Coleman and Ryan, *Globalization*, 257, 262–63.

at discipling new and young believers.' A sizable majority—six in 10—feels that churches are discipling 'not too well.'"[11]

In addition to Groody's thinking on worship and formation, the recent work of James K. A. Smith is stimulating and provocative. First, rejecting worship solely in the service of moral formation or self-improvement, Smith reminds us that "we worship for mission, we gather for sending; we center ourselves in the practice of the body of Christ for the sake of the world; we are reformed in the cathedral to undertake our image-bearing commission to reform the city."[12] If we are to be sent, then worship and formation need to form and enable disciples whose actions or practices reflect the true story of God and God's redemptive and restorative intentions for this world.

Second, Smith addresses the issue of imagination and desire. In the "Worship and Desire" sidebar, he describes how the liturgies of globalization shape our imaginations and desires. He goes on to highlight the link between worship and the (re)shaping of our imaginations and desires: "If we are to be agents of the coming kingdom, *acting* in ways that embody God's desires for the creation, then our imaginations must be conscripted by God. It is not enough to convince our intellects; our imaginations need to be caught by—and caught up into—the Story of God's restorative, reconciling grace for all creation. It won't be enough for us to be convinced; we need to be *moved*."[13] In order to be faithful witnesses within, Smith argues that we need to understand how worship, carefully informed by formational needs of the kind of witnesses that I described earlier in this chapter, can "(re)form" our imaginations, desires, and worldview that in turn determine our practices in daily life.[14]

I believe that a great deal more effort needs to be given to linking the new demands of twenty-first-century mission to revitalizing and enriching worship and spiritual formation. The traditional tools of mission—communication theory, cross-cultural skills, and an understanding of contextualization—alone do not seem up to the challenge.

Recovering the Good News in the Good News

Though it remains the nation's most dominant religion, Christianity faces significant headwind in the court of public opinion. The decades-old trend that

11. Barna Research Group, "New Research."
12. J. Smith, *Imagining the Kingdom*, 154.
13. Ibid., 157 (emphasis original).
14. Ibid.

Christianity is irrelevant is increasingly giving way to the notion that Christianity is bad for society.

—Barna Research Group[15]

Another element of the missiological challenge of globalization comes in the form of a word of caution to evangelicals, especially those of us in the United States and some in the Global South. Somehow we have succumbed to the temptation to express a gospel that focuses on things we believe are wrong. Despite having been told not to judge lest we be judged, we sometimes come across as promoters of a bad-news gospel that offers judgment rather than redemption, presenting an angry, judging God and not the God of grace and love. When we denounce the immorality or lostness of others, we are not pointing to God as much as we are playing God in the lives of those to whom we wish to witness. Sometimes we make it sound like the gospel is not good news except for folks who are just like us.

If we wish to offer the good and needed news of a restored spiritual and moral vision to a fallen world, we need to reclaim and act out the good news of the gospel, the gospel that saves us so that we can be who we most truly are and thus save others. We need to recover the positive gospel of a loving God who has a solution for sin and enables us to love our neighbors, all our neighbors. We need to wrap ourselves, our lives, and our message in the good news—that the gospel is for all people, for their well-being, and is the key to human flourishing.

Recovering Our Confidence

There is a second limitation that the church and Christians need to overcome. Over the last two hundred years, Christians and the church in the West have moved from the center of things to the periphery. Christendom felt good; we were needed and respected. Today we live in a post-Christian world that tells us that we need to learn to live on the edges of the modern world. I've made the case that not only were we relegated to the spiritual realm, but we have seemingly settled in, creating a Christian subculture in which we feel safely Christian, safely apart from a sinful and lost world. In a very real sense, many Christians in the West have lost confidence.

In a survey of evangelical leaders who attended the third international meeting of the Lausanne Movement[16] in Cape Town in 2010, almost 60 percent of

15. Barna Research Group, "Five Ways."
16. In the 1970s, Billy Graham perceived the need for a global congress to reframe evangelical mission in a world of political, economic, intellectual, and religious upheaval. The church, he

Becoming Good News Again

John Dickerson, senior pastor, Cornerstone Church

But we can, and must, adapt the way we hold our beliefs—with grace and humility instead of superior hostility. The core evangelical belief is that love and forgiveness are freely available to all who trust in Jesus Christ. This is the "good news" from which the evangelical name originates. . . . Instead of offering hope, many evangelicals have claimed the role of moral gatekeeper, judge and jury. If we continue in that posture, we will continue to invite opposition and obscure the "good news" we are called to proclaim.

I believe the cultural backlash against evangelical Christianity has less to do with our views—many observant Muslims and Jews, for example, also view homosexual sex as wrong, while Catholics have been at the vanguard of the movement to protect the lives of the unborn—and more to do with our posture. The Scripture calls us "aliens and exiles" (1 Pet. 2:11), but American evangelicals have not acted with the humility and homesickness of aliens. The proper response to our sexualized and hedonistic culture is not to chastise, but to "conduct yourselves honorably among the Gentiles, so that, though they malign you as evildoers, they may see your good deeds and glorify God" (1 Pet. 2:12).

Dickerson, "Decline of Evangelical America"

the leaders from the Global South indicated that evangelical Christians are gaining influence in their countries. In stark contrast, two-thirds of the leaders in the Global North said that "in the societies in which they live, evangelicals are losing influence. U.S. evangelical leaders are especially downbeat about the prospects for evangelical Christianity in their society; over 80 percent say evangelicals are losing influence in the United States today."[17]

I pointed out earlier in this book that Christianity is one of the most enduring globalisms in history and is thus viewed with considerable suspicion by other major globalisms. Such skeptics include Muslims, as we have seen, but also secular humanists who wish to preserve Christianity's relegation to

---

believed, had to grasp the ideas and values behind rapid changes in society. This movement of evangelicals for world evangelization held its first meeting in Lausanne in 1974 and the second in Manila in 1989.

17. Pew Research Center, "Global Survey."

the spiritual world of religion and theology and who deeply distrust the idea of Christianity making any attempt to return to the public material realms of politics, economics, and social change. But here I make a different point. It is we Christians who need to understand, re-embrace, and own our gospel responsibility to act as a globalism. We need to become brave enough and confident enough in our gospel, theology, and practices to insist that a public square without all religions results in a crisis in ethical thinking and ethical behavior. This is the central argument of Sacks, Stackhouse, and Groody.

On what grounds do I make this claim for confidence and boldness? The church has a rather uneven history when it comes to power, ethical behavior, and the like. Why should the world pay any attention to the source of the Crusades, of misdeeds of missionaries during the era of colonial empires, and of religious conflicts throughout history? Surely our expulsion from the public square was richly deserved. I agree in part. There is no question that the church has a history that reflects the impact of original sin in its adherents and its structures.

Even so, two observations are in order. First, the modern world of secular humanism has its own uneven record in terms of genocides, world wars, and social injustice. Second, and more to my point, the story of the church told by secular folk leaves out a broad range of important contributions.

The church has been in the health and healing business for over two thousand years. It created the first asylums for the mentally impaired, hospices to care for the poor and the sick, the first institution to care for the blind, the vocation of nursing, and hospitals as an institution.[18] Rodney Stark has provided a series of books in which he argues for the vital and central role of Christianity in the development of the West,[19] as does Gertrude Himmelfarb.[20] A case can even be made that Christian theology was instrumental in the development of modernity itself.[21]

Yet I am not sure that we Christians are aware enough of this side of our history to be able to embrace it with affection and enthusiasm. Our secular friends have been preaching what amounts to a faith claim that they have the truth and religions do not, and sometimes we act as if we have come to believe what they say. Until we overcome our captivity to the secular faith claim that Christianity has nothing to offer regarding politics, economics, and social issues, we will find it all too easy to operate within a Christian subculture and leave the world to the faith option of secular humanism. We will not be able to

18. Schmidt, *How Christianity Changed the World*, 151–69.
19. Stark, *Victory of Reason*; Stark, *For the Glory of God*.
20. Himmelfarb, *Roads to Modernity*.
21. Gillespie, *Theological Origins of Modernity*.

be faithful disciples within if we cannot begin the hard work of recovering our confidence that our theology, values, and practices have something important to offer the world, something the secular option fails to provide. We need to recover our confidence in the truth of the gospel and the church's mission in the world to witness to Jesus Christ and the emerging kingdom of God.

Are We Up to the Task?

This book has explored the complex and fast-changing world of globalization and its competing offer of "good news." Being faithful witnesses within is a daunting challenge that must involve all of us, and it is not clear that our discipleship and spiritual formation efforts are up to this challenge. It may seem tempting to say that all of this globalization stuff is just too hard and confusing. Can anyone be up to this task of witnessing to Jesus Christ and the emergence of God's kingdom in all facets of where we work, play, consume, and volunteer? Fortunately, there is hope.

At the end of the day, we cannot save the world, and this is not a surprise to God. Nowhere in Scripture are we told that we would be able to banish evil, create justice, or redeem globalization. Only God can save the world, and this will happen in fullness only when Jesus comes again. Only then will all other kingdoms and powers fall away. Only then will we live in a world that truly loves God and all its neighbors. The slain Lamb and God's grace are the final word.

This leads to my first piece of good news. We were never commanded to be successful. We were commanded to love God and our neighbors and to be faithful witnesses to this within the context of our fallen world. Our mission is to be faithful, not successful. No matter our struggle and even failure, God's work will go on and ultimately will succeed. G. K. Chesterton reminds us that "Christianity has died many times and risen again; for it had a God who knew the way out of the grave."[22]

Yet, while the coming of God's kingdom does not depend on us, there is something in God's economy that we need to understand. While we cannot save the world or transform it into the kingdom of God, every kingdom-like action we take, every prayer we utter, every act of kindness and grace, every correction of a small injustice, all are signs of God's emerging kingdom. Somehow our various humble offerings come together as part of God's global work of grace and justice, and the kingdom comes a little bit closer. No matter

22. Chesterton, *Everlasting Man*, 250.

Be Encouraged

Melba Maggay, founder and president, Institute for Studies in Asian Church and Culture

Part of the despair over political questions springs from the sense of futility we feel over our ability to change social structures. The church, we say, is such a struggling minority to take upon itself the task of changing society. This overlooks the fact that the powers of the kingdom are already present. The kingdom is not entirely future, a sudden invasion from outer space at the end of time. It is here, leavening history in a powerful way.

While it is wrong to say that "the world is getting better and better," it is also wrong to say that "the world is getting worse and worse." It may be that the advance of technology has intensified the sense that evil has grown monolithic. But let us not be deceived. It is the dragon making a last desperate assault. For time is running out on it while the mustard seed is growing, hot and rich within and among us.

Maggay, *Transforming Society*, 106

how inefficient or inconsistent you and I may be, God is changing the world through the cumulative faith and actions of all those who love God and daily love their neighbors as best they can. Somehow it all adds up; a mustard seed grows into the world's largest tree. This is the witness of Hebrews 11. This is my second piece of good news: our actions, however meager or flawed, do matter.

My third piece of good news is this. I understand that being asked to be faithful witnesses in a world of over seven billion people, all of whom believe different things, live in different cultures, and follow other religions and ideologies, seems an overwhelming challenge. Being faithful witnesses within our family, city, culture, and nation in the complex, bewildering, ever-changing world of globalization seems even more so. What difference can you or I make, or a church or denomination make?

We need to remember that two thousand years ago Jesus Christ launched a movement with twelve fairly ordinary men supported by a few women. Within three years, these disciples were on their own—no formal education, sophistication, power, or strategic plan, not even a Bible—just their memories of Jesus, a mission, and the Holy Spirit. Yet here we are today with over two billion self-identified Christians on every continent, from every language, tribe, and nation, and from every walk of life. If we simply remain faithful and do what God calls us to do in the moment, however small, if we love God and our neighbors, however erratically, the day will come when even the values, processes, and outcomes of globalization will declare the glory of God.

Bibliography

Abbas, Mohd. "Globalization and the Muslim World." *Journal of Islam in Asia* 8, no. 3 (2011): 275–95.

AfDB Group, OECD Development Centre, and UNDP. *African Economic Outlook 2015*. http://www.africaneconomicoutlook.org/sites/default/files/content-pdf/AEO2015_EN.pdf.

Al-Rodhan, Nayef R. F. *Definitions of Globalization: A Comprehensive Overview and a Proposed Definition*. Geneva: Geneva Centre for Security Policy, 2006.

Archer, Margaret. *Being Human: The Problem of Agency*. Cambridge: Cambridge University Press, 2000.

———. "*Caritas in Veritate* and Social Love." *International Journal of Public Theology* 5, no. 3 (2011): 273–95.

Atherton, John. *Transfiguring Capitalism: An Enquiry into Religion and Global Change*. London: SCM, 2008.

Atherton, John, and Hannah Skinner, eds. *Through the Eye of a Needle: Theological Conversations over Political Economy*. Peterborough, UK: Epworth, 2007.

Avent, Ryan. "The Third Great Wave." *Economist*, October 4, 2014. https://www.economist.com/sites/default/files/20141004_world_economy.pdf.

Bairoch, Paul. *Economics and World History: Myths and Paradoxes*. Chicago: University of Chicago Press, 1993.

Bak, Per. *How Nature Works: The Science of Self-Organized Criticality*. New York: Copernicus, 1996.

Baker, Raymond, and Eva Joly. "Illicit Money: Can It Be Stopped?" *New York Review of Books*, December 3, 2009. http://www.nybooks.com/articles/2009/12/03/illicit-money-can-it-be-stopped.

Banerjee, Abhijit V., and Esther Duflo. *Poor Economics: A Radical Rethinking of the Way to Fight Global Poverty*. New York: Public Affairs, 2011.

Banerjee, Abhijit V., Esther Duflo, Nathanael Goldberg, Dean Karlan, Robert Osei, William Parienté, Jeremy Shapiro, Bram Thuysbaert, and Christopher Udry. "A Multifaceted Program Causes Lasting Progress for the Very Poor: Evidence from Six Countries." *Science* 348, no. 6236 (2015): 772.

Barber, Benjamin R. "Jihad vs. McWorld." *Atlantic Monthly*, March 1992.

———. *Jihad vs. McWorld*. New York: Times Books, 1995.

Barna Research Group. "Five Ways Christianity Is Increasingly Viewed as Extremist: Faith and Christianity." February 23, 2016. https://www.barna.org/research/faith -christianity/research-release/five-ways-christianity-increasingly-viewed-extremist.

———. "New Research on the State of Discipleship: Leaders and Pastors." December 1, 2015. https://www.barna.com/research/new-research-on-the-state-of-discipleship/.

Barnett, Michael N. *Empire of Humanity: A History of Humanitarianism*. Ithaca, NY: Cornell University Press, 2001.

Barrett, David B., George Thomas Kurian, and Todd M. Johnson. *World Christian Encyclopedia: A Comparative Survey of Churches and Religions in the Modern World*. 2nd ed. Oxford: Oxford University Press, 2001.

Bauckham, Richard. "The Bible and Globalization." In *The Gospel and Globalization*, edited by Michael W. Goheen and Erin Glanville, 27–48. Vancouver: Regent College Publishing, 2009.

Bauman, Zygmunt. *Globalization: The Human Consequences*. New York: Columbia University Press, 1998.

Bediako, Kwame. *Christianity in Africa*. Maryknoll, NY: Orbis, 1995.

Benedict XVI. *Caritas in Veritate*. Washington, DC: USCCB, 2009.

———. *Deus Caritas Est*. Washington, DC: USCCB, 2005.

Bernstein, Peter L. *Against the Gods: The Remarkable Story of Risk*. New York: John Wiley & Sons, 1996.

Blocher, Jacques A., and Jacques Blandenier. *The Evangelization of the World: A History of Christian Mission*. Pasadena, CA: William Carey Library, 2013.

Bloesch, Donald G. *Faith and Its Counterfeits*. Downers Grove, IL: InterVarsity, 1981.

Bosch, David J. *Transforming Mission: Paradigm Shifts in Theology of Mission*. Maryknoll, NY: Orbis, 1991.

Bourguignon, François. "Inequality and Globalization." *Foreign Affairs* 95, no. 1 (2016): 11–15.

Brubaker, Pamela. *Globalization at What Price? Economic Change and Daily Life*. Revised and expanded ed. Cleveland: Pilgrim Press, 2007.

Brueggemann, Walter. *Journey to the Common Good*. Louisville: Westminster John Knox, 2010.

Budde, Michael L. "Collecting Praise: Global Culture Industries." In *The Blackwell Companion to Christian Ethics*, edited by Stanley Hauerwas and Samuel Wells, 123–38. Hoboken, NJ: Wiley-Blackwell, 2006.

Butler, Eammon. *Adam Smith—A Primer*. London: Institute of Economic Affairs, 2007.

Calderisi, Robert. *Earthly Mission: The Catholic Church and World Development*. New Haven: Yale University Press, 2013.

Cavanagh, John, ed. *Alternatives to Economic Globalization: A Better World Is Possible*. 2nd ed. Oakland: Berrett-Koehler, 2004.

Central Intelligence Agency. "Country Comparison: Distribution of Family Income—Gini Index." In *The World Factbook 2015*. https://www.cia.gov/library/publications/the-world-factbook/rankorder/2172rank.html.

Chambers, Robert. "Responsible Well-Being—A Personal Agenda for Development." *World Development* 25, no. 11 (1997): 1743–54.

———. *Whose Reality Counts? Putting the First Last*. London: Intermediate Technology, 1997.

Chanda, Nayan. *Bound Together: How Traders, Preachers, Adventurers, and Warriors Shaped Globalization*. New Haven: Yale University Press, 2007.

Chang, Gordon G. "Blue Gold: The Coming Water Wars." *World Affairs*, September/October 2013. http://www.worldaffairsjournal.org/article/blue-gold-coming-water-wars.

Chesterton, G. K. *The Everlasting Man*. San Francisco: Ignatius, 1987.

Clarke, Gerard. "Faith Matters: Faith-Based Organizations, Civil Society and International Development." *Journal of International Development* 18 (2006): 835–48.

Clemens, Michael. "Economics and Emigration: Trillion-Dollar Bills on the Sidewalk?" *Journal of Economic Perspectives* 25, no. 3 (2011): 83–106.

———. "A Labor Mobility Agenda for Development." In *New Ideas on Development after the Financial Crisis*, edited by Nancy Birdsall and Francis Fukuyama, 260–87. Baltimore: Johns Hopkins University Press, 2011.

Coleman, John Aloysius, and William F. Ryan. *Globalization and Catholic Social Thought: Present Crisis, Future Hope*. Maryknoll, NY: Orbis, 2005.

Collier, Paul. *The Bottom Billion: Why the Poorest Countries Are Failing and What Can Be Done about It*. New York: Oxford University Press, 2007.

———. *Exodus: How Migration Is Changing Our World*. Oxford: Oxford University Press, 2013.

Covenant Eyes. *Pornography Statistics*. 2015 ed. http://www.covenanteyes.com/pornography-facts-and-statistics.

Crosby, Alfred W. *Ecological Imperialism: The Biological Expansion of Europe, 900–1900*. 2nd ed. Cambridge: Cambridge University Press, 2004.

Crouch, Andy. *Culture Making: Recovering Our Creative Calling*. Downers Grove, IL: InterVarsity, 2008.

———. "How Not to Change the World." *Books and Culture*, May/June 2010.

Darnton, Robert. *The Kiss of Lamourette: Reflections in Cultural History*. New York: W. W. Norton, 1991.

Deneulin, Séverine, and Masooda Bano. *Religion in Development: Rewriting the Secular Script*. London: Zed, 2009.

de Soto, Hernando. *The Mystery of Capital: Why Capitalism Triumphs in the West and Fails Everywhere Else*. New York: Basic Books, 2000.

———. *The Other Path: The Invisible Revolution in the Third World*. New York: Harper & Row, 1989.

Dickerson, John S. "The Decline of Evangelical America." *New York Times*, December 15, 2012.

Duflo, Esther. "Social Experiments to Fight Poverty." Filmed February 2010. TED video, 16:47. https://www.ted.com/talks/esther_duflo_social_experiments_to_fight_poverty?language=en.

Easterly, William. *The White Man's Burden: Why the West's Efforts to Aid the Rest Have Done So Much Ill and So Little Good*. New York: Penguin, 2006.

Economist. "Amazons of the Dark Net." November 1, 2014.

———. "Investment in Africa." May 30, 2015.

———. "The Paris Agreement on Climate Change: Green Light." December 19, 2015.

———. "The World in 2011." 2011.

Elliott, Charles. *Praying the Kingdom: Towards a Political Spirituality*. London: Darton, Longman & Todd, 1985.

Ellul, Jacques. *The Technological Society*. New York: Vintage, 1964.

Ellyatt, Holly. "Global Drugs Trade 'As Strong as Ever' as Fight Fails." CNBC, August 13, 2013. http://www.cnbc.com/id/100957882.

Escobar, Samuel. *The New Global Mission: The Gospel from Everywhere to Everyone*. Downers Grove, IL: InterVarsity, 2003.

Evans, Alice F., Robert A. Evans, and William Bean Kennedy. *Pedagogies for the Non-Poor*. Maryknoll, NY: Orbis, 1987.

Ferguson, Niall. *Civilization: The West and the Rest*. New York: Penguin, 2011.

———. *Empire: How Britain Made the Modern World*. London: Penguin, 2004.

Fidler, Stephen. "Globalization: Battered, but Not Beaten." *Wall Street Journal*, January 21, 2015, A6.

Fikkert, Brian, and Russell Mask. *From Dependence to Dignity: How to Alleviate Poverty through Church-Centered Microfinance*. Grand Rapids: Zondervan, 2015.

Finley, Moses I. *The Ancient Economy*. Updated ed. Berkeley: University of California Press, 1999.

Freeman, Dena, ed. *Pentecostalism and Development: Churches, NGOs and Social Change in Africa*. Basingstoke, UK: Palgrave Macmillan, 2012.

Freire, Paulo. *Education for Critical Consciousness*. New York: Continuum, 2008.

Friedman, Benjamin M. *The Moral Consequences of Economic Growth*. New York: Knopf, 2005.

Friedman, Thomas L. *Hot, Flat, and Crowded: Why We Need a Green Revolution, and How It Can Renew America.* New York: Farrar, Straus & Giroux, 2008.

———. *Longitudes and Attitudes: The World in the Age of Terrorism.* New York: Anchor Books, 2003.

———. *The World Is Flat: A Brief History of the Twenty-First Century.* New York: Farrar, Straus & Giroux, 2005.

———. "You Break It, You Own It." *New York Times,* June 29, 2016.

Friedmann, John. *Empowerment: The Politics of Alternative Development.* Cambridge, MA: Blackwell, 1992.

Fukuyama, Francis. *The End of History and the Last Man.* New York: Free Press, 1992.

Fund for Peace. "Fragile States Index 2015." http://fsi.fundforpeace.org/rankings-2015.

Gee, Jim, and Mark Button. *The Financial Cost of Fraud 2015.* N.p.: PKF Littlejohn and University of Portsmouth, 2015. http://www.pkf.com/publications/other-publications/the-financial-cost-of-fraud-report-2015.

Geertz, Clifford. "The Bazaar Economy: Information and Search in Peasant Marketing." *American Economic Review* 68 (1978): 28–32.

Gifford, Paul. *Christianity, Development and Modernity in Africa.* London: Hurst, 2015.

———. *Ghana's New Christianity: Pentecostalism in a Globalizing African Economy.* Bloomington: Indiana University Press, 2004.

Gillespie, Michael Allen. *The Theological Origins of Modernity.* Chicago: University of Chicago Press, 2008.

Goheen, Michael W., and Erin Glanville. *The Gospel and Globalization: Exploring the Religious Roots of a Globalized World.* Vancouver: Regent College Publishing, 2009.

Goizueta, Roberto S. *Christ Our Companion: Toward a Theological Aesthetics of Liberation.* Maryknoll, NY: Orbis, 2009.

González, Justo L. Foreword to *Globalization and Grace,* by Max L. Stackhouse. Vol. 4 of *God and Globalization.* New York: Continuum, 2007.

———. *Mañana: Christian Theology from a Hispanic Perspective.* Nashville: Abingdon, 1990.

Gray, John. *False Dawn: The Delusions of Global Capitalism.* New York: New Press, 1998.

Griffin, J. P. "Changing Life Expectancy throughout History." *Journal of the Royal Society of Medicine* 101, no. 12 (2008): 577.

Griffiths, Brian (Lord Griffiths of Fforestfach). *Globalization, Poverty and International Development: Insights from "Centesimus Annus."* Grand Rapids: PovertyCure/Acton Institute, 2012.

Gronewald, Sue. "The Ming Voyages." Asia for Educators, Columbia University, 2009. http://afe.easia.columbia.edu/special/china_1000ce_mingvoyages.htm.

Groody, Daniel G. *Globalization, Spirituality, and Justice: Navigating a Path to Peace.* Maryknoll, NY: Orbis, 2007.

Gunderson, Lance, and C. S. Holling. *Panarchy: Understanding Transformations in Human and Natural Systems.* Washington, DC: Island Press, 2002.

Gupta, Anil. "The Challenge of Scaling Indian Innovation." *Harvard Business Review*, May 11, 2009. https://hbr.org/2009/05/the-challenge-to-scaling-india.

Haidt, Jonathan. "The New Synthesis in Moral Psychology." *Science* 316, no. 5087 (2007): 998–1002.

Han, Deqiang. "Analytical Remarks of Anti-Economic Globalism." In *Chinese Perspectives on Globalization and Autonomy*, edited by Tuo Cai. Leiden: Brill, 2012.

Hanciles, Jehu. *Beyond Christendom: Globalization, African Migration, and the Transformation of the West.* Maryknoll, NY: Orbis, 2008.

Harris, Gardiner. "India Aims to Keep Money for Poor Out of Others' Pockets." *New York Times*, January 5, 2013.

Harrison, Lawrence E. *Underdevelopment Is a State of Mind: The Latin American Case.* Lanham, MD: Center for International Affairs, Harvard University, 1985.

Harrison, Lawrence E., and Samuel P. Huntington, eds. *Culture Matters: How Values Shape Human Progress.* New York: Basic Books, 2000.

Haushofer, Johannes, and Ernst Fehr. "On the Psychology of Poverty." *Science* 344, no. 6186 (2015): 862–67.

Havocscope. "Prostitution Statistics." Accessed August 24, 2016. http://www.havocscope.com/prostitution-statistics/.

Hawke, Gary. "Reinterpretations of the Industrial Revolution." In *The Industrial Revolution and British Society*, edited by Patrick O'Brien and Roland Quinault, 54–78. Cambridge: Cambridge University Press, 1993.

Heilbroner, Robert L. *The Worldly Philosophers: The Lives, Times, and Ideas of the Great Economic Thinkers.* Rev. 7th ed. New York: Simon & Schuster, 1999.

Heilbroner, Robert L., and Lester C. Thurow. *Economics Explained: Everything You Need to Know about How the Economy Works and Where It's Going.* New York: Simon & Schuster, 1998.

Held, David, ed. *A Globalizing World? Culture, Economics, Politics.* 2nd ed. New York: Routledge, 2004.

Held, David, Anthony McGraw, David Goldblatt, and Jonathan Perraton. *Global Transformations: Politics, Economics and Culture.* Stanford, CA: Stanford University Press, 1999.

Hilbert, Martin, and Priscila López. "The World's Technological Capacity to Store, Communicate, and Compute Information." *Science* 332, no. 6025 (2011): 60–65.

Himmelfarb, Gertrude. "The Idea of Compassion: The British vs. the French Enlightenment." *National Affairs* 145 (Fall 2001): 3–24.

———. *The Roads to Modernity: The British, French, and American Enlightenments.* New York: Knopf, 2004.

Hirst, Paul Q., and Grahame Thompson. *Globalization in Question: The International Economy and the Possibilities of Governance.* 2nd ed. Cambridge: Polity, 1999.

Hoffmann, Stanley. "Clash of Globalizations." *Foreign Affairs* 81, no. 4 (2002): 104–15.

Hoksbergen, Roland, Janel Curry, and Tracy Kuperus. "International Development: Christian Reflections on Today's Competing Theories." *Christian Scholars Review* 39, no. 1 (2009): 11–36.

Hoover, Dennis. "What Would Moses Do? Debt Relief in the Jubilee Year." *Religion in the News* 4, no. 1 (2001). http://www.trincoll.edu/depts/csrpl/rinvol4no1/jubilee _2000.htm.

Hughes, Donna Rice. "Internet: Pornography and Predators." White House Briefing, Washington, DC, August 9, 2001. http://www.protectkids.com/donnaricehughes /powerpoints/WhiteHouseBriefing.ppt.

Hunter, James Davison. *To Change the World: The Irony, Tragedy, and Possibility of Christianity in the Late Modern World.* New York: Oxford University Press, 2010.

Huntington, Samuel P. "The Clash of Civilizations?" *Foreign Affairs* 72, no. 3 (1993): 22–49.

Hutton, Will. "The Jubilee Line That Works." *Observer*, October 3, 1999.

Ignatieff, Michael. "The New World Disorder." *New York Review of Books*, September 25, 2014. http://www.nybooks.com/articles/2014/09/25/new-world-dis order/?insrc=toc.

———. *The Warrior's Honor: Ethnic War and the Modern Conscience.* New York: Henry Holt, 1998.

ILO. "Informal Economy." Accessed August 24, 2016. http://www.ilo.org/employment /units/emp-invest/informal-economy/lang--en/index.htm.

IMF. *World Economic Outlook, October 2015: Adjusting to Lower Commodity Prices.* Washington, DC: International Monetary Fund, 2015. http://www.imf.org/external /pubs/ft/weo/2015/02/.

Inglehart, Ronald. *Modernization and Postmodernization: Cultural, Economic, and Political Change in 43 Societies.* Princeton: Princeton University Press, 1997.

International Organization for Migration. "South-South Migration: Partnering Strategically for Development." Background paper, March 24–25, 2014. http:// www.iom.int/files/live/sites/iom/files/What-We-Do/idm/workshops/South-South -Migration-2014/Background-paper-en.pdf.

Internet World Stats. "Internet Users of the World—2016." http://www.internet worldstats.com/stats.htm.

Islamic Human Rights Commission. "UNHCR Statistics Reveal That Around 70% of the Refugees around the World Are Muslim." June 17, 2010. http://www.ihrc .org.uk/activities/alerts/9342-alert-world-unhcr-statistics-reveals-that-around-70 -of-the-refugees-around-the-world-are-muslim.

Jenkins, Philip. "Believers Arrive First; Missionaries Follow." *Books and Culture*, May/June 2016.

————. *The New Faces of Christianity: Believing the Bible in the Global South.* Oxford: Oxford University Press, 2006.

————. *The Next Christendom: The Coming of Global Christianity.* Oxford: Oxford University Press, 2002.

John Paul II. *Centesimus Annus.* London: Catholic Truth Society, 1991.

————. *Ecclesia in America.* Apostolic Exhortation. 1999. http://w2.vatican.va /content/john-paul-ii/en/apost_exhortations/documents/hf_jp-ii_exh_22011999 _ecclesia-in-america.html.

————. "Globalization—What Will People Make of It?" Address to Pontifical Academy of Social Sciences, 2001. https://w2.vatican.va/content/john-paul-ii/en/speeches /2001/april/documents/hf_jp-ii_spe_20010427_pc-social-sciences.html.

————. *Sollicitudo Rei Socialis.* Strathfield, Australia: St Pauls, 1988.

Johnson, Todd M., David B. Barrett, and Peter Crossing. "Christianity 2012: The 200th Anniversary of American Foreign Missions." *IBMR* 36, no. 1 (2011): 28. http://www .internationalbulletin.org/issues/2011-01/2011-01-ibmr.pdf.

Johnson, Todd M., Gina A. Zurlo, Albert W. Hickman, and Peter F. Crossing. "Christianity 2016: Latin America and Projecting Religions to 2050." *IBMR* 40, no. 1 (2016): 22–29.

Jones, E. Stanley. *The Unshakable Kingdom and the Unchanging Person.* Nashville: Abingdon, 1972.

Kalu, Ogbu. *African Pentecostalism: An Introduction.* Oxford: Oxford University Press, 2008.

Kalu, Ogbu, and Alaine M. Low. *Interpreting Contemporary Christianity: Global Processes and Local Identities.* Grand Rapids: Eerdmans, 2008.

Kaplan, Robert D. "The Coming Anarchy." *Atlantic Monthly*, February 1994.

————. *The Coming Anarchy: Shattering the Dreams of the Post-Cold War.* New York: Random House, 2000.

————. "Europe's New Medieval Map." *Wall Street Journal*, January 15, 2016, C1–2. http://www.wsj.com/articles/europes-new-medieval-map-1452875514.

Katongole, Emmanuel. *The Sacrifice of Africa: A Political Theology for Africa.* Grand Rapids: Eerdmans, 2011.

Kaul, Inge, Isabelle Grunberg, and Marc A. Stern. *Global Public Goods: International Cooperation in the 21st Century.* New York: Oxford University Press, 1999.

Kepel, Gilles. *The War for the Muslim Mind.* Cambridge, MA: Belknap Press of Harvard University Press, 2004.

Keynes, John Maynard. *The Economic Consequences of the Peace.* New York: Harcourt, Brace and Howe, 1920.

Kharas, Homi. "The Emerging Middle Class in Developing Countries." OECD Working Paper No. 285, 2010.

Kim, Kirsteen. *The Holy Spirit in the World: A Global Conversation.* Maryknoll, NY: Orbis, 2007.

Kumar, V. S. A. "A Critical Methodology of Globalization: Politics of the 21st Century." *Indiana Journal of Global Legal Studies* 10, no. 2 (2003): 87–111.

Küng, Hans. *A Global Ethic for Global Politics and Economics*. New York: Oxford University Press, 1998.

LaHaye, Laura. "Mercantilism." In *The Concise Encyclopedia of Economics*, edited by David Henderson. Indianapolis: Liberty Fund, 2002. http://www.econlib.org /library/Enc/Mercantilism.html.

Landes, David S. *The Wealth and Poverty of Nations: Why Some Are So Rich and Some So Poor*. New York: W. W. Norton, 1999.

Lapple, Alfred. *The Catholic Church: A Brief History*. New York: Paulist Press, 1982.

LCWE. "Globalization and the Gospel: Rethinking Mission in the Contemporary World." Lausanne Occasional Paper No. 30, 2004. https://www.lausanne.org/wp -content/uploads/2007/06/LOP30_IG1.pdf.

Lee, Hak Joon. *The Great World House: Martin Luther King, Jr., and Global Ethics*. Cleveland: Pilgrim Press, 2011.

Leech, Kenneth. *True Prayer: An Invitation to Christian Spirituality*. San Francisco: Harper & Row, 1980.

Lesaca, Javier. "On Social Media, Isis Uses Modern Cultural Images to Spread Anti-Modern Values." TechTank. *Brookings*, September 24, 2015. http://www.brookings .edu/blogs/techtank/posts/2015/09/24-isis-social-media-engagement.

Long, Jason. "Rural-Urban Migration and Socioeconomic Mobility in Victorian Britain." *Journal of Economic History* 65, no. 1 (2005): 1–35.

Maddison, Angus. *Contours of the World Economy, 1–2030 AD: Essays in Macro-Economic History*. Oxford: Oxford University Press, 2007.

Maggay, Melba. *Transforming Society*. Oxford: Regnum-Lynx, 1994.

Mair, Victor. "Buddhism and the Rise of the Written Vernacular in East Asia: The Making of National Languages." *Journal of Asian Studies* 53 (August 1994): 707–51.

Mann, Charles C. *1493: Uncovering the New World Columbus Created*. New York: Vintage Books, 2012.

Manning, Patrick. *Migration in World History*. 2nd ed. New York: Routledge, 2013.

Marshall, Katherine, and Marisa Van Saanen. *Development and Faith: Where Mind, Heart, and Soul Work Together*. Washington, DC: World Bank, 2007.

McCloskey, Deirdre. *Bourgeois Dignity: Why Economics Can't Explain the Modern World*. Chicago: University of Chicago Press, 2010.

———. *The Bourgeois Virtues: Ethics for an Age of Commerce*. Chicago: University of Chicago Press, 2006.

McKim, Jenifer B. "Privacy Software, Criminal Use." *Boston Globe*, March 8, 2012. http:// archive.boston.com/business/technology/articles/2012/03/08/walpole_companys _anonymity_software_aids_elicit_deals/?page=full.

Middleton, J. Richard. *The Liberating Image: The Imago Dei in Genesis 1*. Grand Rapids: Brazos, 2005.

Milanović, Branko. *The Haves and the Have-Nots: A Brief and Idiosyncratic History of Global Inequality*. New York: Basic Books, 2011.

———. "A Short History of Global Inequality: The Past Two Centuries." *Explorations in Economic History* 48, no. 4 (2011): 494–506.

———. "The Two Faces of Globalization: Against Globalization as We Know It." *World Development* 31, no. 4 (2003): 667–83.

———. "Winners of Globalization: The Rich and the Chinese Middle Class. Losers: The American Middle Class." *World Post*, January 21, 2014. http://www.huffing tonpost.com/branko-milanovic/winners-of-globalization-_b_4603454.html.

Miller, Donald E., and Tetsunao Yamamori. *Global Pentecostalism: The New Face of Christian Social Engagement*. Berkeley: University of California Press, 2007.

Mittelman, James H. *Contesting Global Order: Development, Global Governance, and Globalization*. New York: Routledge, 2011.

———. *The Globalization Syndrome: Transformation and Resistance*. Princeton: Princeton University Press, 2000.

Moe-Lobeda, Cynthia D. *Healing a Broken World: Globalization and God*. Minneapolis: Fortress, 2002.

Mohammadi, Ali, and Muhammad Ahsan. *Globalisation or Recolonisation? The Muslim World in the 21st Century*. London: Ta-Ha, 2002.

Moïsi, Dominique. *The Geopolitics of Emotion: How Cultures of Fear, Humiliation, and Hope Are Reshaping the World*. New York: Doubleday, 2009.

Mokyr, Joel. *The Enlightened Economy: An Economic History of Britain, 1700–1850*. New Haven: Yale University Press, 2009.

Molawi, Afshin. "Straight Up: How Johnnie Walker Conquered the World." *Foreign Policy* 202 (2013). http://foreignpolicy.com/2013/09/03/straight-up.

Morris, David Z. "Will Tech Manufacturing Stay in China?" *Fortune*, August 27, 2015. http://fortune.com/2015/08/27/tech-manufacturing-relocation.

Mugambi, J. N. Kanyua. *Christian Theology and Social Reconstruction*. Nairobi: Acton, 2003.

Musopole, Augustine. "African Worldview." Paper presented at Changing the Story: Christian Witness and Transformational Development, World Vision International, Pasadena, CA, 1997.

Myers, Bryant L. *Exploring World Mission: Context and Challenges*. Monrovia, CA: MARC World Vision International, 2003.

———. "How Did Britain Develop? Adaptive Social Systems and the Development of Nations." *Transformation: An International Journal of Holistic Mission* 33, no. 2 (2015): 136–47.

———. "Isaiah, Which Is It?" In *Reflections: An Exploration of Faith and Development*, 23–26. Monrovia, CA: World Vision International, 2006.

———. "Progressive Pentecostalism, Development, and Christian Development NGOs: A Challenge and an Opportunity." *IBMR* 39, no. 3 (2015): 115–21.

———. *Walking with the Poor: Principles and Practices of Transformational Development.* Revised and updated ed. Maryknoll, NY: Orbis, 2011.

Naím, Moisés. *Illicit: How Smugglers, Traffickers and Copycats Are Hijacking the Global Economy.* New York: Doubleday, 2005.

Nakashima, Ellen, and Andrea Peterson. "Report: Cybercrime and Espionage Costs $445 Billion Annually." *Economist*, June 9, 2014. https://www.washingtonpost.com /world/national-security/report-cybercrime-and-espionage-costs-445-billion -annually/2014/06/08/8995291c-ecce-11e3-9f5c-9075d5508f0a_story.html.

Narayan-Parker, Deepa, Robert Chambers, Meera Shaw, and Patti Petesch. *Crying Out for Change: Voices of the Poor.* New York: Oxford University Press, 2000.

Narayan-Parker, Deepa, Raj Patel, Kai Schafft, Anne Rademacher, and Sarah Koch-Schulte. *Can Anyone Hear Us?* New York: Oxford University Press, 2000.

Narayan-Parker, Deepa, and Patti L. Petesch, eds. *From Many Lands.* Washington, DC: Oxford University Press, 2002.

National Human Genome Research Institute. "DNA Sequencing Costs." 2015. http:// www.genome.gov/images/content/cost_per_genome_oct2015.jpg.

NationMaster. "Population below Poverty Line." 2015. http://www.nationmaster .com/country-info/stats/Economy/Population-below-poverty-line.

Neill, Stephen. *History of Christian Missions.* New York: Penguin, 1964.

Newbigin, Lesslie. *The Gospel in a Pluralist Society.* Grand Rapids: Eerdmans, 1989.

———. *The Household of God: Lectures on the Nature of the Church.* New York: Friendship Press, 1954.

North, Douglass C., and Robert P. Thomas. *The Rise of the Western World: A New Economic History.* Cambridge: Cambridge University Press, 1973.

Nurullah, Abu Sadat. "Globalisation as a Challenge to Islamic Cultural Identity." *International Journal of Interdisciplinary Sciences* 3, no. 6 (2008): 45–52.

O'Brien, David J., and Thomas A. Shannon. *Catholic Social Thought: The Documentary Heritage.* Maryknoll, NY: Orbis, 1992.

OECD. "The Rationale for Fighting Corruption." *CleanGovBiz Integrity in Practice*, 2014. http://www.oecd.org/cleangovbiz/49693613.pdf.

Offutt, Stephen, F. David Bronkema, Krisanne Vaillancourt Murphy, Robb Davis, and Gregg Okesson. *Advocating for Justice: An Evangelical Vision for Transforming Systems and Structures.* Grand Rapids: Baker Academic, 2016.

Oldham, J. H., and W. A. Visser 't Hooft. *The Church and Its Function in Society.* New York: Willet, Clark, 1937.

Parris, Brett. *Development and Wealth Creation: Why Redistribution Is Only Part of the Answer to Poverty.* Melbourne: World Vision Australia, 2005.

Paul VI. *Octogesima Adveniens.* Available at http://w2.vatican.va/content/paul-vi /en/apost_letters/documents/hf_p-vi_apl_19710514_octogesima-adveniens.html.

———. *Populorum Progressio*. Boston: Daughters of St. Paul, 1967.

Peasgood, Sean. "The Counterfeiting Conundrum: How Technology Will Slam the Scam." *Cantech Letter*, October 27, 2014. http://www.cantechletter.com/2014/10/counterfeiting/.

Peet, Richard, and Elaine R. Hartwick. *Theories of Development*. New York: Guilford, 1999.

Pew Research Center. "Cell Phones in Africa: Communication Lifeline." April 15, 2015. http://www.pewglobal.org/2015/04/15/cell-phones-in-africa-communication-lifeline.

———. "Faith on the Move: The Religious Affiliation of International Migrants." March 8, 2012. http://www.pewforum.org/2012/03/08/religious-migration-exec.

———. *Global Christianity: A Report on the Size and Distribution of the World's Christian Population*. Washington, DC: Pew Research Center's Forum on Religion & Public Life, 2011. http://www.pewforum.org/files/2011/12/Christianity-fullreport-web.pdf.

———. "Global Religious Landscape." December 18, 2012. http://www.pewforum.org/2012/12/18/global-religious-landscape-exec.

———. "Global Survey of Evangelical Protestant Leaders." June 22, 2011. http://www.pewforum.org/2011/06/22/global-survey-of-evangelical-protestant-leaders.

Pinker, Steven. *The Better Angels of Our Nature: Why Violence Has Declined*. New York: Viking, 2011.

Pius XI. *Quadragesimo Anno*. New York: Paulist Press, 1939.

Quah, Danny. "The Global Economy's Shifting Centre of Gravity." *Global Policy* 2, no. 1 (2011): 3–10.

Ramalingam, Ben. *Aid on the Edge of Chaos: Rethinking International Cooperation in a Complex World*. Oxford: Oxford University Press, 2013.

Raustiala, Kal, and Chris Sprigman. "How Much Do Music and Movie Piracy Really Hurt the U.S. Economy?" *Freakonomics* (blog), January 12, 2012. http://freakonomics.com/2012/01/12/how-much-do-music-and-movie-piracy-really-hurt-the-u-s-economy/.

Reisacher, Evelyne A. *Joyful Witness in the Muslim World*. Grand Rapids: Baker Academic, 2016.

Reiser, William E. *To Hear God's Word, Listen to the World: The Liberation of Spirituality*. New York: Paulist Press, 1997.

Richards, Larry. *New International Encyclopedia of Bible Words*. Grand Rapids: Zondervan, 1999.

Rodrik, Dani. "Goodbye Washington Consensus, Hello Washington Confusion? A Review of the World Bank's Economic Growth in the 1990s: Learning from a Decade of Reform." *Journal of Economic Literature* 44, no. 4 (2006): 973–87.

———. "The Past, Present, and Future of Economic Growth." Working Paper 1, Global Citizen Foundation, June 2013. http://drodrik.scholar.harvard.edu/files/dani -rodrik/files/gcf_rodrik-working-paper-1_-6-24-13.pdf.

Roodman, David. "The Arc of the Jubilee." Essay, Center for Global Development, October 2010. http://cgdev.org.488elwb02.blackmesh.com/sites/default/files/1424539 _file_Roodman_Jubilee_FINAL.pdf.

Rosenau, James N. *Turbulence in World Politics: A Theory of Change and Continuity.* Princeton: Princeton University Press, 1990.

Rosling, Hans. "Wealth and Health of Nations." 2015. www.bit.ly/1GjrNRo.

Rostow, W. W. *The Stages of Economic Growth: A Non-Communist Manifesto.* Cambridge: Cambridge University Press, 1960.

Roy, Olivier. *Holy Ignorance: When Religion and Culture Part Ways.* New York: Columbia University Press, 2010.

Sachs, Jeffrey. *The End of Poverty: Economic Possibilities for Our Time.* New York: Penguin Press, 2005.

Sacks, Jonathan. "Dignity of Difference." *Review of Faith and International Affairs* 7, no. 2 (Summer 2009): 37–42.

———. *Not in God's Name: Confronting Religious Violence.* First American ed. New York: Schocken Books, 2015.

———. *The Persistence of Faith: Religion, Morality and Society in a Secular Age.* New York: Continuum, 2005.

———. "Swords into Plowshares." *Wall Street Journal*, October 3–4, 2015.

Sanger, David, and Nicole Perlroth. "Senate Approves a Cybersecurity Bill Long in the Works and Largely Dated." *New York Times*, October 27, 2015.

Sanneh, Lamin. "Christian Missions and the Western Guilt Complex." *Christian Century*, April 8, 1987, 331–34. http://www.religion-online.org/showarticle.asp ?title=143.

Schmidt, Alvin J. *How Christianity Changed the World.* Grand Rapids: Zondervan, 2004.

Sen, Amartya. *Development as Freedom.* New York: Knopf, 1999.

Shaw, Anuj, Sendhil Mullainathan, and Eldar Shafir. "Some Consequences of Having Too Little." *Science* 338, no. 602 (2012): 682–85.

Singh, Puneet Pal. "How Does Illegal Sports Betting Work and What Are the Fears?" *BBC News*, February 19, 2013. http://www.bbc.com/news/business-21501858.

Sirota, Brent. "The First Big Society: Eighteenth Century Britain's Age of Benevolence." *ABC Religion and Ethics*, January 9, 2014. http://www.abc.net.au/religion /articles/2014/01/09/3922667.htm.

Smilde, David. *Reason to Believe: Cultural Agency in Latin American Evangelicalism.* Berkeley: University of California Press, 2007.

Smillie, Ian, and Larry Minear. *The Charity of Nations: Humanitarian Action in a Calculating World.* Bloomfield, CT: Kumarian, 2004.

Smith, Christian. *Moral, Believing Animals: Human Personhood and Culture*. New York: Oxford University Press, 2003.

———. *What Is a Person? Rethinking Humanity, Social Life, and the Moral Good from the Person Up*. Chicago: University of Chicago Press, 2010.

Smith, James K. A. *Desiring the Kingdom: Worship, Worldview, and Cultural Formation*. Grand Rapids: Baker Academic, 2009.

———. *Imagining the Kingdom: How Worship Works*. Grand Rapids: Baker Academic, 2013.

Soysal, Yaseman, and David Strong. "Construction of the First Mass Educational Systems in 19th Century Europe." *Sociology of Education* 62 (1989): 277–88.

Stackhouse, Max L. *Globalization and Grace*. Vol. 4 of *God and Globalization*. New York: Continuum, 2007.

Stackhouse, Max L., with Don S. Browning, eds. *The Spirit and the Modern Authorities*. Vol. 2 of *God and Globalization*. Harrisburg, PA: Trinity Press International, 2001.

Stackhouse, Max L., with Diane B. Obenchain, eds. *Christ and the Dominions of Civilization*. Vol. 3 of *God and Globalization*. Harrisburg, PA: Trinity Press International, 2002.

Stackhouse, Max L., with Peter J. Paris, eds. *Religion and the Powers of the Common Life*. Vol. 1 of *God and Globalization*. Harrisburg, PA: Trinity Press International, 2000.

Stark, Rodney. *For the Glory of God: How Monotheism Led to Reformations, Science, Witch-Hunts, and the End of Slavery*. Princeton: Princeton University Press, 2004.

———. "The Truth about the Catholic Church and Slavery." *Christianity Today*, July 1, 2003.

———. *The Victory of Reason: How Christianity Led to Freedom, Capitalism, and Western Success*. New York: Random House, 2005.

Statista. "Size of the Online Gaming Market from 2003 to 2015." Accessed 2015. http://www.statista.com (subscription required).

Steger, Manfred B. *Globalization: A Very Short Introduction*. 3rd ed. Oxford: Oxford University Press, 2013.

Stiglitz, Joseph. "The Future of Europe." Lecture presented for UBS International Center of Economics in Society, Basel, Switzerland, January 27, 2014. Available at https://www.youtube.com/watch?v=LaRW5jix_ic.

Street, Nick. *Moved by the Spirit: Pentecostal and Charismatic Christianity in the Global South*. Los Angeles: Center for Religion and Civic Culture, University of Southern California, 2013.

Summer, Andy. "Where Do the World's Poor Live? A New Update." IDS Working Paper, vol. 2012, no. 393, Institute of Development Studies, June 2012. https://www.ids.ac.uk/files/dmfile/Wp393.pdf.

Sznaider, Natan. "The Sociology of Compassion: A Study in the Sociology of Morals." *Cultural Values* 2, no. 1 (1998): 117–39.

Táíwò, Olúfẹ́mi. *How Colonialism Preempted Modernity in Africa.* Bloomington: Indiana University Press, 2010.

Tanner, Kathryn. *Economy of Grace.* Minneapolis: Fortress, 2005.

Tennent, Timothy C. *Invitation to World Missions: A Trinitarian Missiology for the Twenty-First Century.* Grand Rapids: Kregel, 2010.

———. *Theology in the Context of World Christianity: How the Global Church Is Influencing the Way We Think About and Discuss Theology.* Grand Rapids: Zondervan, 2007.

Transparency International. "Corruption Perceptions Index 2015: Results." Accessed September 20, 2016. http://www.transparency.org/cpi2015#results-table.

Tucci, Serena, and Joshua M. Akey. "Population Genetics: A Map of Human Wanderlust." *Nature* 538 (October 13, 2016): 179–80. http://www.nature.com/nature/journal /vaop/ncurrent/full/nature19472.html.

Tyndale, Wendy, ed. *Visions of Development: Faith-Based Initiatives.* Burlington, VT: Ashgate, 2006.

UN. *The Millennium Development Goals Report 2015.* New York: United Nations, 2015. http://www.un.org/millenniumgoals/2015_MDG_Report/pdf/MDG%202015% 20rev%20%28July%201%29.pdf.

UNCTAD. *World Investment Report 2014: Investing in the SDGs; An Action Plan.* New York: United Nations, 2014. http://unctad.org/en/PublicationsLibrary/wir 2014_en.pdf.

UNDP. *Human Development Report 2013: The Rise of the South; Human Progress in a Diverse World.* New York: United Nations Development Programme, 2013. http://hdr.undp.org/en/2013-report.

———. *Human Development Report 2015: Rethinking Work for Human Development.* New York: United Nations Development Programme, 2015. http://hdr.undp .org/sites/default/files/2015_human_development_report_1.pdf.

UNFPA. "How Has the World Changed in the Last 20 Years?" April 7, 2014. http:// www.unfpa.org/news/how-has-world-changed-last-20-years.

UNHCR. "Worldwide Displacement Hits All-Time High as War and Persecution Increase." June 18, 2015. http://www.unhcr.org/558193896.html.

United States Department for Health and Human Services. "Poverty Guidelines." January 25, 2016. https://aspe.hhs.gov/poverty-guidelines.

UNODC. "Illicit Money: How Much Is Out There?" October 25, 2011. https://www .unodc.org/unodc/en/frontpage/2011/October/illicit-money_-how-much-is-out -there.html.

———. "New UNODC Campaign Highlights Transnational Organized Crime as a US$870 Billion a Year Business." July 16, 2012. https://www.unodc.org/unodc /en/frontpage/2012/July/new-unodc-campaign-highlights-transnational-organized -crime-as-an-us-870-billion-a-year-business.html.

Waliggo, John Mary. "A Call for Prophetic Action." In *Catholic Theological Ethics in the World Church*, edited by James F. Keenan, 254. New York: Continuum, 2007.

Walls, Andrew F. "Christian Mission in a Five-Hundred-Year Context." In *Mission in the 21st Century*, edited by Andrew F. Walls and Cathy Ross, 193–204. London: Darton, Longman and Todd, 2008.

———. *The Missionary Movement in Christian History: Studies in the Transmission of Faith*. Maryknoll, NY: Orbis, 1996.

Wariboko, Nimi. "Pentecostal Paradigms of National Economic Prosperity in Africa." In *Pentecostalism and Prosperity: The Socioeconomics of the Global Charismatic Movement*, edited by Amos Yong and Katherine Attanasi, 35–59. New York: Palgrave Macmillan, 2012.

Wexler, Alexandra. "Startup Fuels Africa's Mobile-Payment Boom." *Wall Street Journal*, November 15, 2015.

WHO. "Under-Five Mortality." Accessed September 20, 2016. http://www.who.int /gho/child_health/mortality/mortality_under_five_text/en.

Williams, Rowan. "New Perspectives on Faith and Development." Lecture presented at the Royal Society of the Arts, London, November 12, 2009. http://rowanwilliams.arch bishopofcanterbury.org/articles.php/768/new-perspectives-on-faith-and-development.

Wink, Walter. *Engaging the Powers: Discernment and Resistance in a World of Domination*. Minneapolis: Fortress, 1992.

———. *Unmasking the Powers: The Invisible Forces That Determine Human Existence*. Philadelphia: Fortress, 1986.

Wolf, Martin. *Why Globalization Works*. New Haven: Yale University Press, 2004.

Wolterstorff, Nicholas. *Justice: Rights and Wrongs*. Princeton: Princeton University Press, 2008.

———. *Until Justice and Peace Embrace*. Grand Rapids: Eerdmans, 1983.

Woodberry, Robert. "The Missionary Roots of Liberal Democracy." *American Political Science Review* 106, no. 2 (2012): 246–74.

Wootton, David. *The Invention of Science: A New History of the Scientific Revolution*. New York: HarperCollins, 2015.

World Bank. "Fragility, Conflict and Violence: Overview." Accessed September 22, 2016. http://www.worldbank.org/en/topic/fragilityconflictviolence/overview#1 (last updated September 21, 2016).

———. "Migration and Remittances: Recent Developments and Outlook." In *Migration and Development Brief* 26 (April 2016). http://pubdocs.worldbank.org /en/661301460400427908/MigrationandDevelopmentBrief26.pdf.

———. "Poverty: Overview." Accessed September 20, 2016. http://www.worldbank.org /en/topic/poverty/overview (last updated April 13, 2016).

———. *World Development Indicators 2015*. Washington, DC: World Bank, 2015. https://openknowledge.worldbank.org/handle/10986/21634.

———. *World Development Report 2009: Reshaping Economic Geography*. Washington, DC: World Bank, 2009. https://openknowledge.worldbank.org/handle /10986/5991.

———. *World Development Report 2011: Conflict, Security, and Development*. Washington, DC: World Bank, 2011. https://openknowledge.worldbank.org/handle /10986/4389.

WTO. *World Trade Report 2013: Factors Shaping the Future of World Trade*. Geneva: World Trade Organization, 2013. https://www.wto.org/english/res_e/booksp_e /world_trade_report13_e.pdf.

Yergin, Daniel, and Joseph Stanislaw. *The Commanding Heights: The Battle for the World Economy*. New York: Touchstone, 2002.

Yoder, John Howard. *The Priestly Kingdom: Social Ethics as Gospel*. Notre Dame, IN: University of Notre Dame Press, 1984.

Yong, Amos. *Hospitality and the Other: Pentecost, Christian Practices, and the Neighbor*. Maryknoll, NY: Orbis, 2008.

Yunus, Muhammad. *Creating a World without Poverty: Social Business and the Future of Capitalism*. New York: Public Affairs, 2009.

Yunus, Muhammad, with Alan Jolis. *Banker to the Poor: Micro-Lending and the Battle against World Poverty*. New York: PublicAffairs, 2007.

Zak, Paul J. *The Moral Molecule: The Source of Love and Prosperity*. New York: Dutton, 2012.

Zakaria, Fareed. *The Post-American World: Release 2.0*. New York: W. W. Norton, 2012.

Zalanga, Samuel. "Religion, Economic Development and Cultural Change: The Contradictory Role of Pentecostal Christianity in Sub-Saharan Africa." *Journal of Third World Studies* 27, no. 1 (2010): 43–62.

Zwane, Alix Peterson. "Implications of Scarcity." *Science* 338, no. 6107 (2012): 617–18.

Index